The

RANGE
BUCKET
LIST

— • —

THE GOLF
ADVENTURE
of a
LIFETIME

JAMES DODSON

Illustrations by Harry Blair

Simon & Schuster Paperbacks

NEW YORK · LONDON · TORONTO · SYDNEY · NEW DELHI

Simon & Schuster Paperbacks
An Imprint of Simon & Schuster, Inc.
1230 Avenue of the Americas
New York, NY 10020

First Simon & Schuster trade paperback edition May 2018

SIMON & SCHUSTER PAPERBACKS and colophon are registered trademarks
of Simon & Schuster, Inc.

For information about special discounts for bulk purchases,
please contact Simon & Schuster Special Sales at 1-866-506-1949
or business@simonandschuster.com.

The Simon & Schuster Speakers Bureau can bring authors to your
live event. For more information, or to book an event, contact the
Simon & Schuster Speakers Bureau at 1-866-248-3049
or visit our website at www.simonspeakers.com.

Interior design by Paul Dippolito

Manufactured in the United States of America

1 3 5 7 9 10 8 6 4 2

Library of Congress Cataloging-in-Publication Data is available.

ISBN 978-1-4767-4671-5
ISBN 978-1-4767-4672-2 (pbk)
ISBN 978-1-4767-4673-9 (ebook)

To Wendy

CONTENTS

The

RANGE
BUCKET
LIST

THINGS TO DO IN GOLF

Several years ago I made a nice discovery while going through an old footlocker from my mother's attic that contained various objects from my teenage years. Beneath camping gear and a well-worn Wilson fielder's glove autographed by Orioles Hall of Famer Brooks Robinson, I found a trio of golf books and a small green spiral notebook marked "Things to Do in Golf" in large adolescent block letters.

The golf books—gifts from my father—were the first I ever owned. They included an autographed 1962 first-edition hardcover copy of Sam Snead's folksy *The Education of a Golfer*, written with Al Stump; a 1967 paperback biography of Arnold Palmer by the editors of *Golf Digest* magazine ("An inside look at the most fabulous player in golf history!"); and a well-worn, water-stained edition of Ben Hogan's *Five Lessons: The Modern Fundamentals of Golf*, the best-selling golf instruction book of all time.

As you might expect, it was a pleasure to sit and leaf through my first golf books, noting passages I found important enough to underline in pencil, remembering what it was like to be a skinny Carolina kid falling in love with his old man's game. My first sports heroes were indeed Arnold Palmer and Brooks Robinson. I'd tagged after Arnold many times at my hometown Greater Greensboro Open (GGO)—now the Wyndham Championship—and though I

2 • THE RANGE BUCKET LIST

would never see Ben Hogan play golf in person, my father believed his instruction book, written in collaboration with the great Herbert Warren Wind, to be the best and simplest analysis of a golf swing in print. As for Brooks Robinson, the finest third baseman in Major League history, the Human Vacuum Cleaner was the person I hoped to be like in the unlikely event that my plan to be the next Arnold Palmer failed to bear fruit.

The pocket-size notebook marked "Things to Do in Golf," however, was really what brought those memories rushing back. It was a Range Bucket List thirty-five years before I coined the phrase, begun because I'd read somewhere that as a kid, Arnold Palmer recorded his golf goals in a small notebook he kept in his golf bag. Decades later, when I was working with Arnold on his memoirs, I actually confirmed this with him during an early-morning chat in his Latrobe workshop. "Oh, for sure," he said with a warm chuckle, "I had *plenty* of big golf dreams in those days. And, come to think of it, I did write them down. I wanted to get good enough at golf, first of all, to impress Pap [Deacon, his father]. Then I wanted to win the state amateur championship. I was probably twelve or thirteen at the time. Frankly, I never thought about turning pro in those days—there was no real money in it—though I did secretly dream about somehow winning the Masters or a US Open. I never could have imagined . . ."

His voice trailed off. Arnold was sixty-eight years old then and stood in the before-hours quiet of his modest Latrobe office workshop regripping a favorite driver as he revealed this, sounding almost as dreamy as a Pennsylvania teenager. We'd just begun collaborating on *A Golfer's Life*, a two-year partnership that would reveal his incomparable life and transform mine—a writer's version, if you like, of playing in the Masters or the US Open. Arnold had recently undergone surgery for prostate cancer. His wife, Winnie, had been diagnosed with ovarian cancer. The dimensions of his world were suddenly much narrower and more precious than ever.

He stared off into the ether and more than six decades of memories, then took a moment to compose himself. He glanced over at me, eyes wet with emotion, cleared his voice, and smiled. "Of course, every kid has those kinds of golf dreams, Shakespeare. I just never imagined mine would come true the way they did—or go so quickly."

I knew exactly what he meant, but didn't know what to say—and couldn't have found my voice regardless. Suffice it to say, discovering my "Things to Do in Golf" list in an attic trunk a decade or so later brought on my own rush of memory and emotion. The game of golf will do that.

Here's the list, such as it is:

Things to Do in Golf

1. Meet Arnold Palmer and Mr. Bobby Jones
2. Play the Old Course at St Andrews, Scotland
3. Make a hole in one
4. Play on the PGA Tour
5. Get new clubs
6. Break 80 (soon!)
7. Live in Pinehurst
8. Find golf buddies like Bill, Alex, and Richard
   [*my dad's Saturday-morning regulars*]
9. Caddie at the GGO
10. Have a girlfriend who plays golf
11. Play golf in Brazil

That's it: eleven items, short and sweet. It's obvious why Palmer and Jones top the list. They were the reigning gods of American golf, both of whom had a strong connection to my hometown. Jones's daughter lived in Greensboro, and one of Arnold's early college buddies, Charlie Teague, was my dad's best friend's younger brother and ran the Gate City's best sporting-goods store, where I purchased my Brooks Robinson fielder's glove with my lawn-mowing earnings shortly before I got it autographed by the Human Vacuum Cleaner himself at my first Orioles game. Our voyaging, Henry Thoreau said, is only a great circle-sailing.

The other items on the list were the kinds of things any twelve-year-old boy in Palmer's 1960s America might have placed high on his golf to-do list—the forerunner of what, nearly four decades later, I would come to call my Range Bucket List of things I still wanted to do in golf. To this day, however, I have no clue why I was so eager to play golf in Brazil. Might have just been the pretty, dark-haired exchange student in my eighth-grade earth science class. Her name was Juliana. But I can't be sure.

In any case, had a magical genie appeared to me when I re-corded this beginner's short list—I place it anywhere from late 1965 to early 1967—and informed me that I would in time accomplish, in one form or another, almost every item on that list and a great deal more, growing up to know many of the great players, golf writ-ers, teachers, design pioneers, and architects of the game's modern era—not to mention be recruited to help the most charismatic player in the game's history produce his best-selling memoir—I probably would have laughed out loud at such a crazy notion, or simply passed out from pure, glandular teenage joy.

But such is the transformative power of golf. For me, this ex-traordinary ancient game has not only been an unexpected career shaper but also introduced me to my best friends, and has even been something of a spiritual lifesaver over many years.

Just after I started that first list, you see, I was banished from my father's course in Greensboro for half the summer by a color-ful club professional named Aubrey Apple for losing my cool and burying my new Bulls Eye putter in the flesh of the fourteenth green after missing a two-foot birdie putt. This happened during my first-ever round on a regulation eighteen-hole golf course. I was playing with my father and his buddies Bill Mims and Alex Roberts. Visibly disappointed at my behavior, my father calmly showed me how to repair the green, then insisted that I walk all the way back to the clubhouse and report my crime to Mr. Apple, who unplugged the smoldering stogie that anchored the southwest corner of his mouth long enough to issue a stream of profanity that raised the hair on my skinny chicken neck. He pointed me to the door, warning that I'd better not show my bleeping face around the club until "after the *God-damned* Fourth of *Joo*-lie!"

Which explains item number 7: "Live in Pinehurst."

The day after this unfortunate incident, I was moping around in the backyard after church, smacking Wiffle golf balls over the roof of our house with my father's old Spalding Bobby Jones pitching wedge, when my dad suddenly appeared wearing golf clothes and instructed me to grab my clubs from the garage and follow him.

We drove ninety minutes due south from the rolling Piedmont into the lonesome longleaf pines of the Carolina Sandhills. As I recall, my father didn't say much during the ride on that beautiful May afternoon. My (not entirely kind) nickname for my relentlessly cheerful and incorruptibly upbeat father was Opti the Mystic. He was an adman with a poet's heart who always seemed to have some nugget of wisdom reserved for any occasion and who viewed one's transgressions against man or nature as timely opportunities to teach lessons about character and personal growth. Opti possessed an unsinkable belief in the power of human optimism and gratitude that shaped his life and, ultimately, mine, a belief perhaps most tellingly revealed through the life lessons of his favorite game: golf.

It was Opti who taught me the protocols of the ancient game and patiently endured my early eruptions of teenage angst as I struggled to control my hot temper and learn to play proficiently. It was Opti who placed those iconic golf books in my hands and gracefully spoke about the game's "higher properties," explaining how it is both an ever-changing journey into the unknown and a wonderful test of skill, character, and imagination that reveals who you really are and what you aspire to be.

This was pure Opti-speak, a few almost fairy-tale words that my older brother, Dicky, and I heard many versions of while growing up in North Carolina, the code by which our funny, philosophical, straight-arrow old man lived his life. Back then, neither my brother nor I could fully divine the deeper meanings of such lofty phrasings, and especially how they applied to a seemingly simple game like golf.

Our father, for instance, was the first person I heard say that golf is a metaphor for life, with its unexpected ups and downs, unfair breaks, and sudden breakthroughs, a game played by uniform rules of conduct that "apply to all" and that are older (and even more commendably democratic) than the US Constitution. Above all else, it was a "gentleman's game" that offered challenges that tested, shaped, and ultimately "revealed one's grit under fire." The stories he loved to tell about taking up the game in England and Scotland during the Second World War, highlighted by his pilgrimage to the "Birthplace of Golf" at St Andrews just before D-Day, were magical to me.

Opti even told us how golf was something of "a mental anchor and lifesaver" during those years of war and uncertainty, a game he discovered as a homesick Carolina boy stationed on England's Lancashire coast not far from the entrance gates of Royal Lytham & St Annes Golf Club, where Bobby Jones captured the 1926 British Open title. The club had a civilized wartime policy that allowed American servicemen to borrow the clubs of absent members and play the course for a few shillings. Shortly before he shipped out in the second wave of Operation Overlord, Opti and a second lieutenant buddy from South Carolina hopped a train to St Andrews just to play the Old Course. I still have a faded photograph of them posing on the first tee, the solemn facade of the Royal and Ancient clubhouse rising in the background. Befitting the occasion, Opti and his pal are both dressed in their Eighth Army Air Corps uniforms, neckties tucked into shirts, grinning like excited teenagers. Afterward, young tech sergeant Braxton Dodson mailed this photograph home to my mother, his war bride, a former Maryland beauty queen who was doing her part to save democracy by being chased around a desk by an admiral in Annapolis. At the bottom of the photo Opti jotted in ink: "A couple good eggs at the Home of Golf."

Weeks later, a terrible tragedy occurred at the air base where my father was stationed that prevented him from piloting a troop glider into Normandy, an event he never spoke of until he and I took a trip to England and Scotland during the summer of the fiftieth anniversary of D-Day to play the courses where he fell hard for the game. It was then and there that I unwittingly exhumed an unspeakable event that had dramatically changed his life and that explained so much about his unsinkable optimism and passion for living, his determination never to waste a day. "Life promises us sorrow," he said to me one evening as we walked together across the Old Course at dusk, repeating something I'd heard him say many times but never before understood. "It's up to us to provide the joy. The game ends far too soon, Bo. But if you're lucky, the journey will bring you safely home."

═══ • ═══

In a manner of speaking, my own long journey to such opti-mystic awareness began the day after I got booted from Green Valley Golf Club in May of 1966, a golf awakening that began on the beautiful Sunday afternoon we rolled into sleepy Pinehurst, the so-called Home of American Golf.

We drove past a magnificent white hotel with a copper roof drowsing in the longleaf pines, and I saw, out the window of the Oldsmobile, golfers and caddies dressed all in white moving along a baize-green fairway while a church somewhere chimed a familiar hymn.

"Beautiful, isn't it?" Opti remarked. "That's Pinehurst No. 2, Donald Ross's masterpiece. One of the most famous golf courses in the world. It's right up there with the Old Course at St Andrews. Every legend of the modern game has played it, including Bobby Jones, Arnold Palmer, and Sam Snead. Unfortunately, unless you learn to control your temper on the golf course, you'll never get to play there."

With that, he fell silent as we rolled on past the course, leaving me both dazzled and crestfallen.

A few minutes later, though, we wheeled into a charming smaller hotel called the Mid Pines Inn and Golf Club, and my father suggested we step inside to say hello to an old friend named Ernie Boros. He explained that Ernie was the younger brother of recent US Open winner Julius Boros. Julius was Mid Pine's touring professional and my father's favorite golfer. Earlier that spring, Opti and I had followed Boros at the Greater Greensboro Open, amazed by his buttermilk-smooth golf swing.

In the pro shop, Ernie Boros greeted us warmly and chatted with my dad about mutual friends from Greensboro. When the subject of his famous brother came up, Boros mentioned that Julius just happened to be on the property that afternoon, and was presently having lunch alone in the inn dining room. Ernie Boros offered me a Mid Pines visor and wondered if I wished to meet his brother and maybe get his autograph. Looking back, I remember how he glanced at my old man, smiled, and winked.

The encounter was brief. Julius Boros couldn't have been nicer. He asked me a few questions about my game and offered to autograph my new visor. He thanked us for coming and observed, as we departed, "You know, son, golf is a game for gentlemen and ladies. It'll teach you a great deal about life and can take you a lot of great places."

Had I been in less of a daze, I might have heard the echoes of Opti's own words coming from the great man's lips. As it was, we then strolled out to take a look at the spectacular final hole of Mid

Pines, and Opti pleasantly remarked, "Wasn't that something? You just never know who you'll meet in golf. That alone is a good reason to calm down and behave on the golf course."

He let that soak in for a moment. "Tell you what," he added, as if undergoing a change of heart, "if you think you can knock off the temper tantrums, maybe we can play the golf course here today. It's also a fine Donald Ross course, by the way. One of his best."

With that, we fetched our clubs and played Mid Pines, my first full eighteen holes on a championship golf course. To this day, though nearby Pinehurst No. 2 rightfully calls itself the Home of American Golf and is every bit Ross's masterpiece, Mid Pines still holds a special place in my heart, second only to Greensboro, the birthplace of my love affair with golf.

For the record, it took many years (and my mother finally spilling the beans) for me to learn that the unexpected meeting with Julius Boros was a prearranged deal, an artful teaching moment designed by my father to have maximum impact on his hardheaded son.

I never tossed a club or buried a putter in anger again.

At least, not with Opti the Mystic—or, worse, Aubrey Apple—anywhere in view.

═ ● ═

The first time I heard the phrase "bucket list" was in the fall of 1999, almost a decade before it gained popular currency from the 2007 Morgan Freeman film of the same name. It came from the lips of my friend and mentor John Derr, the former head of CBS Sports who was instrumental in bringing the Masters to television and who broadcasted the action from Augusta for decades.

We were dining with the great Carolina amateur Harvie Ward at the homey Pine Crest Inn in Pinehurst. I was making one of my occasional passes through my boyhood stomping grounds, ostensibly to sign copies of *Final Rounds*—a surprise bestseller that evolved from that final golf trip to Britain with my dying father—and to give a speech at the Art of Golf convention put on by the Tufts Archives and the Old Sport Gallery in Pinehurst at Pine Needles Resort. The other reason I was there was to interview Harvie Ward for my monthly Golf Life column in *Golf* magazine.

Long before Tiger Woods captured three US Amateur titles, Harvie Ward won two National Amateurs in a row and likely would have secured a record third had he not been singled out and sanctioned by the USGA for accepting outside financial support to play in the Masters, a scandal that sent perhaps the most promising amateur player of his time into a long tailspin of booze and failed marriages and nearly drove him from the game. Marriage to the right woman and a return to Pinehurst, where his amateur career began with an upset victory over the volatile Frank Stranahan at the 1948 North and South Amateur, was, as he'd told me just that morning, "like finding my way home. It was the cure I needed."

Now sober and teaching some of the state's most promising young players at Pine Needles Resort, Harvie was regarded by many—myself among them—as the greatest player who never was, the man whose painful fall from grace heralded the end of the golden age of amateurs and sent a flood of young, collegiate talents into the professional ranks, lest they suffer a similar fate. This included Harvie's greatest college rival, a fellow named Arnold Daniel Palmer.

On the heels of cowriting Arnold's *A Golfer's Life*, I'd been approached by the heirs of Ben Hogan to write an authorized biography of golf's most elusive superstar. In every conceivable way, dark and introverted Ben Hogan was as different as could be from sunny and smiling Arnold Palmer. Yet both men unmistakably fueled my early love affair with golf. And on the plus side of the equation, Hogan's heirs promised complete access to his personal papers, closest friends, and surviving family members, all of whom up till then had kept up a code of silence equivalent to a mafia *omertà*.

For additional insight on this opportunity, I'd come to Pinehurst from my longtime home in Maine to seek the counsel of the ageless John Derr, then eighty years old, a newsman who'd been a close friend to both Sam Snead and Ben Hogan. Derr had accompanied the ailing Hogan on every step of his historic fortnight at Carnoustie in 1953, for instance, which was the Hawk's final triumph before disappearing from public view to start his golf equipment company. Derr, I'd been reliably informed by his friend Sam Snead, was a walking encyclopedia on the postwar era of American golf.

Also dining with us that night was Tom Stewart, a former head professional at several leading clubs, Michigan PGA section chief, and a cheerful Irishman who owned the Old Sport Gallery in the heart of Pinehurst Village. In time I would come to think of Tom's shop as the golf world's version of Dickens's Old Curiosity Shop, and of genial Tom Stewart as the de facto Lord Mayor of Pinehurst. That very morning, as if to illustrate the point, he'd put another beguiling idea into my head by proposing that after I completed my Hogan project, Harvie and I should collaborate on a book about his rags-to-riches-to-rags golf career and call it *The Last Amateur.* I'd even gone so far as to broach the idea to Harvie and his wife, Joanne, that afternoon, and both thought it was indeed time for Harvie to finally tell his side of the biggest scandal of golf's modern era.

"If you're going to write books about Hogan *and* Harvie," Tom said that evening at the Pine Crest, after learning that I hailed from just seventy miles up the road in Greensboro, "you ought to think of actually moving home to the Sandhills."

Harvie smiled and said he agreed. "You should come take the Pinehurst cure the way I did," he added, explaining that in the early days of Pinehurst, the longleaf pines were believed to emit a mysterious healing "ozone" capable of curing anything from plantar warts to ailing golf swings. He was convinced of the phenomenon's authenticity.

"Haven't you heard?" said the redoubtable Derr in his best broadcaster's voice. "Old golf writers never die. They just move to Pinehurst and lose their balls!" He ticked off a list of famous golf scribes who'd spent some of their best years living and working in the Home of American Golf: Bob Harlow, Dick Taylor, Charles Price, Bob Drum, and even Herb Wind, who returned on a regular basis to see his pal Dick Tufts at his cottage off Pinehurst No. 2.

I admitted that the idea was awfully tempting and briefly recounted my teenage epiphany in the Pines and an old desire to call Pinehurst home.

"I'll bet your father would tell you it's time to do that," Derr said.

I was more than a little surprised to hear my father brought into the discussion. Opti had been gone for four years at that point, a loss I still felt keenly almost every day of my life; I missed his voice, his humor, his good-hearted wisdom, and his upbeat take on every bump and hurdle of life.

"You knew him?" I asked John.

Derr smiled. "We started our careers together on the newspaper in Greensboro. That was either 1937 or '38. I was an assistant sports editor, totally wet behind the ears, and he was a local boy selling advertising and writing an aviation column. The war took us our separate ways. But I always liked your dad very much." A roguish smile appeared. "We were both Golden Glove boxers and snappy dressers who had an eye for the ladies. My ring name was 'Dirty Derr.' Don't remember your dad's"—it was "Bomber Brax"—"but I know he moved to Maryland and married a beauty queen: your mother, I presume. Which reminds me, I've just started dating a lovely widow in her late seventies who cooks like a Michelin chef, sings opera, plays golf, and likes to take midnight swims in the nude. Best of all, she can drive at night! She keeps me so young that I've added a dozen new things to my bucket list."

"What's a bucket list?" I asked.

"That's a list of things you have to do before you kick the bucket," John explained. "Everyone should have one, dear boy—especially golfers."

"I have one," quipped Harvie. "I plan to go back and win the Masters someday. I need a green jacket to complete my wardrobe."

Tom said, "Mine is to convince you to move home to North Carolina so I'll have a regular golf buddy before I get too old to play. Best remember what I tell visitors to my shop—that life and golf are both subject to change without notice."

"That's so true," Harvie agreed, striking a wistful tone. "Better come on home, son, before you reach the final clubhouse turn."

For the rest of the evening, I simply sat and soaked up this trio's delightful stories from their long journeys through an ancient game, thinking about my own bucket list. On the long drive home to Maine, in the spirit of Opti and John Derr, I decided I would call mine a "Range Bucket List" (RBL) and populate it with things I hoped to do in golf—maybe even including figuring out a way to eventually return to the place where my golfing life began.

═══ • ═══

Every golfer's Range Bucket List is different, of course—as individual as one's thumbprint or golf swing. That's part of an RBL's endless attraction. As one item is checked off the list, another may take its place. Some dream of playing the planet's top one hundred golf courses or participating in a pro-am with their favorite PGA Tour star. Others merely hope to someday shoot their age or win their club championship. Some—like me—to paraphrase Bobby Jones, simply wish to chase Old Man Par until our legs give out.

Since I'm the son of an incurable optimist who believed that golf provides the best opportunities for competitive fun and friendship in a complex world, I've always felt the game to be about its remarkable people, places, and traditions far more than a good score on the card.

I have an abiding passion for old clubhouses and vintage courses, as well as the deep friendships and diverse landscapes that have enriched my own peculiar golf IQ along with the game's incomparable history of colorful characters and assorted heroes and rogues, all linked by an incurable addiction to chasing a tiny ball all over God's green earth, discovering whatever adventure lies just around the next dogleg.

═══ • ═══

At the end of the day, when I look back on a deeply rewarding life in golf that I never expected to have, I can think of no other activity that has provided me more fun and friendship. Maybe it has for you, too. This book is about that, and maybe something more—the highlights of a grateful everyman's Range Bucket Lists past and present, peak experiences and favorite bits of golf lore, unforgettable characters and moments that made my travels through the game so fun and enriching, and even a few remaining "Things to Do in Golf" before reaching Harvie Ward's final clubhouse turn. In some ways, it's simply a universal tale about a kid whose wildest golf dreams, jotted down long ago in a small notebook, somehow came true, and a grown man's love letter to the finest game of all.

Above all, dear old John Derr was on to something when he declared that every true son or daughter of the game should keep a Range Bucket List, regardless of age, because such a list will keep its owner young in spirit and forever "on the right side of the sod," as he liked to say.

And Opti the Mystic was surely right when he pointed out that this splendid game ends far too soon but that it can take you far and bring you safely home again.

CHAPTER ONE

MEETING BOBBY JONES

In the spring of 1983, I didn't have a Range Bucket List—or even a golf game to speak of.

For six years I'd been a staff writer for the *Atlanta Journal-Constitution Sunday Magazine,* the oldest such magazine in the nation, chasing after New South con men and political empire builders by day and spending my nights in the company of police informants and repo kings in the hometown of Robert Tyre Jones.

Whenever my father was passing through Atlanta on business, he never failed to playfully remind me of what was missing from my life. "This is sacred ground, Bo—the city where Bobby Jones learned the game. When was the last time *you* played golf?"

I never managed a good answer. But he knew the truth anyway—that I was in a rush to be the next Bob Woodward or Carl Bernstein, ideally working at the same *Washington Post* where my father was working in the advertising department when I was born in 1953.

"I'll bring your clubs next time I'm in town," he offered more than once.

"Don't," I said. "They'll just remind me that I don't have time to play."

In some ways I felt exiled from the life I'd known before becoming an essayist and investigative reporter in the Gotham City of the South. Many nights I woke up with an oppressive weight in the center of my chest, sweating and panicked and gasping for breath, wondering if I might actually be dying. I'd just turned thirty years old.

Something had to give. Ironically, it did so a few days before I was scheduled fly to Washington, DC, for a long-hoped-for job interview with an editor at the *Post*. I was sitting in my office at the newspaper when a man named Tommy Barnes phoned me.

"You don't know me," Barnes said, "but I hear from our mutual friend Furman Bisher that you're a young fellow who loves golf." Furman Bisher was the legendary sports editor of the *Atlanta Journal-Constitution* and a North Carolinian who took me under his wing when I arrived on the same magazine where Margaret Mitchell and a who's who of fine southern authors had worked, still wide-eyed and wet behind the ears from my rookie year as a reporter and feature writer in Greensboro.

"That's true," I admitted. "But I don't get to play much anymore." *Or ever*, I came close to adding.

"Well," said Barnes, "I'm here to change that."

He asked me if I'd ever been out to East Lake Golf Club, the course where young Bobby Jones learned the game from Scotsman Stewart Maiden, and which was owned by the Atlanta Athletic Club. I'd passed the club's gates many times but had never been inside the grounds, an oasis of green surrounded by a tall chain-link fence topped with barbed wire, a golf course surrounded by a neighborhood principally known for a decaying federal housing project called East Lake Meadows, which was so violent that the beat cops called it "Little Vietnam."

"A man named Charlie Yates and I would like to buy you lunch and talk," Tommy explained. "We can even play a little golf."

"My clubs are back in North Carolina," I pointed out.

"Don't worry about clubs," he said. "We'll fix you up."

From Furman Bisher I learned that Barnes and Yates were Georgia golf legends. Barnes was a former Georgia Tech star, Southern Amateur champ, and multiple Georgia state champion; Yates was the elegant patriarch of a distinguished golfing clan, a major patron of the arts, and a lynchpin of Atlanta's philanthropic community. He was perhaps Bobby Jones's closest boyhood friend, a man who as a kid crawled under the East Lake fence just to watch his older pal play.

Frankly, I was shocked to see how run-down East Lake's grand neo-Gothic clubhouse was on the cool spring afternoon I arrived inside the fenced perimeter. Almost nobody was around. Part of the building was actually boarded up, and the golf course appeared to my eye to be in equally poor condition.

My gracious hosts explained that East Lake was in a life-and-death struggle and about to go on the auction block. The Atlanta Athletic Club had decided to sell the property and move to a much larger site in the northern suburbs. According to Yates, a man who owned a demolition and construction company hoped to buy East Lake and use it as a staging area for his dump trucks.

"Can you imagine that?" Barnes said, shaking his head. "This is sacred ground, the place that produced America's most important golfer."

Charlie Yates smiled and explained that that's why they had called me, hoping I might help spread the word and try to save East Lake from the wrecking ball.

I thought it was curious that Tommy Barnes used the same words as my father to talk about the hometown of Bobby Jones: "sacred ground." For that matter, Barnes even looked and acted like my dad, and could have been Opti the Mystic's long-lost brother.

The three of us ate sandwiches in the elegant but empty dining room, where, I noticed, the handsome wallpaper was starting to peel. Together Barnes and Yates outlined their plan to rally local civic and corporate support to save East Lake and their hope that I might, given my love for the game, be willing to write about their quest.

I told them I would happily help in any way and admitted that meeting Bobby Jones was a boyhood goal of mine that had failed to materialize. Jones died in 1971, the year I finished high school in Greensboro.

"Well, that's all going to change today," said Barnes. "You're going to meet Bobby Jones. His spirit is everywhere at East Lake."

They shared their memories of young Bobby Jones and Alexa Stirling and Perry Adair, the so-called Dixie Whiz Kids, who also grew up at East Lake and helped stoke the nation's early passion for the game through dozens of exhibitions around the country that attracted thousands of curious newcomers to the game. After lunch, Yates apologized for being unable to join us for golf, as he had an important doctor's appointment. But the unsinkable Tommy Barnes suggested we go tee it up and continue our conversation.

We had the course to ourselves, and it didn't really matter that I was using borrowed clubs. My game was beyond awful, rusted up like a bicycle left in the rain. But my upbeat host hardly seemed to notice or care, regaling me with more delightful stories that brought Bobby Jones alive and rekindled something that had lain dormant in me for far too long. Fortunately, we didn't even bother to keep score. Mine would have been an embarrassment.

As we walked back to the clubhouse terrace for a farewell beer, I actually apologized to my host for my game being in such woeful shape.

Barnes stopped me with a hand on my arm. "Let me tell you something, son. We've all been where you are. Bob Jones once told me something important: Golf will never forget you. It's never too late to begin again. The game will always be here waiting for you to come back. Your age or score are irrelevant. Mr. Jones genuinely believed that."

=== • ===

A few days later, I phoned my father from the outer office of Vice President George H. W. Bush, whom I'd dropped in to see after my big job interview at the *Post*, hoping to say hello. Bush and I had traveled extensively together during the primary season of the 1980 presidential campaign, from Iowa's frozen tundra to balmy Puerto Rico, having some great conversations about golf, family, Yale baseball, politics, and the state of Maine, his favorite getaway place.

Bush was traveling that day, but his outer-office secretary agreed to let me use her desk phone to call my dad back in Greensboro. Opti was his old self, eager to hear about my job interview and pleased to learn that it had seemingly gone well. The editor particularly liked my neo-Gothic tales of murder and political mayhem in the New South and said a job on the feature staff could be mine if I was willing to move right away. He pointed out that jobs at the *Washington Post* were precious and highly competitive. "Most reporters here will tell you that you'll need two things to succeed," he quipped. "A good literary agent to sell your stories to Hollywood, and a *great* personal therapist to help you handle the pressure." He advised me not to take too long deciding. I told him I needed a few weeks to think and thanked him for the opportunity.

"So what's up?" Opti asked, always able to read my moods, even across time and distance.

"I'm not sure I want the job," I admitted. Truthfully, I was embarrassed to say this, thinking my father might be disappointed in me.

"I have an idea," he suggested lightly. "Why don't you change your flight and stop off in Raleigh on your way home to Atlanta?"

I agreed to do so, and asked why.

"Because I want to take you somewhere you always loved. It may help."

═══ • ═══

The next afternoon he picked me up at Raleigh's airport and we drove to Pinehurst. My Haig Ultra golf clubs were in his trunk.

He'd secured us a tee time on No. 2. We played with a friendly older couple, the Rizzos, from New Jersey. Seeing Pinehurst had long been on Herb Rizzo's list of things to do in golf.

Opti played his usual chip-and-run game and shot in the high 80s. I played miserably and barely broke 100.

We didn't speak at all about my sudden quarter-life career crisis during the round but simply enjoyed chatting with the Rizzos about their grown grandchildren and other friendly matters until we reached the safety of the Donald Ross Porch for a parting beer, at which point the truth came tumbling out of me.

I confided—and these are my exact words—that I was "sick of being a writer trafficking in the tragedies of others" and feared that going to the *Post* or any other big-city newspaper would mean more of the same, turning me into a cynical cuss, or something even darker. I recounted sharing a drink during the 1980 presidential campaign with celebrated columnist Jack Germond of the *Baltimore Sun* at which he poked a blunt finger in my face and growled, "Here's some good career advice for you, kid. Get out of this racket while you still can, or risk becoming me!" We'd both laughed and ordered another round of Scotch whiskeys. I didn't have to wonder what he meant. Finally, I admitted how my chest hurt at night and that I thought I might be dying.

My father calmly listened, drinking his beer and managing not to laugh at my Hamletian angst. He knew what was really bothering me, even if I didn't. During my junior year of college, the girl I'd loved since I was fourteen and dated through high school before each going off to separate colleges was murdered by a fifteen-year-old kid during a botched holdup at a country club in the western hill country of North Carolina where she worked as the weekend hostess. Her violent and incomprehensible death—which made sensational news across North Carolina—had effectively ended my youth and shaken every faith I had grown up believing in, including—maybe especially—golf. Part of the allure of accepting the job at the Sunday magazine in Atlanta, though it took me years to actually realize this, was a subliminal desire to investigate the darkest corners of the human psyche.

It's amazing how many stories I ended up writing about young women who found their way to the "Sodom of the South" only to lose their lives. Repo kings, discredited politicians, and Alabama Klansmen were a close second. Save for my travels with George H. W. Bush and the mostly black baseball team I coached to the Midtown city championship (twice), mine was a personal odyssey through the heart of New South darkness. Bobby Jones belonged to another time, another life.

"To begin with, sport, you're not dying," Opti quietly reassured me. "But here's what I think might be the problem: maybe you're just writing about the wrong things."

I think I laughed. He sipped his beer.

"You're a storyteller," he added. "A pretty promising one, in fact. But maybe you should write about things you love instead of things you don't."

This was vintage Opti. The principle of creating joy, the power of positive thinking and living, ruled his life; it was a gift that would take me years to fully appreciate and begin to emulate. I remember gazing out at the famous golf course where so many giants had stridden to fame and glory, a place where my own modest start in the game came at age thirteen. Ross's No. 2 was a beautiful sight under the long afternoon shadows. "I love golf," I heard myself say. "But clearly I can barely even play it anymore."

"You might be surprised how quickly it will come back to you. Once you learn, you never forget."

This struck a familiar chord. I told Opti about a man I'd recently met in Atlanta who told me pretty much the same thing. "He said golf will never forget you—that the game is always waiting for you to come back and begin again."

Opti smiled. "Smart fellow."

I told him more about my afternoon with Tommy Barnes and Charlie Yates at East Lake Golf Club, about their personal quest to save Jones's birthing ground from destruction, and how through them I felt that I'd finally "met" Bobby Jones by walking East Lake's hallowed ground with a man who dearly loved it. Indeed, I was almost finished writing a story about their efforts and hoped it might help the cause in some small way. It would turn out to be my final story for the magazine.

Opti smiled. "Good for you. Maybe you should write about golf. Who knows? You could become America's answer to Henry Longhurst."

This was an old joke between us. The spring after graduating from East Carolina University in late 1975 I went home, hoping to snag a job with my hometown *Greensboro News & Record*, and ventured out to sign up to caddy at the Greater Greensboro Open the last year the venerable tournament was held at Sedgefield Country Club. I wound up caddying in the celebrity pro-am for a tubby TV comedian who never hit a fairway and cracked up the galleries by inviting the prettiest girl on the green to pull his finger and surprising each startled victim with a courtly kiss to the hand. On the final hole, however, my jolly client let loose a loud fart that made the gallery roar with laughter, completing my humiliation. To make matters worse, he handed me a two-dollar tip and advised me not to spend it all in one place.

But I did just that by making straight for the bar in the stately Sedgefield Inn, where I ordered a Miller High Life and saw an older man nursing a drink in the corner shadows. "Young man," growled a cultured English voice that I instantly recognized, "you look as terrible as I feel upon rising most mornings nowadays."

It was Henry Longhurst himself, my favorite golf writer. I couldn't believe my good fortune. Two volumes of his collected golf columns from the *Sunday Times* of London sat on my bedroom bookshelf. After I poured out my little tale of caddying woe—how my dismal afternoon had dashed my secret plan to try to spend a year caddying on the Tour before going off to graduate school—we chatted briefly about my hoped-for job at the newspaper until the great man finally rose and slowly made his way around the bar, pausing to place an avuncular hand on my shoulder. "Young man, I have just two things to say to you. First, it is never too late to ponder a career in the insurance racket. That way, you will have plenty of time to hone your game. More important, if you stick to the journalism racket and sadly someday find yourself writing about golf and having to eat your words, as I have done for nigh on half a century, I promise that you shall never meet a collection of more glorious rogues, liars, and flat-out thieves—plus the occasional truly inspiring hero—than in the wide world of golf. Of that you can be *supremely* assured."

With that, Henry Longhurst lifted his hand and was gone. That spring of 1976, I learned years later from John Derr, was the last time Longhurst anchored his famous post at Augusta's sixteenth green for CBS. He retired after that season and passed away just two years later.

"He probably would find that funny," I conceded, adding that I would *love* to write about golf. Unfortunately, I didn't know a soul in the golf-writing world and might just as easily decide I wanted to be a NASA astronaut.

Predictably, Opti nodded and smiled.

"For what it's worth—and laugh if you must—I've found that if you tell the universe what's honestly in your heart, you may be surprised by what happens. That probably sounds a bit corny to you."

I looked at my funny, philosophical father, grayer than I remembered but still up to his old Socratic tricks, and mused for the second time in as many weeks that he and Tommy Barnes could have been brothers of the sod. I later realized that they were, in fact, exactly the same age—sixty-three, the age I am as I write this. In any case, it did sound rather corny to me, a young man under the influence of dark ambition gone awry.

"It couldn't possibly be as simple as that," I said.

Opti shrugged and finished his beer. I suddenly felt thirteen years old again.

"Don't take my word for it," he said. "You're the one who just met Bobby Jones. You might be surprised how far writing about something you love can take you. Especially when that thing is golf."

CHAPTER TWO

DRIVING MISS GLENNA

S o I did.

Not long after I wrote that final small piece for the *Atlanta Journal-Constitution Sunday Magazine*, I took my old man's *and* Bobby Jones's advice, politely withdrew my name from consideration in Washington, and went to work instead for *Yankee Magazine*, becoming the first southerner and senior writer in that iconic magazine's seventy-five-year history.

Smartest career move I ever made. Even smarter life move.

For starters, that next November I found a small cabin heated by a woodstove on the banks of the winding Green River just southwest of Brattleboro, Vermont, where I adopted a yellow pup from the Windham County Humane Society, purchased a second-hand L.L.Bean fly rod, and took a few rudimentary casting lessons from a crusty retired Presbyterian minister I nicknamed Saint Cecil, a terrible golfer and a living terror upon the local trout population. When Saint Cecil informed me that Rudyard Kipling had played Brattleboro's nine-hole golf course while finishing work on his *Just So Stories*, I showed up there and began beating years of accumulated rust off my game just as the first snowflakes fell. By Christmas, heating my tiny cabin with hardwood I split myself, crunching over snow-covered roads with my dog in the blue winter dusk, sleeping beneath quilts of glittering northern stars, I realized that my racing pulse had slowed and that the oppressive weight had disappeared from the center of my chest. I felt completely alive again. Even reborn. The people at *Yankee* were the best colleagues ever, and I was suddenly writing stories that were meaningful and life-affirming.

The northern New England spring—all three days of it—found *Yankee*'s senior editor Tim Clark and me chasing golf balls over a wonderful public course called Bretwood, just north of Keene, New Hampshire. I was in possession of a new secondhand set of Hogan clubs and a fierce hunger to get my game back in shape.

One crisp morning in late autumn, a beautiful young woman wearing scuffed saddle shoes brought me my office mail. She was Alison, a recent Radcliffe graduate and one of the magazine's talented winter interns. She laughed when I commented that I liked her shoes because they resembled golf shoes and made me want to drop everything and hop a plane to Scotland.

"My family is Scottish," she said, but I thought she was joking.

A year later, we got married in an old church on the North Shore of Boston, with a bagpiper playing "Scotland the Brave."

Hurricane David had brushed the New England coast earlier that week, flooding the salt marsh in the coastal village of Essex, Massachusetts, where we shared a modest, weathered cottage with a golden retriever and two barn cats brought from Alison's family's sprawling farm in the highlands of central Maine. Her folks were indeed proud Scots, a stern superintendent of local schools named Kathleen and her brilliant, globe-trotting scientist husband, Sam. I was relieved that Sam seemed to like me straightaway, perhaps because he'd spent a great deal of time living in the South. But I wasn't at all sure Kathleen Bennie—"Mum," as everyone in tiny Harmony, Maine, where Alison grew up, called her—approved of her younger daughter's choice of husband.

On the Friday before our wedding, in any case, the weather suddenly cleared and grew bracingly cool, and Opti and I managed to slip off with my fiancée's younger brother, Ian, to play a quick nine holes at the modest Cape Ann Golf Course on the coast road between Essex and Ipswich. It was the first round my father and I had played since the fateful Pinehurst conversation that changed my life. Upon learning that I worked for *Yankee*, the man who owned the course informed us that writer John Updike had revived his game at the humble little nine-hole course, though he was now a member at Myopia Hunt Club in nearby Hamilton and seldom returned to Cape Ann.

We didn't bother keeping score that afternoon. We just hit shots and talked our way around the course. Opti looked happy but a little tired to me, his hair a little thinner and grayer. When I privately commented on this fact, he shrugged it off but casually mentioned that he was scheduled to have a "small prostate trim" upon returning to North Carolina. He assured me it was nothing to be concerned about and insisted that we concentrate on the wedding. Several of my old golf pals had flown up from Carolina, and a number of Alison's college friends and Scottish family members had come to help us celebrate in true Hibernian style.

The rowdy reception was held in our yard overlooking the vast salt marsh and Choate Island. The October evening was mild and the dance floor sank in the mud, but the highland reels and Dixieland blues went on until well after midnight. At one point late in the festivities my father and I found ourselves standing together on a darkened deck overlooking the marsh beneath a moon that hung like a theatrical prop in the sky, good French brandies in hand. I thanked him for giving me such good advice that afternoon at Pinehurst, and the courage to follow my heart rather than my head. "Among other things, my golf game has returned," I added.

"And you have the most beautiful bride in America tonight," he pointed out, a tad tipsy but clearly elated. "Even better, she's promised me a dance."

"I sometimes think none of this would have happened if we hadn't gone to Pinehurst," I said.

He sipped his brandy. "Oh, I don't know. You just needed a little friendly nudge from Bobby Jones and me."

He asked if I'd ever heard from Tommy Barnes again. I was happy to tell him that Barnes and Yates had successfully put together a coalition of Atlanta business interests that had saved East Lake from the wrecking ball. An ambitious development plan was in the works to restore the course and clubhouse, and maybe even expand the restoration fever to the surrounding neighborhood. Atlanta developer Tom Cousins was interested in a much broader concept to restore East Lake and its environs.

"That must make you feel good," he said.

"You have no idea," I replied.

But my dad's "small prostate trim" was weighing on my mind that night. "I've been thinking," I said, with this worry in mind. "Maybe we should take that trip to England and Scotland. The one we've always talked about taking."

He looked at me and smiled. "We'll do that someday soon. Now let me go dance with your bride before the band quits."

═══ • ═══

As my second New England summer dawned, Tim Clark stepped into my office at *Yankee* waving an item clipped from the *Providence Journal*.

"You're a student of golf history," he said. "Ever heard of a lady named Glenna Collett Vare?"

"Sure. They called her the female Bobby Jones because she won five or six US Women's Amateur Championships." I pointed out that the LPGA's Vare Trophy, for the lowest scoring average, was named for her, adding, "I think she died not long ago."

Tim smiled. "Guess someone forgot to tell her. According to this, Glenna Vare is about to play in her sixty-second-straight Point Judith Invitational down in Rhode Island. She's eighty-three and still has a fifteen handicap. Thought you might like to mosey down and see if she'd let you caddie for her. Could be a fun story, right up your fairway."

A few days later, I parked in front of a rambling shingled mansion overlooking a sunlit Narragansett Bay and knocked on the screen door.

A husky, no-nonsense voice commanded me to enter. I did so and found a stocky, deeply tanned elderly woman standing dangerously on the highest step of a very tall wooden stepladder. She was thumping the business end of a vintage wooden "spoon" (fairway club) against the ceiling. She glanced down at me and demanded, "Young man, have you ever had raccoon piddle in your rafters?"

"Not lately," I admitted truthfully.

"Well, come up this ladder and thump the ceiling until the critter man gets here."

Miss Glenna came down, and I went up as instructed and took over the thumping. Miss Glenna left me alone in the room.

A little while later, the critter man showed up and I came down, placing the spoon back in an umbrella rack beside the front door that contained a number of clubs from a faraway era. On the nearby foyer table sat a beautiful bronze statue of a woman dressed fashionably in late-1920s style, cloche and all, making a beautiful, compact swing: Miss Glenna Collett in her prime, frozen in time. I wandered off after my elusive subject, passed by a young maid who was busy thumping a hallway molding with her broom, and eventually found Miss Glenna standing in her kitchen, violently chopping up carrots.

She gave me a hard look with deep sea-blue eyes.

"The critter man just arrived," I explained.

"Good. Do you know how to use a knife without fatally injuring yourself?"

"Yes, ma'am." I explained that I was an Eagle Scout.

Unimpressed, she handed me the large knife. "Splendid. Finish cutting up these carrots and onions, dear, and place them in the soup pot. You can do the celery next."

Then she disappeared again. I seemed to be chasing one of golf's greatest if slightly forgotten legends through her own house.

A little while later she came back to inspect my work. "I'm trying a new tomato vegetable recipe from a friend in Jupiter Island," she explained. "I have friends coming tomorrow for lunch."

Somewhere there is a wing of the Golf Journalism Hall of Fame dedicated to stupid opening questions. I was about to make the first of my many contributions. Out of the blue I said, "I was hoping I could ask you a few questions about golf. Do you remember the first ball you ever hit?"

"Of course I don't," she snapped. "Do *you*?" Before I could reply, she added with testy vigor, "Listen here, young man: I don't like to talk about golf. I have a terrible memory, and everything I did was so very long ago. Besides, nobody remembers who I am, or really should anymore. If you want to know something about me, I suppose there are dusty history books that can tell you what you need to know. Don't waste your time and mine."

That, I decided, was that. I was about to be dismissed completely, or sent back to help with the raccoon piddle.

But Glenna Collett Vare was full of surprises. She left the room but reappeared a few minutes later, frowning at me.

"You'd better come along with me to the porch."

I followed, and we sat in large wicker chairs on her sunny veranda overlooking the ocean and a blue horizon set on infinity. Red geraniums blazed in pots. A maid brought us glasses of cold, tart lemonade.

"Tell me about yourself," she insisted, sounding like a grand dame from an Edith Wharton tale, chastely sipping her refreshment.

I told her I hailed from North Carolina, had been married for eight months, and had just moved to a small coastal town in Maine.

Miss Glenna's broad, freckled face softened. She asked where in North Carolina.

"Greensboro. But I grew up playing golf in Southern Pines and Pinehurst."

"I won a tournament once at Pine Needles. Can't recall its name. I even sold real estate there for Mr. Ross and his friends for a time. You must know Mrs. Peggy Bell and her family."

I'd met Peggy Kirk Bell, I replied, though she wouldn't know me. Mrs. Bell was a Sandhills legend, after all, a pioneering teacher and pal of Babe Zaharias who helped establish the LPGA Tour in the early 1950s. The Bell family owned the cozy Pine Needles Resort and had recently acquired its sister property, Mid Pines Hotel, along with its historic Donald Ross golf course, just across Midland Road in the Pines, my golfing ground zero.

"I assume you play?" Miss Glenna asked.

I told her I was a ten handicap on a good day, even better with the moon in the right phase when using a lucky number 3 Titleist ball and wearing my favorite white polo shirt and khakis. "But I'm not superstitious or anything," I joked.

Miss Glenna didn't seem to get my prod. I knew that during her salad days, Glenna Collett was so superstitious about golf that she wore the same clothes anytime she was near the lead of a tournament and often pocketed four-leaf clovers she found on the course for additional good luck.

"I suppose I'm about a fifteen now," she said, sounding wistful.

I decided this was my opening—also known as my second big mistake.

"I'd love to see you play," I said. "In fact, I just read in the paper that you're playing in the Point Judith Invitational next week. It would be my honor to caddie for you."

She shook her head, sipping her lemonade. "Don't be ridiculous. No one should have to see my golf swing now."

A silence fell between us. Out in Narragansett Bay, a huge sailboat was heading for open water. I'd had easier times with indicted politicians and murder suspects. Miss Glenna was one hard nut to crack. But I'd come too far, in more ways than one, to give up now.

Braving her further wrath, I inquired whether I might at least come out and follow her around the Point Judith links—though mostly just to view the golf course. Having grown up in the Donald Ross Fertile Crescent of North Carolina, I explained, I'd recently made up my mind to try to play every Ross course in America, or at least in my home state. Point Judith was one of Donald's oldest, dating back to 1894, just before his first work at Pinehurst.

"Absolutely not. I forbid it."

We sat for a moment more. Miss Glenna clearly wasn't going to yield to my raccoon-rattling, veggie-chopping southern charm. But I tried one final gambit.

"I read somewhere that you drove your family car at age ten."

She sighed and gave me a lengthy, stern look. "If you are determined to do this, let's at least make an agreement," she said.

"Yes, ma'am?"

Miss Glenna offered her terms. If I agreed *not* to show up at Point Judith, she would agree to be interviewed for a story in *Yankee*—but only because she loved the magazine. If I wished to see Point Judith for myself, she would arrange for me to go there and play at some later date.

"One more thing. Do *not*, under any circumstances, mention that you found me on top of that stepladder when you came in. My son, Neddy, will have my head about that. He's always going on about me falling. You must change that or leave it out altogether. Agreed?"

I consented to that, too. Invisible fingers crossed.

Miss Glenna sighed, settling back in her chair. "Very well; ask your questions. I shall tell you whatever I'm able to remember, which I promise won't be much."

=== • ===

By age twelve, young Glenna Collett was playing baseball with the boys of East Providence and had already won several junior tennis tournaments at the Metacomet Country Club, where her family belonged, home to its own Donald Ross gem. About this same time, she took in her first golf exhibition featuring three teenage stars named Alexa Stirling, Perry Adair, and Bobby Jones, East Lake's Dixie Whiz Kids.

One summer day when she was thirteen, her father, George, a wealthy industrialist, invited a couple of his cronies to watch his willowy daughter hit a golf ball from the first tee. Glenna might have weighed seventy pounds. She slugged her ball well over one hundred yards down the fairway.

One of the men reportedly whistled. "George, that girl should play competitive golf," he remarked.

"Don't try to stop her," agreed George Collett.

The next spring, Collett took his daughter to see Alex Smith, the Scottish teaching pro who had twice won the US Open. "Alex was a real go-getter," Glenna remembered. "He insisted that I practice all the time. Without him, I might not have gone very far at all."

But go far she did, and fast.

In 1922, at just nineteen years old, Glenna won the US Women's

Amateur Championship at White Sulphur Springs, West Virginia. It was a watershed year in golf. Brash Gene Sarazen, just one year Glenna's senior, won both the US Open and PGA Championship, the first man to win both in the same year; and flashy Walter Hagen popularized the use of a wooden golf tee by winning the first of his four British Opens at Royal St Georges, Sandwich. The first Walker Cup matches were also played at the National Golf Links of America, pitting the finest amateur players of Great Britain and America, won by the Americans in a romp, 8 to 4. The formidable squad was led by Bobby Jones, Chick Evans, and that year's US Amateur champion, Jess Sweetser.

The sporting press, however, was equally taken with young Glenna Collett, the slim and politely restrained young woman with the simple, compact swing who could drive a golf ball farther than most male club champions. They hungered to know every detail about the engaging schoolgirl from East Providence, discovering the curious fact she was so superstitious that she wore the same ensemble anytime she was near the lead—the same deep red fingernail polish, too.

In 1924, Miss Collett played in sixty golf matches and won fifty-nine of them, most by wide margins. The next year she fulfilled an important criterion of greatness by winning the Women's Amateur for a second time, at St. Louis. Over the next five years she nailed down three more national championships and developed a passionate international following thanks to her celebrated matches against Britain's finest female champion, Joyce Wethered. Glenna was invited to write about their friendship and spirited rivalry for the *Saturday Evening Post* and *Liberty Magazine* and did so charmingly, becoming a groundbreaking advocate for women in sports in the process. Someone in the national press began calling her "the female Bobby Jones." The nickname stuck.

In 1931, she married Edwin Vare, a wealthy Philadelphia businessman, and played less competitive golf as she developed a keen interest in trapshooting and bridge, becoming nationally respected at both. She took up needlepoint and had two children, a boy and girl, Neddy and Glenna.

But golf, as Tommy Barnes liked to say, never forgets you and is always waiting for your return. In 1935, the female Bobby Jones mounted a historic comeback. At Interlachen, in Minneapolis, where Jones won his final US Open in 1930, the third leg of his grand slam, Glenna was matched against a popular hometown girl named Patricia Jane Berg in the final. Glenna was old guard; Patty was part of a new breed of young women who saw golf as another barrier just waiting to be demolished. Along with Babe Zaharias, Louise Suggs, and a friendly young woman from middle Ohio named Peggy Ann Kirk, Berg would play a pivotal role in forming the Ladies Professional Golf Association fifteen years later, rewriting the record books in the process.

An estimated 6,500 fans swarmed after the pair at Interlachen. On the thirty-fourth hole of their match, Glenna dropped a heart-stopping putt to salvage par, capturing the championship for a record sixth time.

Modest and restrained to the end, she thanked the fans and the press for their support and quietly slipped back to her very private Philadelphia life, making far fewer public appearances as the decades progressed, becoming all but invisible.

"I couldn't wait to get back to bridge and shooting," she confided.

— • —

Miss Glenna was sitting so still with the sun on her face that I wondered if perhaps the woman who felt she had outlived her own history had fallen asleep. Immortals must dream, too. But suddenly her sea-blue eyes fluttered open. She glared at her wristwatch.

"Oh my goodness. We must get Jimmy!"

She invited me to come along. Actually, she ordered me to come along.

Jimmy, it emerged, was her closest companion since Edwin's death ten years earlier—a small beige Norwich terrier who was being groomed at a local pet shop. As her Cadillac Fleetwood gunned out of the driveway, causing the driver of a service van to swerve and lay on the horn, Miss Glenna explained that she preferred driving up the entire East Coast from her winter home in Delray Beach, Florida, every spring, rather than flying. Her daughter, Glenny, who resided in Venezuela, worried about her mother making such a long drive alone. "My eyes aren't so great anymore," Miss Glenna sniffed, bumping over the raised median to get around a station wagon turning left into Narragansett's sluggish noon traffic. "But I love driving and hate flying. Jimmy would hate it, too," she added. "He loves to sit by the car window and watch the world whiz by."

If the golf world at large had basically whizzed past the female Bobby Jones, Miss Glenna Vare—for the moment, at least—didn't appear to care all that much. "It's been ages since a reporter called me," she confided as we rode along. "They used to call just to ask what Bobby Jones was really like, and other silly questions. Mr. Jones was very courtly, I told them, a true southern gentleman. And, like his good friend Jess Sweetser, quite a handsome fellow!"

She asked if I'd ever met Bobby Jones.

"In a way," I said, telling her about the unexpected afternoon at East Lake that sent me to live in rural New England. I also told her about the fateful conversation with my father on the Donald Ross Porch at Pinehurst that had led me to her doorstep.

She smiled. "So I have your father to blame for your being such a nuisance."

"Yes, ma'am. Just me and the raccoon in your attic." I told her my nickname for my old man, and why.

"You're lucky to have a father like that," she said. "Everything in this life is connected, you know. Just like a round of golf, you'll find in time, it's all one big circle. We end up where we started. I forget who said that."

I knew a couple of variations on the quote, and shouldn't have been surprised that Miss Glenna had her own. Her house was filled with books. But I didn't dare suggest either Thoreau or Eliot's *Four Quartets* lest she stop and put me out on the street.

"You sound like Opti the Mystic," I remarked.

She simply smiled.

Fortunately, Miss Glenna suggested that I drive the car home from the groomer's. Soon Jimmy was sitting on the seat between us with a nice blue bow in his hair. He hopped into his owner's lap and poked his head out her open window. As she stroked his head, Miss Glenna told me about how she and Edwin purchased their big shingled home above Narragansett Bay just weeks before the historic hurricane of 1938 struck Rhode Island's coast a direct blow. Edwin was playing backgammon down at the Dunes Club that evening, she remembered. "He left the club just before the storm hit and drove home to Providence. Otherwise he would have been gone. The club was washed completely out to sea. So was most of our house."

The Great New England Hurricane of 1938—sometimes called "The Wind That Shook the World"—struck without warning on the evening of September 21, a category-3 sea monster with winds topping 120 mph that produced a seventeen-foot storm surge that flooded the streets of Providence, killing seven hundred people and injuring five thousand more and destroying more than nine thousand homes and businesses in its path, leaving sixty-three thousand homeless and doing $51 billion (present-day dollars) worth of damage, the most destructive storm to strike the region during the twentieth century.

"That seems so long ago . . ." Miss Glenna said, her voice trailing off as we sat down together again on her porch to have lunch. Jimmy went off to make his inspection of the premises, and the maid brought us bowls of newly made tomato vegetable soup. The critter man and the girl who was thumping walls were gone. The house had grown peaceful and silent. I imagined the raccoons were finally getting some rest.

"How's the soup?" Miss Glenna demanded, brightening.

"Excellent," I said. "You do good work."

"You helped," she said, taking a cautious sip.

There was no more discussion of her illustrious golf past—at least, not that day. The subject, I sensed, was either too painful or too familiar, like a once-beautiful yard overgrown with weeds. Instead, over the next hour or so, we talked about the sailboat races she could watch from her porch and my recent nuptials.

Days later, I risked her wrath and sneaked out to watch Glenna Vare play in the Point Judith Invitational. It was a cool, misty morning, and I was careful to stay out of her line of sight, following just close enough to see that famous, compact swing. Miss Glenna was dressed head to foot in cheerful bright yellow, a human canary in the Narragansett mist. A small group of locals followed her, including a Newport insurance man who told me he'd once caddied for her in the US Women's Amateur. "I was fifteen. She was amazing. She tipped me twenty dollars, if you can believe it." After a few holes I peeled off the course and drove home to Maine. My last view of the female Bobby Jones at play was as she struck a fine fairway wood and marched up a long hill after her ball like a yellow bird vanishing in the sea mist.

═ • ═

Weeks after my story about making soup with Glenna Vare appeared in *Yankee*, Bob Sommers from the USGA's *Golf Journal* tracked me down to see if he could purchase the profile for his magazine. "I don't think any of us realized Glenna Vare was still alive," he admitted sheepishly.

But that was only the beginning. Something happened that I still marvel over today. Corny as it sounds, it was proof of Opti's universe at work.

After the Miss Glenna piece appeared in *Golf Journal*, an editor for Britain's largest golf publication phoned to ask if he could purchase the story as well. By this point I'd also been contacted by an editor named David Earl, who wondered if I would be interested in writing for *Golf* magazine. He sent me down to Sea Island, Georgia, to spend time with Davis Love Jr. and his son Davis III, a fellow Carolinian and promising young player who'd just completed his rookie year on PGA Tour. After that story appeared, the Duke of Earl—as a small group of budding golf writers David nurtured took to calling him—proposed that I take on writing *Golf*'s Tour profiles and essays, which I was thrilled to do.

Equally meaningful to me, I saw Miss Glenna Vare every year upon her return to Narragansett until her death in 1989. She took me to lunch at her club and always made me drive us there in her big Cadillac. As good as her word, she also arranged for me to play both Point Judith and Metacomet Country Club with members who knew their lore and histories, feeding my growing passion for golf-course architecture. The last time I went to see Miss Glenna was in October 1988, when she agreed to allow me to do a follow-up conversation with her for *Golf*.

Once again, this time in early autumn, we sat together on her sun-splashed veranda watching sailboats cross the bay, catching up like old friends do. I got the impression that she was secretly pleased that she hadn't outlived her own glorious history, and that her excellent soup-making had brought me to her doorstep. She never let me leave without a gift of some kind. Over the years these gifts had included a program from an early women's tournament in Southern

Pines; an excellent instruction guide written by her son, Ned; and potted Martha Washington geraniums for my pregnant wife.

During all our time together, though, I never worked up the courage to admit that I'd sneaked out to briefly watch her play that day in the sea mist at Point Judith.

I did, however, thank her for what she had done for me—opening an unexpected second door to the world of golf writing.

She patted my hand like an approving great aunt. "I think you are a good writer," she said, "and an excellent driver. That combination ought to take you wherever you wish to go."

Miss Glenna never saw our conversation in print. She passed away the day after my birthday the following February, just days after my only daughter, Maggie, was born on a snowy morning in Maine, just hours before our conversation about her historic career reached the newsstand.

CHAPTER THREE

THE ART OF GRONKLE

My first glimpse of John Updike came at church. The Molière of America's suburbs often sat near my wife and me in a middle left-hand pew at the eight o'clock service at St. John's Episcopal Church in Beverly Farms, Massachusetts, Rabbit Angstrom in the flesh, sometimes gazing thoughtfully and unnervingly over at us—newcomers in the church where we'd just been married—with a bemused expression on his pale, beaky face.

Updike later told me—his words—that he was simply admiring my bride's beauty and envying our "unmolested youth"; that seeing us reminded him of the early days of his own marriage and struggling writing life. For what it's worth, my favorite Updike novel is *Marry Me*, a tender tale that evolved out of those years living on the coast of Cape Ann.

In any case, we spoke for the first time at one of the coffee hours following a late-autumn morning service. Rector Jim Purdy had evidently told him I was a writer for *Yankee* and a new contributor to *Golf* magazine. The courtly Mr. Updike sidled over and pleasantly remarked that he thought I might have the perfect job, roaming New England for a great magazine but also writing about his favorite game, which prompted me to inquire if it was true that he once played the Cape Ann Golf Course on the coast road between Essex and Ipswich, a mere driver and seven-iron combo from our cottage on Island Road. "It's true," he confirmed. "That's where I played when we first moved to the North Shore. My game was pretty bad in those days, but I loved playing that little course. Sometimes I miss those days." Then, almost as an afterthought, he added, "You'll have to come over and play sometime at Myopia."

I thanked him, hoping this might happen, though I assumed he was just being polite to a fellow parishioner over coffee. Unfortunately, I didn't see Updike at church again until the end of the following summer. That year he won the National Book Award and a second Pulitzer Prize, and was reportedly traveling abroad. Though I feared golf with Rabbit Angstrom was probably a missed opportunity, I spent the summer rereading his Rabbit books, happy that I'd had a passing acquaintance with one of my literary heroes. Then one morning in late October, he was at coffee hour after the early-morning service and reminded me that we'd never had our golf date.

"Say, do you think you could play next Thursday afternoon?" he wondered. "The course is scheduled to close in a week or so, but I'm sure I can rustle up a couple of my regulars, if you don't mind the cold." I assured him this wouldn't be a problem, excited at the prospect of getting to play Myopia in the bargain, a top-one-hundred layout designed by amateur architect Herbert Leeds in the same spirit that created Hugh Wilson's Merion and Henry Fownes's Oakmont. Myopia had hosted four US Opens between 1898 and 1908, two of them won by Willie Anderson.

"Very good," Updike said. "We'll have lunch and then a little gronkle."

"Gronkle?" I wondered if that might be some unique home-grown game played only by the Yankee bluebloods at Myopia.

"That's from Shakespeare—my word for bad but enjoyable golf."

A few days later, however, my new friend phoned to let me know his mother had passed away and he needed to postpone our round. "The club is closing, so let's try again when it reopens in the spring," he suggested.

When cold and rainy April appeared once more on the calendar, a postcard arrived from the Arnold Palmer of American letters, proposing that we meet at Myopia in two weeks' time. By then, however, my pregnant wife and I had moved to Maine and the card had been forwarded, arriving just four days before the proposed meeting.

I showed up at Myopia just before noon, straight from my first working trip to the 1990 Masters. Unfortunately, my golf clubs failed to make the flight back to Boston, putting me in something of a panic until I discovered my wife's new (and rarely played) Lady Tiara clubs in the trunk of my car.

I hoped my host would at the least appreciate the amusing irony of this development, especially after I explained to him that my best-ever round happened with a borrowed set of women's clubs on a challenging golf course down in Rhode Island not long after I moved to New England. A friend's wife loaned me her Patty Berg model irons and woods one early spring afternoon at Quanset Point, and I somehow broke 70 for the first time, scoring a 68 that could easily have been a few strokes better if I'd had my trusty Zebra putter. It was an unexpected gift from the golf gods.

As I raced north from Logan Airport to horsey Hamilton, I told myself that maybe this kind of magic could happen a second time; at the very least, I hoped I wouldn't embarrass myself and prompt my host to regret his invitation.

Silly me. It was far worse than that.

To begin with, the day was classic springtime in northern New England, meaning miserably cold and misty, which perhaps explained why Myopia Hunt Club was shuttered up like a Whitney estate about to be auctioned off by Christie's when I splashed into the empty parking lot just before noon. Nary a human was in sight, though a lone chestnut horse hung his curious head over the paddock fence, so I walked over to commiserate with Old Dobbin, wondering if I'd managed to get the day wrong. Just then a gray Ford Taurus wheeled into the parking lot, and John Updike hopped out dressed in baggy green cargo pants, a camel sweater, and a moss-green turtleneck; he opened his trunk, hoisted a small carry bag, and strode toward me smiling and apologizing for being late while pulling on a white bucket hat. He explained that the two buddies he hoped might join us were sadly scratches. One had yet to return from Florida, and the other was down with a nasty spring head cold.

"I'm fighting off one myself," Updike admitted, blowing his nose as he glanced around the vacant premises, looking surprised. "Oh my. I guess the club doesn't actually open until *next* week. But let's muddle along, just the two of us, shall we? There won't be any tee markers or flags out, but how bad could that be? It's April, and we're playing golf. Let's see how far we get."

We hoisted our bags and set off for the first tee, wherever it was. I saw him glance at my clubs and smile.

"They belong to my wife," I said, explaining how my fate happened to be in the hands of Lady Tiara. "My clubs are probably halfway to Bermuda by now. I didn't want to postpone my chance to see Myopia. Besides, I'm already in the grip of Masters Fever."

"What's Masters Fever? I thought you were just in Augusta."

"I was indeed, on Wednesday and Thursday. But that was for work. That only made my Masters Fever worse."

It was now Friday of Masters week, and I was in the grip of a full-blown seasonal malady common to geographically displaced golf-mad southerners accustomed to the sight of green grass and blooming dogwoods and azaleas in early April. For those of us who lived in the Great Frozen North—defined more or less as anything above Fenway Park—Masters Fever reached its peak with the annual telecast of the Masters and was characterized by a frenzied desire to hit a golf ball off living grass after the long winter layoff.

Teeing up a high-optic yellow golf ball, my host laughed. He withdrew an old Lynx driver from his bag and began making stiff warm-up swings. "That's why I go to Florida for the winter," he explained, wondering what I did for the ailment when Masters Fever struck.

I told him about a private little ritual I'd developed during my first wintry spring in New England, inspired by a game I made up as a kid growing up in North Carolina called "Ace." The northern version of Ace involved placing a brand-new Titleist (ideally a lucky number 3) golf ball on anything resembling turf in front of my house and seeing if I could knock the ball safely over the roof with one cold swing using my sand wedge. In my preteen version I'd always used a Whiffle ball and pretended to be playing the famed No. 12 at Augusta National. Every time the ball cleared the roof of my parents' house, I scored an ace. In the Great Frozen North, however, the act was far more symbolic—a statement of personal meteorological defiance—with potentially grave consequences to an innocent house and domestic harmony.

Updike looked delighted by this peculiar ritual, wondering with a note of boyish glee if I'd ever shanked a ball into the house or maybe knocked out a picture window.

"Not yet," I said. "Luckily, I'm four for four in the northern version of Ace."

He was also curious if I'd ever scored a hole in one. I admitted that I had come close so many times that I'd basically given up, because every twenty handicapper I'd ever met had four or five aces under their belt. I was now a six handicap with no ace to show for my trouble—which was why, I added, I'd founded the Hole-in-None Society for long-suffering golfers like me.

"I wish I could join," he said almost wistfully.

"So you've gotten one?"

"Two, actually. But one happened when I was playing all by my-self in the twilight, hitting two practice balls. So I guess it doesn't count."

"We might be able to get you in under the rarely used grand-father clause that you didn't intend to make an ace and are genuinely sorry it happened. I'll take it up with the committee. Did you at least buy yourself a drink afterward?"

Updike smiled. "I did indeed. A nice ginger beer."

He invited me to play away, and I said it was my pleasure to follow him.

There was no flag in the distance, but my host took dead aim up the hill toward a spot where an actual green presumably lay. He made a firm cut, and the ball dribbled off thirty yards to the right, throwing up a rooster's tale of water before it vanished into thick tufted grass at the edge of the bare woods. Rabbit slid me a wry look.

"Mulligans for Masters Fever?"

"Absolutely," I agreed. "This is golf's spring training."

His next shot flew a couple hundred yards up the fairway, a sweet little fade that seemed to please him. My opening drive wound up just thirty yards below the green I hadn't known was there.

"Marvelous shot!" said Updike, replacing his bucket hat with a stocking cap as he set off up the hill at a surprisingly brisk pace. I almost had to run to keep up with him, in fact, as he explained: "My wife and I got to play only twice over the winter, so I know what you mean about Masters Fever. When you live in New England, you learn to cherish any golf day you get."

No moss grew under John Updike's FootJoys. He strode straight up to his ball, whipped out a mid-iron, and gave the ball a solid whack before I'd fully caught up. I saw his bright-yellow ball scamper onto the green, where there was no flag in the cup, or, really, no cup to speak of—only a ragged hole where someone perhaps had intended to place a cup or had taken one out. I aimed my ball at where I guessed the cup might be, were there a cup, and pitched my ball ten feet over the green, chipped back, and three-putted for a six, while my gracious partner made par.

"I'm afraid you're seeing Myopia in her winter underwear," Updike said as we stepped to the tee on the second hole, a soulful 485-yard par-five aptly named "Lookout," whose fairway was covered with practice balls. "Some of the members like to use this hole as their practice range in the winter."

He hooked his drive toward a clump of young saplings, and I faded mine deep into the golf ball graveyard. Unlike my host in his spikes, I had to wear my Topsiders, which slipped on the soggy turf about every fourth shot. Still, what a sight Myopia's pale-yellow clubhouse presented in the greening springtime gloom, glowing peacefully in a grove of ancient, just-budding oak trees, surrounded by century-old forests and white-fenced pastures just beginning to display shoots of tender green, all of it framed by majestic rolling hills.

As we searched for my ball, he told me about his start in the game.

"I was in my midtwenties. I'd just moved to New England from New York, and was trying to become a freelance writer. My former wife had an aunt, Dotty, who lived in Wellesley. Quite a faithful golfer, Aunt Dotty was. She took me out in the backyard and said, 'Oh, John. What a lovely natural swing you have.' Like a fool, I believed her. I started playing small public courses like Cape Ann and got hooked. For a while I thought I might even try to become a freelance golfer instead."

We never found my ball. So I dropped a new one and took a two-stroke penalty, hitting a decent three-iron shot my host praised lavishly, an ill-deserved courtesy he would keep up all afternoon.

We walked over to John's ball and he settled over it, mumbling, "So here goes another gronkle."

Ah, there was that word again. "Remind me about gronkles," I said.

Still over his ball, he aimed an amused eye at me. "You remember Shakespeare's *Two Gentlemen of Verona.* 'Why dost thou gronkle so much!' I think that was it. Or maybe it was *As You Like It.* In any case, a gronkle is when you hit it hard but the ball sputters miserably along the ground. It's the perfect name for what we're doing today—soggy spring golf in New England."

And with that, he struck a perfectly lovely fairway wood down the hill.

Updike's swing featured an unconventionally deep bend of his left knee, but at age fifty-eight he also exhibited the general suppleness any man my age would envy. As a fine shot left his club, I supportively quipped, "No gronkle that; perhaps more of a Stadler."

Rabbit grinned, clearly pleased. "I'll show you gronkles aplenty yet, young blood."

I frankly hadn't expected my host to be so fun-loving and amusing, a man who clearly relished the fellowship and sweet unpredictability of the game. In other words, my kind of guy. So onward we played, our noses leaking and our light banter becoming a kind of bonding element and mutual defense system against the miserable weather. We chatted amicably about a host of related subjects— wives and children, my new friendship with Glenna Vare and his old one with Herbert Warren Wind, shared hopes for the new Red Sox season, and talk of our favorite golf books. He wondered if I'd ever read *The Mystery of Golf* by Arnold Haultain; there was a new Classics of Golf edition for which he'd recently written the afterword. I admitted that I had not.

"You must get a copy." He explained that Haultain analyzed

the confounding appeal of the game by quoting everybody from Saint Paul to Lao Tzu, ruminating on everything from the physiology of the golf swing to our social addiction to competition and the contradiction between the game's solitary nature and its incomparable knack for forging friendships. The author also dipped into metaphysics and hard science, declaring that golf was not so much a simple game as it was a creed and a quasi-religion—all told in the amused, fancy, antique language of another century. "It's really quite extraordinary," Updike added. "It's almost as if Henry David Thoreau had taken up the game on weekends off from Walden Pond."

I wondered if he actually solved the mystery of golf.

Updike smiled. "Not in the least, which makes it so completely wonderful. I'll make sure you get a copy."

Suddenly we found ourselves standing at the ninth hole's teeing ground, looking down upon a gorgeous postage stamp of a par-three set behind a perfectly still pond that would have delighted brother Thoreau. Behind us lay a string of double and triple bogeys that made me wonder why on earth we'd kept a card—yet another beguiling mystery of the game.

"So how does your wife like Maine?" he asked out of the blue, sounding a tad more like Rabbit Angstrom than John Updike. I explained that Alison had grown up the middle child of Glaswegian Scots. We'd moved to a coastal town ninety minutes below their sprawling farm in the central Maine highlands at the end of the previous summer to have our first child, a girl named Margaret, after both her grandmothers. Now a second babe was on the way, due in August. We'd recently learned that the baby was a boy.

My host seemed pleased by this news. "So you'll be able to use those Lady Tiaras for a while yet," he needled gently, the way he might have done with one of his normal golf pals.

Earlier, as we'd gronkled along, he'd told me about his golf buddies and an essay on the subject of golf companions he'd recently submitted to *Golf Digest*, prompting me to admit that I did not have a regular group, and hadn't really ever had one to speak of.

"I would advise you to find a good group of men to play with— cheaper and far more fun than group therapy in the church basement," he'd said with a chuckle.

We both buried shots in the bunker by the ninth green. My host made a triple bogey, while I scraped out yet another thrilling double.

As we walked off the green, I feared this might be all the golf for one day. There was still no sign of humanity around Myopia's darkened clubhouse, so no lunch, or even a friendly warm-up toddy. I totaled up our scores. The Master of Gronkle made 51, his apprentice 48.

"Shall we continue the pain?" I felt obliged to ask.

Just then the sun appeared, flooding the pretty hills around us.

"There's a sign," said Updike, peeling off his stocking cap and the all-weather jacket he'd put on several holes back. The bucket hat went back on his head. "I think you always learn something from a bad round—to keep going, if nothing else. The back nine is bound to improve us. Game?"

"Absolutely," I said, squishing after him in my water-filled Topsiders.

══ • ══

John Updike's best drive of the day came on the tenth hole, mysteriously nicknamed "Alps," where he unleashed a 230-yard scorcher with the sweetest hint of a draw.

"I'm your basic left-to-right golfer who's been unsuccessfully trying to cultivate a reliable draw for years," he explained after watching me drill my drive into a grassy mound on the right. "The real mystery of golf is that sometimes things you're trying to do really happen. The gods give you a momentary taste of heaven."

After foolishly trying to hack my way through the nettles, I took two more shots just to reach the fairway, then sent a fourth into a pot bunker and a fifth whistling over the green and past a small stone fence, disappearing into a valley of handsome old trees and tangled, just-budding vines.

"Don't worry. I've got it marked!" cried my thoughtful partner, nimbly hopping the wall and disappearing into the bosom of nature. There followed a great deal of enthusiastic cracking and thrashing about, while I simply stood there like a dolt having a small out-of-body experience, hoping the Arnie of American letters didn't injure himself on my behalf.

"Excuse me, sir," came a polite voice from the rear. "May I ask what you're doing out here?"

I turned around to find a suntanned young man wearing a green windbreaker with the Myopia club emblem on its breast.

"I'm asking myself that very question," I admitted with a weak smile.

"The course is officially closed until next week," he said in a tone as cool as the weather, obviously running my flushed mug through his mental Rolodex of members and coming up empty. The sun had disappeared, and so had my hopes for at least seeing Myopia's fabled back nine.

"I think I've got it!" came a triumphant cry from over the wall. "You might even be able to get a club on it!"

"That's okay, John," I called back. "I think we may be finished anyway."

Moments later my companion climbed up from the forest primeval, winded and grinning like a man who'd found more than a golf ball in the brambles. He handed me my errant Titleist and greeted the assistant pro warmly by name and explained we were just out for a little "April exercise—spring training for golf. This is, after all, Masters week." Still catching his breath, he added cheerfully,

"Hope that's okay. My friend here wanted to try out his wife's new golf clubs."

The young fellow didn't appear particularly amused. But he managed a polite smile. "Absolutely, Mr. Updike. We should have the course ready for real play by next weekend. Enjoy your exercise."

So onward we went, into the succession of holes whose beauty befitted their having been shaped by a gifted amateur rather than some machine, ingeniously simple affairs that hugged the contours of the land like a well-tailored glove.

After my disastrous 10 on ten, I'd basically given up chasing Old Man Par and focused on the pleasure of getting to know my fellow golfer and churchgoer even better. On a hole called "Valley," we paused to watch a squadron of hungry robins descend on an adjacent meadow and a small boy scouting for lost balls in the rough. We talked about English weather, Renaissance popes, Boston real estate, and my favorite of his novels, *Marry Me*, which he explained was written during a difficult period in his first marriage—and which may have given birth to Rabbit Angstrom.

The sun bobbed out on the sixteenth hole, another short and handsome par-three. Updike stroked a masterful four-iron to the center of the green and nearly made birdie. I bunkered for another double bogey. On hole seventeen, however, my amiable companion nailed his tee shot OB (out of bounds) over a stone wall and issued the only swearword I heard him say all afternoon, a gentlemanly "Sonofabitch."

On the eighteenth tee, he told me about his new novel, due out sometime in the autumn, *Rabbit at Rest*. He hit his final drive of the day, and we watched it bounce out of bounds as well.

"Rabbit is tired," he quipped wearily, "and so is his creator."

Indeed, it felt like we'd slogged through four different seasons in as many hours. But what an unforgettable Masters Friday—better than anything happening down in Augusta, Georgia, I decided.

Even better, there was a light on in the club bar, where we found a bald sergeant-major type who gruffly greeted us as we shuffled in. He brought us a couple of restorative beers. Mine was a German girl named St. Pauli; John's was a ginger beer.

"Good to have one of the regulars back, Mr. Updike," the barman declared. "Awful brave of you men to be out there today."

My host was grimacing at the card.

"What's your handicap?" he asked.

I had no official handicap, because I had no club, no regular game, and no golf buddies. But I typically shot around 78.

"I'm a sixteen," he said, and showed me the untidy results of his math, smiling like an amused Borgia pope. He finished with a score of 100 to my 101.

We touched glasses. "Terrible golf for us both. But here's to an excellent round of gronkle," he said with a wry smile.

As we walked out to our cars—still the only ones in the members' parking lot—he told me that he'd read somewhere that Vice President Dan Quayle took the game so seriously that he brooded for days over a bad round.

"Do you think we should take this game more seriously?" he asked.

"Not unless you plan to be vice president," I said.

He laughed. "We could just throw away the card and try again in June."

"I'd like that very much," I said. "Good thing Quayle isn't president, with a thumb on the button. A round like ours could mean the end of the world."

My companion put his clubs in his trunk, removed his bucket hat, and offered me his hand.

"You're right. I find that sharing pleasure and pain with a friend is one of golf's great compensations. No mystery about that."

I thanked him for a delightful afternoon.

Two weeks to the day after our Myopian adventure, a postcard arrived in Maine.

Dear Jim,

I played there yesterday with another awful head cold, and got 91. So, by simple linear projection, I will get an 82 the next time, followed by a 73. Since 64 is the course record, I can hardly wait for my fifth round of the year. It was a fun round, with its ups and downs, as is the way. We'll play again sometime soon.

Best Wishes, John.

A few days after that, a new edition of Haultain's *The Mystery of Golf* with an afterword by John Updike appeared in our rural Maine postbox. It became one of my favorite books.

Rabbit and I never teed it up again, though we did exchange handwritten notes from time to time.

But I look back on that dreary spring afternoon of gronkle as a highlight of my evolving Range Bucket List, proof that you never meet a stranger on a golf course.

As Rabbit—finally at rest—might say, no mystery about that.

CHAPTER FOUR

THE QUEEN MUM'S ACE

Just days after my round with John Updike, I made my first and only ace.

Well, sort of. In truth, it wasn't a hole in one in the conventional sense—the kind every hacker dreams of making, and Tour players statistically accomplish every 2,700 swings or so. But it did involve an extraordinary shot that found the cup with one fortuitous swing that once again changed my life for the better.

An ace is not the rarest shot in golf—an albatross (a two on a par-five) owns that distinction. But an ace is easily the most mythic and desired shot, something every golfer hopes to someday check off his or her RBL. According to USHoleInOne.com, a company that insures hole in one contests, the odds of bagging a hole in one for a skilled amateur are roughly 12,500 to 1, and approximately 7,500 to 1 for a touring professional. *Golf Digest* estimates that a single-digit handicapper will make only one or two in his or her lifetime, but more than 95 percent of the golf population will never make one.

For the record, Jack Nicklaus claimed twenty aces on his way to eighteen major championships, his last coming during a practice round at the 2003 Senior British Open. Rivals Gary Player and Arnold Palmer scored nineteen and twenty aces, respectively. Tiger

Woods made his first one at age six, followed by seventeen more as his outstanding career unfolded. Only three presidents, all Republicans, scored aces: Eisenhower, Ford, and Nixon, who made his with a five-iron on the second hole at Bel-Air Country Club in 1961. Afterward, Nixon described his lone hole in one as "the biggest thrill of my life—even better than getting elected."

For better or worse, my lengthy quest for an ace came to a shattering end on April 15, 1990, a cold but sunny Sunday afternoon that also happened to be two days shy of my Scottish mother-in-law's fifty-eighth birthday. It was just one week after Nick Faldo edged out Raymond Floyd to capture his second consecutive green jacket at the Masters and John Updike and I gronkled our way around Myopia.

My mother-in-law's full name was Kathleen Sinclair Bennie, and she was a formidable Scottish lady, a crack gardener and rural Maine school superintendent who, early in our acquaintance, informed me in no uncertain terms that "March in Maine—and most of April, too—is still wintertime. The sooner you accept this, James, the happier you'll be. Spring will eventually arrive, just not anytime soon."

I liked Mum, as some in tiny Harmony, Maine, affectionately called her. But I wasn't convinced that Mum liked me, her son-in-law of five years. Though perfectly polite, Kate Bennie's Glasgow-accented body English seemed to indicate we had little or nothing in common save her beautiful daughter, Alison, and a pair of infants, one of whom was on the way.

Mum was a no-nonsense daughter of Glasgow's working-class Netherlee neighborhood, a dedicated socialist and self-declared atheist who detested peanut butter (my favorite food) and Republicans of any persuasion (guilty again). I also understood that Kathleen Bennie hadn't enjoyed the easiest of lives. After losing one parent before the war and one a decade later, she got a brilliant education at Glasgow University; and married a fellow scientist named Sam

Bennie and followed his work on the Distant Early Warning Line to Canada and Alaska before settling down in a rambling two-hundred-year-old farmhouse above beautiful Moose Pond in the highlands of central Maine with three small children. The house originally had an outhouse and later a toilet in the middle of the living room and was heated exclusively by woodstoves. Thankfully, by my first visit in 1985, an actual bathroom and other useful conveniences had been installed—though there was still a shocking absence of peanut butter anywhere on the premises.

Coming as I did from a gentrified southern background, stepping into the Bennie home felt a little like entering a Thomas Hardy novel. Sam made me feel welcome right away, however, plying me with tales of his Scottish homeland and his eccentric golfing uncles whenever we enjoyed a wee dram by the woodstove, which was basically every time I saw him during those years. Much of the time he was traveling to exotic locales to consult on national security, a charming son of Paisley who looked and sounded a bit like Peter O'Toole and was, or so I imagined, a brilliant spook. Mum was left to run the local primary school—serving dually as superintendent of schools—and tend the home fires, raising three very bright children and looking after everything in their rambling nineteenth-century farmhouse.

Darkening the mood that weekend was the fact that Sam had passed away from cancer at the farm weeks before the rest of the family descended for the birthday weekend. But Scots are nothing if not an emotionally durable race, constitutionally equipped to expect the worst weather in life and ready to push on regardless of the obstacles, chin up and no complaining. As usual, good Scottish meals were served and polite political debates were conducted by the fire. Neighbors popped in to say hello to Mum and to see her beautiful new infant granddaughter, Margaret Sinclair, named for both Scottish and southern great-grandmothers. Not long before he died, Sam actually got to hold his first grandchild and presented her with a sack full of adorable stuffed animals he'd gathered from his travels around the globe. He called them "the Stardust Fan Club."

Good Eisenhower Republican that I was, I brought a gift, too, a birthday present with which I hoped to finally break the ice with Mum—the latest novel by her favorite writer, A. S. Byatt. She thanked me and placed the book on the reading table by her favorite armchair near the large farmhouse window close to the kitchen woodstove.

Not long after the others cleared out for the two-hour drive back to Boston late that Sunday, as my wife gathered up our belongings and our daughter for the shorter trip home to Maine's Midcoast, Mum finished cleaning up the kitchen, loaded up her woodstove, and finally sat down with A. S. Byatt.

Still suffering from Masters Fever and my embarrassing showing at Myopia, I used the lull to slip out to our car, fetch my new Titleist irons—delivered that very week, too late to help at Myopia, but a true sign of Easter rebirth—and a brand-new Titleist ball, and hustle over to the far side of the small pond that fronted the ancient farmhouse and barn. A game of Ace was exactly what I needed, I decided—just the thing to sort myself out and start the season off on the right foot.

To properly establish the scene: wood smoke rose serenely from the great-room chimney and golden sunlight fell across the surrounding Maine highlands, making it easy to imagine I was actually teed up to play at, say, the mighty eleventh at the Old Course at St Andrews, the famous par-three hard by the Eden estuary where young Bobby Jones hit his tee shot into the menacing Strath bunker, took several shots to get out, tore up his card in disgust, and stalked off the course—a moment of self-immolation that changed both Jones and the future of the game. Deeply embarrassed, the young man took a silent oath to become a symbol of golf's integrity and sportsmanship going forward and turned himself into an immortal in the process.

In any case, I judged the distance to clear Mum's tall shingled farmhouse roof to be a whisker over 155 yards, roughly the same distance as Old Course No. 11. The weather was clear and brisk—not unlike St Andrews in mid-April—with a helpful breeze off Moose Pond rather than the Eden Estuary at my back.

Placing the ball on a tuft of hard brown grass, holding this image in my mind, I took dead aim at the chimney and made a really nice golf swing, if I may say so myself. I looked up to see my ball soaring beautifully into the pale blue sky.

Unfortunately, it came down directly through one of the large windowpanes where Mum happened to be sitting with her book and a cup of tea.

Frozen in disbelief, horrified by the potential consequences, I considered two viable options. One was to get into my car and flee, never to show my face again in Harmony, Maine—though this would mean abandoning my wife and two heirs and certain banishment from the clan even before I got my first taste of Mum's famous haggis.

I chose option two: to immediately go and face the music, which would undoubtedly be a Scottish dirge. Rushing inside, I found Mum sitting perfectly still in her armchair, still holding her Byatt book, her teacup undisturbed beside her. Shards of window glass, however, were everywhere.

She silenced my stream of babbling apologies with a lifted hand, motioning me to come forward. I carefully approached, bracing for a reproach worthy of Mary, Queen of Scots, when she discovered her worthless husband, Lord Darnley, skipping archery practice in favor of golf, shortly before she had him blown to bits by royal assassins.

Weirdly, Mum silently pointed to her teacup.

In it, to my astonishment, sat my new Titleist number 3 golf ball, marinating in good Scottish black tea.

"James," she said gravely, "I have just one thing to say to you."

Inwardly, I cowered like Lord Darnley.

She spoke the words like a Queen Mum officially pronouncing the ultimate penalty. "I sincerely doubt whether, given the opportunity to do so, you could hit that shot again if your very life depended upon it."

And with this, she smiled.

You could have knocked me over with a tea bag.

She instructed me to pull up a chair and sit. We talked for quite a while. I learned that she actually liked me and thought I had the makings of a fine husband and father. She thanked me for her birthday book and pointed out that, despite our differences on peanut butter and Republicans, we had several important things in common, including a taste for good literature and a love of gardens, political debate, expensive English gin, classical music, and even golf.

Her uncle Eddie, she revealed, had been the champion golfer of Williamwood Golf Club several times during his life. She invited me to visit with his widow, Aunt Dorothy, on my upcoming trip to Scotland. I promised I would—and I did.

In the end, more than ice and an old farmhouse window were broken that early spring Sunday. A deep and enduring friendship of the first order was born.

Among other things, the Queen Mum—as I soon dubbed her—became the first reader of my first six books, making invaluable corrections and suggestions before they went off to the publisher. We never reached a rapprochement on the subject of peanut butter, but we found abundant pleasure in each other's company and common ground on almost every other subject, ranging from grandchildren to garden roses. We never lost our tastes for gently arguing politics and religion and sharing great books, and rarely missed a telecast of a major golf championship in each other's company. Moreover, wherever I wandered in the wide world of golf—and especially when that was to golf's Holy Land—the Queen Mum was the first to demand a full account of my activities, especially after I took Aunt

Dorothy to supper in Edinburgh and looked up, as instructed, several of Mum's old school chums during subsequent visits. Eventually we even traveled together across her homeland.

More important, Kathleen Sinclair Bennie guided our family through many happy years and only one truly difficult one, serving as the wise and gentle matriarch who steered us all through an amicable separation and divorce that seemed to come out of nowhere a dozen years into our marriage. Thanks to the Queen Mum's steadfast guidance, Alison and I worked hard to minimize the negative impact upon our children—if such a thing can ever be truly accomplished—allowing us to not only recover our equilibrium and honor our years together but also to grow into something new and enduring, a true extended family that continues to this day.

Not surprisingly, when I got married again a few years down the road, Kate was among the first to welcome my new wife, Wendy, into that extended family, remaining one of my closest friends and advisors for the next two decades.

As a bonus, she even consented to let me have her famous recipe for proper Glaswegian haggis, quoting the great French chef Chateaubriand, who remarked, upon taking his first bite of the fabled Scottish dish: "I thought it merely looked and smelled like shit."

THE QUEEN MUM'S FAMOUS HAGGIS

1 sheep stomach
1 sheep liver
1 sheep lung
1 sheep heart
1 sheep tongue
1/2 pound suet, minced
4 onions, minced
1/2 pound rolled oats

1 week-old edition of the *Glasgow Evening News*, finely shredded
3 pairs of lightly soiled cotton athletic kneesocks from the University of Glasgow women's field hockey team
1/2 teaspoon salt
1/2 teaspoon pepper

1/2 teaspoon nutmeg	1 cup of fine Scottish Drambuie, as first served to Charles Edward Stuart by Clan MacKinnon after the Battle of Culloden in 1746
1/2 teaspoon mace	
1 cup of cheap French brandy	

1. Cook liver, lung, heart, and tongue in a pot of boiling water and mince thoroughly before combining with suet, onions, oats, shredded newspaper, athletic socks, and herbs. Place mixture inside stomach and put stomach in a large pot of boiling water and cook for three hours, being careful to avoid premature explosion.

2. Remove and allow to briefly cool before pouring cheap French brandy over haggis and setting on fire, preferably accompanied by a recording of Jean Redpath singing "Skipping Barefoot Through the Heather."

3. Recite Burns's "Address to a Haggis," throw away haggis, and drink a toast to Scotland the Brave with Drambuie.

(Champit tatties and bashit neeps optional.)

A final note on the Queen Mum's Ace:

Not long ago, while sharing her memories of that fateful Easter Sunday in 1990, Alison reminded me that the very next year, my silly game of Ace came to an abrupt and permanent conclusion after I skulled a wedge shot through the large and expensive bathroom window of our new post-and-beam house, nearly giving her a heart attack.

"Mum found that endlessly amusing," she reported.

CHAPTER FIVE

GOLF PALS

Not long after we moved to Maine, started a family, and began building a house on a forested hill near the coast, I dropped into the semiprivate Brunswick Golf Club to investigate the cost of joining my first-ever golf club—a true Range Bucket List moment. Apples don't drop far from their trees, after all, and since my earliest days in golf I'd hoped to someday find a regular group of golf pals like my father had with Bill Mims, Bob Tilden, Richard Childress, and Alex the Englishman. Every Saturday morning for more than a decade, they were the first off the tee at Pine Tree Golf Club just outside Greensboro, true Dewsweepers who seemed to take such pleasure in the lively camaraderie of their weekend matches.

It was a crisp late September afternoon when I showed up at Brunswick Golf Club. The summer tourist invasion was mercifully over for another year—neatly halving the price of shore dinners and allowing locals to venture safely back into the town center—and there was only one gentleman preparing to play on BGC's inviting first tee. With its simple white clapboard clubhouse and a settled air found only at clubs of a certain age (this was one of New England's oldest courses, dating from 1888), BGC featured an unfussy back nine reportedly laid out by Bowdoin College professors and Civil War veterans and a new front nine designed by Brian Silva. I would come in time to regard it as a workingman's Pine Valley, where the membership boasts everyone from Bath Iron Works pipefitters to Fortune 500 CEOs, an egalitarian club composition you will find across Scotland and Ireland especially.

Brunswick's head professional was a friendly fellow named Mal Strange, who not only warmly welcomed me to the premises but encouraged me to hustle on out and join the older gentleman just then teeing off.

His name was Tom Dugan, a dapper and fit fellow wearing a crimson cashmere sweater and impressively carrying his own bag. As I walked up, he pegged a perfectly straight shot to the heart of the wide first fairway.

"Won't you join me?" he said with a pleasant smile.

"If you don't mind," I said, "that would be great."

It turned out to be more than great, however—a moment I regard as almost providential in the larger scheme of my lucky life in golf.

Tom Dugan turned out to be a charming, witty Irishman and retired athletic equipment salesman who'd grown up playing ice hockey and caddying at Brae Burn (Massachusetts) Country Club for Densmore "Denny" Shute, the three-time major champion who won consecutive PGA Championships beginning at Pinehurst in 1936. Newspapers nicknamed the English-born Shute "The Human Icicle" owing to his visible discomfort when playing in the public eye. According to Tom Dugan, Shute was so naturally retiring in nature that his wife, Hettie, often accepted prize checks and tournament hardware in his behalf.

"A lot of people thought poor Denny was just aloof and cold, a social misfit, but it was really almost a pathological shyness on his part. I'll tell you this: no one ever hit a one- or two-iron better than Denny Shute," Tom explained as we enjoyed beers on BGC's wide porch overlooking the club's picturesque ninth hole. "I always heard that Ben Hogan, Snead, Nelson, and many others watched Denny just to learn the art of hitting low irons."

Among the many things that drew me to Tom Dugan was the fact that he was a veteran of the Second World War and of the same Eighth Army Air Corps in which my old man had served. Beginning at just age nineteen, Tom served as the radar operator on twenty-nine bombing raids over occupied France and Germany, including the infamous daylight raid on Germany's Schweinfurt ball-bearing plant that resulted in more than half of the attacking Allied crews being lost. When I casually mentioned to Tom that he reminded me of my father, also a veteran of the "Flying Eighth," he simply smiled and said, "I'd very much like to meet your father sometime."

Even better, my new friend invited me to join him and two of his regular playing pals for a round the following Wednesday afternoon. "But be warned, one's a crusty old-timer like me, and the other's a bright young buck like you," he said with a smile. "I think you might enjoy them both."

That next Wednesday I was introduced to Sid Watson and Terry Meagher. The former was a living sports legend, the other merely a legend in the making. It was Sid who confided that Tom's nickname as a hockey-playing Olympian was "Bunny Dugan," owing to his remarkable speed and friendly disposition.

Sidney J. Watson was Bowdoin's athletic director and the school's legendary former hockey coach, one of the winningest college hockey coaches in American history. Between 1969 and 1983, Sid's Bowdoin Polar Bears missed the ECAC playoffs only once and won the league championship a record six times, amassing a record of 326-210. In 2001, Sid received the Hobey Baker Legends of College Hockey Award and was inducted into the US Hockey Hall of

Fame. In 1983, he became Bowdoin's athletic director and hired his replacement, a genial Canadian and former Boston University hockey standout named Terry Meagher.

Terry, only a year older than me, was already on course to over-take his Hall of Fame boss and mentor in terms of championships and wins.

Our first time out, Sid and I teamed up to play Terry and Tom. Eager to acquit myself decently, I quickly lost track of the crazy game due to the rapid pace at which they played. The wager was two bits per hole, with side bets on everything from greenies to sandies, long drives to closest to the pin, with constant barbs flying between Sid and Terry. All I knew at the end was that Sid and I were each roughly one dollar richer and had somehow beaten long-driving Terry and straight-driving Tom. When I innocently proposed that next Wednesday Tom and I team up against Terry and Sid, Sid-ney violently shook his head and growled, "Hell no. That will *never* happen."

Terry laughed, pointing to his boss. "Sid refuses to play with me because he loves trying to beat me. I inspire him. He lives to beat me."

"That's completely ridiculous. It's the other way around!" Sidney snapped, offering the tiniest of smiles.

"The poles may reverse, and the world will certainly end," Tom explained, "if those two are ever allowed to play on the same team."

And so it went for the next fifteen years, give or take a rainy or sleety Wednesday off. From early April's soggy opening day to No-vember's sharp winds and barren links, ours was a delightful four-part fellowship—sometimes made a fifth when joined by Bowdoin's beloved athletic trainer Mike Linkovich—that ripened incredibly as the years passed, providing yours truly with the only standing game he's ever had.

Among other things, Terry and I both carried a six handicap

and quickly established an automatic side bet for one million dollars per round, and were almost always dead even when we showed up on closing day to play just ahead of the crew that was busy taking out the flags for the long winter. Whenever Terry was up, I joked that the million I owed him was in Canadian dollars, because the unfavorable exchange rate made the debt worth roughly half that. Whenever he was up, he insisted that we were playing for whichever exchange happened to be worth more at that moment. Neither of us was ever up more than a million or two by season's end. And the bet always carried over.

A funny and unforgettable moment came somewhere near the end of our faithful company, a month or so before the club closed down for the winter. Terry and I were playing Sid and Tom, as usual—Old Farts versus Young Fools, as Sid liked to call this configuration—when we reached BGC's challenging fourth hole, a midlength par-three with a kidney-shaped pond on the right and a deep bunker protecting the front left.

Terry and I had the honors. I hit first, knocking my ball into the pond. As Terry set up to play, Sid began needling him about his mismatched socks, which quickly devolved into their usual debate over which was a better shot on this hole, a fade or a draw. Sid argued that a fade was far better than a natural draw, because a fade, at least, could be controlled. Terry naturally disagreed, because his preferred shot was a beautiful draw, which he argued always went farther and allowed for the use of a shorter club and thus better accuracy. According to Bunny Dugan, the two of them had been having this disagreement since Terry played hockey for Sid in the mid-1970s. To prove his point, Terry struck a nicely drawing shot that placed his ball in the center of the green, ten feet from the cup.

"See what I mean?" Terry teased Sid. "That's the power of a working draw."

Sid grumbled, "*That's* a lucky shot."

"Listen to them," Tom said to me, shaking his head with amusement. He teed up, took dead aim at the green, and made one of his simple, graceful swings—sending a rare topped ball scampering along the ground toward the green.

"Oh heavens," he said. "*That's* not good."

"I don't know," I said. "That might work out nicely."

As he and I watched and our mates debated, Tom's ball ran into and out of the left-side bunker and jumped onto the green, curling sweetly from left to right as it rolled toward the rear flag, dropping into the hole.

It was the first—and only—ace I'd ever witnessed live. I let out a bark of joy and offered a blushing Bunny Dugan my hand. Both Sid and Terry fell silent and stared at us.

"What the hell just happened?" Sid demanded.

"You guys just missed Bunny Dugan's first ace."

"Actually, it's my fourth," Tom explained modestly. "But this one was pure luck."

The next year, my parents came to Maine for the first of their many annual summer visits, and Tom and my dad finally got to meet and play golf. They rode in a cart, while I walked along listening to the two old soldiers swapping memories of the war years, a conversation that continued through drinks afterward and supper at our favorite seaside restaurant.

Nothing lasts *but* forever, as I once heard a famous preacher say.

Our sacred golf group began to fall apart when Tom and Jane Dugan moved permanently to their winter home in Port Charlotte, Florida, not long before the new millennium dawned. Terry, Sid, and I continued as a threesome for another season or two, sometimes joined by Bowdoin squash coach Tomas Fortson, but something unspoken was clearly missing—a walking fellowship that had carried me though marriage and fatherhood and even through the hardest days of a marriage that inexplicably came apart at the seams.

Sid passed away in 2004, shortly before I moved home to North Carolina. Bowdoin named its handsome new ice rink the Sidney J. Watson Arena in honor of him. His memorial service was like a family gathering of his former players and colleagues from the worlds of football and hockey.

=== • ===

Not long after I arrived in Pinehurst, Bunny Dugan stopped off to see me on his way back to Florida from a brief visit to Maine. I took him to lunch at the Pinehurst members' club, and we played No. 2, the course where his old boss Denny Shute captured the first of his two Wanamaker Trophies. We caught up on children and grand-children and recalled all the good times with Sid and Terry and Mike Linkovich. At one point I asked Tom how his golf life in Port Charlotte had turned out. He smiled and shrugged. "Oh, it's fine. I play with a group of retired guys who complain about their wives or kidneys or the weather and then go home to nap and watch Fox News all afternoon." He added, a touch wistfully, "But it's really not the same. I miss our Brunswick group—Sid and Terry and you."

I walked him to his car in the parking lot. I remember he was wearing a dark-green cashmere sweater that made him look like an Irish aristocrat. We grasped hands, then hugged, and I waved as he drove off, headed for his new home in Florida. Watching him go, I was overwhelmed with both gratitude and not a little sadness.

Tom passed away the next spring.

I sat with Terry Meagher at his memorial service up in Maine. He admitted that his game had really slumped since our sacred four-some broke up.

"I play with Link and Tomas and Barry [Mills, then Bowdoin's president] once in a while, but it's just not the same," he said, eerily echoing Bunny Dugan's words on the subject, and explained that he was even considering dropping out of the club. Then he grinned, flashing a glimpse of the old Coach Terry. "But I might reconsider if you'd come back to Maine. Besides, I think you still owe me half a million dollars—Canadian, now that the exchange rate is slightly higher than the American dollar."

"Don't tempt me," I said.

The funny thing is, we both meant it.

Maybe, like first love, golf-group camaraderie is an ephemeral experience meant to be savored while it lasts and stored away for the cold winds of old age, when one's game has vanished and good memories are like warming coals from a once-blazing fire.

"Golf camaraderie," wrote my friend John Updike in his lovely meditation on the subject in *Golf Dreams*, "like that of astronauts and Antarctic explorers, is based on a common experience of transcendence; fat or thin, scratch or duffer, we have been somewhere together where nongolfers never go."

Amen, John. *Amen.*

CHAPTER SIX

UNFINISHED BUSINESS

As my father approached eighty, he lost his own longtime golf group. Bob Tilden died, Alex the Englishman moved to South Carolina, and Richard Childress married a new younger wife who reportedly demanded his entire weekends. According to my mother, good old Bill Mims and my father soldiered on together for a while, even though Bill had developed a heart condition and was playing less and less. "Your father has been playing with younger fellows, but I don't think he likes it very much," she said during one of our weekly Sunday-evening phone calls. "He says they take the game way too seriously, and he really misses his buddies. I'm afraid he might just quit playing."

Unable to accept this verdict, I sent him a new set of the latest high-tech "super senior" graphite-shafted golf clubs that my friend Barney Adams made up expressly for him, designed to put distance and zip back into an elderly golf swing.

Two weeks later, the fancy clubs came back to Maine with a thank-you note and a joke about my dad's loyalty to his old Wilson irons. "They've gotten me this far," Opti wrote. "I think they deserve to finish the round." Included was a check for the cost of the new sticks, along with a suggestion that I donate them to the annual summer church auction or find some "determined older fella who can really use and enjoy them."

I tore up the check and did just that—put them in the church summer auction. I think they fetched a nice price, too.

That next October, on a raw and windy day during one of my occasional passes through the Sandhills, Opti and I met at Pinehurst No. 2 to play with a couple of my colleagues from *Golf* magazine. Neither of us played particularly well, but at least we laughed about it on the short ride home through the pines to Greensboro. I gently needled my dad that we would surely have beaten our opponents if he'd only kept those super senior clubs, and offered condolences over the loss of his regular golf group. He smiled and told me about a new routine that had replaced his Saturday-morning Dewsweeping sessions—how he and my mom rose early to be the first through the door of the downtown farmers' market and then went to breakfast at Tex & Shirley's Pancake House.

"Emerson said life always has compensations. We've also started driving up to the mountains on weekends," he confided, warming to the topic. "I play golf, and your mom just rides along, taking in the scenery. We've been up to Blowing Rock and the Grove Park Inn in Asheville a couple of times. Last weekend we even went to the old Lake Lure Inn. That's where your mom and I had a second honeymoon before I shipped out to England in early 1943. They have a nine-hole course. It's not very fancy, but they say Donald Ross built it. I had fun playing it. They made a movie there, you know—at the hotel, I mean. I can't remember the name of the movie."

"*Dirty Dancing*," I provided.

"Beg pardon?"

"The movie is called *Dirty Dancing.*"

"Right," he said, and promptly changed the subject to his grand-children.

When a patch of silence fell between us, I said, "Hey, let's take that golf trip we always talked about. Just us."

"You want to play Lake Lure, too?"

"No. Unfinished business."

Opti knew exactly what I was talking about: a trip to play the courses in England and Scotland where he'd learned to play the game during the Second World War, retracing his steps up the Lancashire coast from Lytham & St Annes to St Andrews. We'd talked about making this trip since I was a club-tossing kid.

"What fun would that be for you," Opti said. "You go to England and Scotland pretty regularly now."

"I go there regularly all *alone*," I pointed out. "But I've never been there with you."

Though I didn't say so—or need to—a pilgrimage with him to Lytham and Scotland had been a key item on my Range Bucket List even before it officially existed.

"Next summer is the fiftieth anniversary of D-Day," I said. "What a perfect time to go."

Opti nodded, mysteriously managing to conceal his enthusiasm for the idea. "Maybe so," he agreed vaguely. "Let's see how we feel when we get to summer."

═══ • ═══

When my folks made their annual summer visit to Maine that next July, the heart of the D-Day anniversary summer, Opti seemed to thoroughly enjoy playing a round at my club with Tom Dugan and Terry Meagher, displaying bits of his old chip-and-run magic. Stories about the golden anniversary of D-Day were all over the news. Old Eighth Army airmen Dugan and Dodson had a particularly good time talking about their years of service.

As we sat on the terrace of our favorite seafood joint overlooking Casco Bay that evening, drinking wine with Tom Dugan and his wife, Jane, I quietly raised the idea of a golf trip to golf's Holy Land one more time—fearing that our window to make the trip was rapidly narrowing.

"How many times have you been to St Andrews?" Opti asked.

"Who's counting?" I replied. "But as I told you down in Pinehurst, that's not the point."

I knew I'd become a gentle pest on this subject, but, given his feelings about golf and St Andrews, I was mystified by his reluctance to do something we'd been talking about doing forever. I explained that I would arrange everything—plane tickets, tee times, car rental, hotels, and even scouting out the best pubs along the way, ticking off a golf nut's dream itinerary that included Sunningdale Old, Royal Birkdale, Lytham & St Annes, Turnberry, Gleneagles, St Andrews, and "whatever glorious Scottish goat farms we happen to find in between."

He listened, smiling as if amused, gazing out to sea, hopefully seeing those places in his mind. Finally, he sipped his wine and looked at me, clearly turning something over in his head. I thought he was going to say no, but Opti was a man of constant surprise.

"Okay, Bo. I've got a little time in early September. Let me mention this to your mama and see what she says. She likes her getaway weekends in the fall."

"Great," I said. "If you like, we can go on to Compiègne after Scotland—maybe find that beech tree in the forest."

After landing in France shortly before the liberation of Paris, Opti was put in charge of a German POW camp near the ancient river city of Compiègne, where the Germans had surrendered the First World War in a railcar on the edge of the town's famous medieval forest. My brother and I had grown up hearing about how somewhere in that magical forest by an arched stone bridge stood a centuries-old beech tree in which generations of lovers had carved their initials—and our dad supposedly added his and our mom's names one October afternoon not long before he shipped home with a duffel bag full of French perfume for his war bride.

"That might be a bridge too far," he said, smiling. "Let's just aim for England and maybe Scotland and see how far we get."

=== • ===

Not surprisingly, my mother was firmly opposed to the trip from the start. At the airport seeing us off, she took my arm and said in the quiet but unmistakable voice of a true steel-belted magnolia, "Darling, I personally feel this is the craziest idea you two have ever hatched. He won't tell you, but Steve [his cancer surgeon] has given him only a few months to live—maybe even weeks. You have no idea what his daily struggle is like. He never lets on. But I hate to think what could happen with you two walking golf courses in the rain and eating bad English food and drinking beer for nine or ten days. The hospitals are said to be very poor, and they drive like crazy people on the left-hand side of those tiny Scottish roads. But he wants to do this *entirely* because you do, honey."

Her words weren't a complete shock. My dad had phoned me a few weeks after our itinerary was officially set in mid-August to tell me he'd had some sudden, unusual bleeding, had gone in to check it out, and was advised by his friend and surgeon Steve Blevinieck that he needed to begin getting his final affairs in order; the trip would have to be postponed indefinitely so he could explore additional treatment options.

A day or two later, however, Opti phoned back to say he'd decided to skip any further treatments and to "let nature take its course." We would go, he said, but only on his terms of departure: "We go to have laughs and hit a few good shots, see some places for old times' sake, and take some of the Queen's currency from each other's pockets. No complaints, no long faces, no talk of endings. But when I say it's time to go home, I go home. I still have things to do. But I do want to pin your ears back one more time—if only so you'll remember me."

He laughed, and I laughed. Only Opti could have made us both laugh at such a daunting proposition. He also made me swear not to tell my mother that I knew any of this.

Hoping to ease her worries as she saw us off in Atlanta, I assured my mother that I would watch over her husband of fifty-three years like a hawk, carefully mind what we ate and drank—only the *best* British ales, I said—and skip golf if there was either cold or rain. The long-range forecast for Scotland was for clear skies and decent temperatures. As for crazy Scottish drivers, I added, I was an old hand at driving British back roads, and rarely hit a hedgerow or farm animal.

She smiled, but was not terribly mollified. "I'm sure you will look after him, darling. But if something unfortunate happens while you two are over there, you may wish to seek citizenship in Scotland. Maybe Kate Bennie can help you with that."

I suppose that was her idea of a joke. Though to this day, I'm pretty sure she wasn't joking.

═ • ═

Naturally, almost everything went wrong from the start.

We arrived in London in a downpour and were forced to settle for an impromptu putting match on a splotchy putting green in Hyde Park, and then had to abandon a scheduled round at Sunningdale Old, where a friend's brother was club secretary and Bobby Jones recorded his perfect round, a smooth 33 on each nine.

The rain followed us to Royal Birkdale on the Lancashire coast, where in 1961 Arnold Palmer captured the Claret Jug just one year after making his Open debut at St Andrews and narrowly losing out to Kel Nagle. On our brief visit, we met a friendly local caddie named Fred who claimed to have followed Palmer during his triumphant march to the championship, a moment widely credited with reviving public interest in the British Open and creating Britain's version of Palmer mania. Fred wondered if I'd ever met Arnold Palmer. I had indeed, but only once. My father's best friend's little brother had been one of the King's best chums at Wake Forest University. Only one or two degrees of separation existed between Arnold and his army, I joked.

This conversation took place in a light Lancashire rain that quickly became a bone-chilling downpour somewhere around the fifteenth tee, where Arnold pulled off the shot of the tournament. With the worsening rain, we'd decided to simply walk out to the famous spot and play in. Fred the caddie followed us, talking the whole way.

As we hurried back to the clubhouse, I picked up a lovely bit of golf trivia from Fred, namely that three-time Open champion Henry Cotton made his final appearance in the Open the year Arnie captured the jug at Birkdale, and that the oldest man in the field that week also happened to be an American, a delightful fellow I'd recently interviewed and played a round with in California for my column in *Departures* magazine. During his prime, the ageless Paul Runyan was nicknamed "Little Poison," owing to his extraordinary short-game skills. During our afternoon together at his club in Pasadena, Little Poison told me how he beat Sam Snead out of the PGA Championship in 1938 purely by dint of short-game wizardry. "Sam outdrove me by fifty yards or more on every hole. But I needed just twenty-seven putts, and chipped in twice for birdie," he explained during a much-needed chipping lesson following our round. At Birkdale in 1961, Runyan, then fifty-three, finished a respectable eighteenth in the field that Arnold Palmer lapped to claim his first Claret Jug.

The golf gods smiled on us up the coast road at Lytham, where a charming former club captain named Tony Nickson sent us out on a clear, cool Wednesday morning and invited us for lunch afterward. Nickson, a debonair man and fellow WWII veteran who had served in Burma and was somehow convinced, due to the club's generous policy of allowing American servicemen stationed at a base in the adjacent village of Freckleton to use the clubs of absent members, that my father had used *his* clubs at Lytham. Whatever the truth of this conviction, we had a nice leisurely round, and I even learned about the spunky ginger-haired teenage girl—the pro's daughter, as it happened—who caddied for my old man during his interlude at Lytham and even gave him useful swing tips.

"So you learned to play golf from a girl?" I needled Opti over a pint with Tony Nickson after the round.

"These young ones have no respect for their elders, Braxton," Tony said, winking at my dad. "She was a very fine player, young Nicky Ferguson, who went on to claim several ladies' championships in the area. You weren't the first golfer she took in hand and sorted out." The two old soldiers spent the next hour sharing wartime memories as I sat nearby and soaked it all in, taking mental photographs.

What had been a thoroughly grand day turned dark, however, when I proposed we check out a popular pub before we headed to supper. The pub was a low-beamed affair buzzing with thirsty patrons. Signs welcoming Americans for the village's D-Day reunion earlier that summer still adorned the walls. I went off to the gents' and returned to find a drunken Irishman named Jimmy gently haranguing my dad about a terrible accident involving a bomber that missed the runway during a freak summer thunderstorm and crashed into the school annex of the local Anglican church, killing dozens and setting the central square of Freckleton on fire. On my way to the loo, I'd paused to examine a framed newspaper that showed rubble and featured the headline THE DAY FRECKLETON WEPT.

When I came back, my old man looked as if he'd seen a ghost.

He motioned me to follow him outside, and paused only a moment to get his bearings before heading off toward the aforementioned church. I wordlessly followed him through an iron gate to a large memorial set off by itself in the burying ground. There were twenty-seven names carved into the memorial.

Standing there in the evening light, I learned my father's deepest secret—the reason he'd become Opti the Mystic.

Coming out of flight training at Chanute Field in Chicago, he was one of the highest-rated glider pilots and was scheduled to fly a troop glider into occupied France when the liberation effort commenced. He was also a parachute-packing instructor and the photographer for the base newspaper, double duty that meant he'd been up all night with packing crews when a refitted heavy bomber missed the runway and crashed into the neighboring church annex, killing two dozen five- and six-year-olds and setting the village square on fire, additionally killing several servicemen and villagers. Because the tragedy occurred just months before the start of Operation Overlord, government censors prevented any mention of the Freckleton tragedy from leaking into the press. My dad, it turned out, had been one of the first responders on the scene, burning his hands so badly that he was briefly hospitalized.

Our trip could easily have ended right there in that silent churchyard. But it didn't. Sitting quietly in the empty breakfast nook at the Clifton Arms Hotel the next morning, he opened up and talked about the darkest moment of his life for the first time, sharing every detail of the tragedy that had long haunted him, especially the memory of a particular little girl he called "Lady Sunshine," whose mother was one of several grieving parents who approached him during his recuperation, hoping he might have taken photographs of their children. He arranged for all his photos to be given away, but kept one of Lady Sunshine sitting on a stone wall beside her bicycle.

He told me that his spunky granddaughter, Maggie, reminded him of Lady Sunshine.

It was suddenly, abundantly clear to me that Opti the Mystic had risen from the ashes of that unspeakable event, vowing to never have a bad day again if he could help it. It explained why he believed "Life promises us sorrow. It's up to us to add the joy."

Opti's unburdening led to my own. Though I'd spent two decades trying to put the tragedy of my murdered girlfriend, Kristin, behind me, it was suddenly obvious to me, as we drove up the coast to Scotland talking about both tragedies, that I'd immersed myself in every tragic story I could find simply to plumb the heart of human darkness during my strange passage through the murder capital of the South. This explained why the summons from Tommy Barnes to help publicize the plight of the East Lake Golf Club was such a welcome surprise, and a redeeming glimpse of what could be—and the reason, after my hearing Opti's thoughts at Pinehurst, I turned down Washington, DC, in favor of a Vermont trout stream.

Fortunately, the sun bobbed out and the mood brightened dramatically at Turnberry, where a pair of dentists from Alabama spotted my *Golf* magazine cap and somehow lured us into a team match for fifty quid over the mighty Ailsa course. They won the first five holes before we found our games and won five out of the next eleven, a fantastic comeback inspired by my dad's near ace on the par-three eighth hole and a chip-in birdie at the eleventh, both of which would have delighted Little Poison. The cocky dentists fell silent, and their heads looked ready to explode with rage. Unfortunately my father's colostomy bag beat them to the punch, rupturing as we hiked up the hill to the seventeenth tee. We conceded the match and sent them on, and just sat together on a bench, gazing over the beautiful Irish sea and saying very little, because so little needed saying.

We grabbed lunch the next day at Royal Troon, where Arnold captured his second and final Open in 1962, and pushed on to the Gleneagles Hotel, where my friend Jimmy Kidd, the resort's superintendent, joined us for a round on the King's Course, after which we sprung for supper in the dining room. One of my nicest memories of that evening was meeting Jimmy's young son, David, a skinny teenager who would grow up to become one of the world's leading golf course designers.

Perhaps our best day of golf came at Muirfield, where local historian Archie Baird showed us around his charming golf museum in the center of golf-mad Gullane and somehow scrounged up the only riding cart in the village so the two old soldiers, trailed by Archie's terrier, Niblick, could play Muirfield that afternoon in gorgeous autumn weather. I carried my bag silently in their wake, happy to be in their company.

Our finish at St Andrews had a surprise ending worthy of O. Henry, the famous writer who hailed from my hometown. A friend who managed the Old Course Hotel arranged for my dad and me to avoid the daily lottery for tee times that the governing St Andrews Links Trust had recently instituted. My straight-arrow dad, however, felt this was an unfair advantage and a breach of the rules, and therefore insisted we submit to the lottery, just the same as any visiting pilgrims. As a result, we waited two full days but never drew a tee time.

In the end, we wound up simply walking the most famous golf course in the world together at dusk, playing a round of "air golf" and clearing the air of any remaining things—unfinished business— left hitherto unspoken. Opti told me how he gave up flying after nearly crashing a plane with my infant older brother on board, and gave me firm instructions on how my brother and I were to take care of our mother after he was gone. I told him for the first time about my quietly unraveling marriage, and how both of us seemed helpless to stop it from doing so. He listened without judgment and advised me to make sure that I conducted myself with the utmost dignity and kindness, whatever was to come. "Life promises us sorrow," he repeated somewhere around the Road Hole, where he once made a miraculous sand save from the infamous bunker there. "It's up to us to add the joy."

Opti went home to his deeply relieved war bride, and I went on to France, where, rather amazingly, I managed to find that ancient graffitied beech tree in the forest of Compiègne. I took a photograph of my mother's and father's initials and sent it to them. Then I went home, too.

My father beat the odds and lived longer than expected. We all gathered for Christmas in Greensboro, where my mom cooked a feast, and Opti ironically gave me a second copy of Haultain's *The Mystery of Golf* and spent most of his time reading to his grandchildren. As we set off for New Year's Eve in Maine, which the Scots call Hogmanay, one might have been forgiven for thinking—as I tried to do—that time hadn't expired. But a few weeks later, toward the end of February, Opti thanked his half dozen employees, closed his office in Greensboro, and went home to Dogwood Drive for the final time.

I joined him a few days later. With the aid of a thoughtful hospice technician, I became my father's personal caretaker for the last four weeks of his life. We moved his bed to my old bedroom so he could look out the window at the back garden. We sat and talked about many things as his days and nights reversed, including old golf matches and our trip to golf's Holy Land. He wondered how the book I was writing about the trip was coming along, and I admitted that, save for the one chapter I'd written detailing our delightful day with Archie Baird at Muirfield, which I called "The Mystery of the Hole," the project had pretty much stalled.

I read him that chapter and apologized that we hadn't been able to play the Old Course or the three other Open venues I'd arranged.

"It seems like we just drank and talked our way in pubs from London to St Andrews," I said, pointing out how I'd managed to check us into the worst hotels with the lumpiest beds and get us repeatedly lost on rainy back roads, to say nothing of the terrible emotions I unwittingly exhumed.

"I think that was just what we both needed," Opti said quietly.

"You're such a crazy optimist," I pointed out.

"I know," he agreed. "Perhaps you will be, too, in time. Besides, you're talking about a trip that had a few challenging moments. I'm talking about a journey I won't forget. And you won't, either."

That evening he asked me to help him down the hall so he could sleep with my mother in their own bed. I remember hearing her make a sweet fuss over him, tucking him in properly as I gently closed their bedroom door behind me.

The next night, sleet ticked the windows. My dad woke up long enough to ask me about this and to assure me the weather would be "just fine in the morning." He began making funny little lip purses, like air kisses.

"What are you doing?" I asked.

"Kissing your babies good night."

I simply could not speak. So he spoke for me.

"Go kiss your wife and the babies," he said a few minutes later, the last words I heard my father say.

The next morning was indeed beautiful, a gorgeous March morning in Old Catawba. After his body had been taken away to be cremated, my closest friend and oldest golf pal, Patrick McDaid, showed up out of the blue and suggested we grab our clubs and go play Longview, the glorious goat farm out by the Piedmont Triad International Airport where we had played as boys and argued about everything from orange golf balls to which Bond girl we would someday marry.

"Opti would approve," Patrick assured me. "He might even insist."

And he was right. We had a fine time playing and talking. Glorious Goat Farming—as we loved to call it—was just what I needed, though to this day I have no idea what either of us scored.

CHAPTER SEVEN

A BOOK WITH A HEARTBEAT

Shortly before the publication of *Final Rounds* in November of 1996, I joked to the aforementioned Patrick McDaid that if all my rednecked, pink-eyed, lint-eared cousins in the five central North Carolina counties purchased a copy of the book (and my mom bought the hundred or so copies I knew she would buy), my tales of travel with Opti might easily sell two hundred copies.

The first few weeks out, the book didn't even do that well.

On a frigid morning in early December, however, I was in my barn office writing a column for *Golf* when a publicist from Bantam Books called to say that, thanks to a flurry of strong reviews, the book had jumped onto several regional and independent bestseller lists, and was even rising on the extended *New York Times* list. She wondered if I might be willing to go on a national book tour to boost the book for the holidays. Naturally I agreed, figuring that would make for a fun couple of days. But she had at least two weeks and a dozen stops in mind, almost a complete circle around the United States that would get me home to Maine a few days before Christmas Eve.

In some ways, the opportunity couldn't have come at a better moment. By then I was a single father sharing joint custody of my two children. They shuffled uncomplaining between two houses—their mother's on a watery cove in Phippsburg, mine on a forested hilltop west of Brunswick—every fortnight, performing a civilized ritual common to millions of modern American families. The parting was still almost unimaginable to me, and, lacking clearer answers and enough time to fully comprehend how this sad event had come to pass, was doubly devastating in such close proximity to my father's death. I'd at least managed to show an optimistic face and keep moving forward, uncertain what the universe had in mind next, determined to get through on little more than faith and the unerring counsel of the Queen Mum, who never wavered in her devotion to us all. "James, I think you should go," she said when I phoned to tell her about the book tour and wondered if I should travel so close to the holidays. "It's a beautiful book, and you'll have fun talking about your father." Not surprisingly, she agreed to look after our dogs and my house while I was away.

The first big night came in Greensboro, where friends and family turned out in surprisingly large numbers, including my elementary school teachers and my dad's closest golf pal, Bill Mims, who told me he cried as he read the book. Strangely, the next night in Charlotte—where I knew maybe six people, including college roommates and an old girlfriend—the crowds were even larger, a mystery that resolved itself when an elderly couple waiting patiently in the long line at Park Road Books discovered that I *wasn't* James Dobson, the Christian broadcaster. (He was apparently scheduled to speak at a big Christian conference in town that week.) When I playfully offered to sign one of his books in his absence, the couple did an about-face and marched straight out of the shop, taking every third disappointed person in line with them.

As usual, the Queen Mum was right. The tour, which took me

on a circuitous route around the United States, was an unexpected tonic. I met hundreds of nice folks and golfers of every stripe, and even played once or twice with colleagues and old friends at distinguished golf clubs I'd long wished to visit during the California segment of the tour, arriving home a few nights before Christmas exhausted but happy to be home, and determined to keep my chin up and carry on as a snowless holiday descended.

I'd promised the dear lady who ran our local independent bookshop that I would do a final book talk and signing on the eve of Christmas Eve, even though I was fairly certain the turnout would be minimal. Not only are Mainers fanatically frugal—buying new books, even by local authors, isn't high on their list of priorities when a single copy at the town library will do nicely—but the first true snowstorm of the season was rapidly bearing down on the Pine Tree State, rendering the proposition of leaving a warm hutch simply to collect a local author's signature a laughable exercise.

This explains why I pulled up in front of the bookshop just as sleet began pelting the windshield to discover only two cars parked there. I sat for a moment, wondering if I should even bother to go inside or just go home and make a big fire, pour a nice aged bourbon, and read a good book. My kids weren't scheduled to come back to my house until Christmas Day.

Just then, the phone attached to the dash of my aging Blazer rang. I considered ignoring it, but answered in order to stall for a few more minutes.

A cheerful woman's voice said, "Hello—is this Jim Dodson?"

"Yes, ma'am," I replied, "unless perhaps you're looking for James Dobson."

She laughed. "Oh, no. You're the one I'm looking for. Jim, this is Winnie Palmer calling. I wanted to tell you that Arnie and I just finished reading *Final Rounds* and thought it was the sweetest book we've ever read. You know, Arnie was very close to his father, too. Deacon took Arnie to Pinehurst when he was a teenager—just like Opti the Mystic did with you."

Pleasantly startled, I thanked her. But I also wondered if this really was Winnie Palmer, or just someone pulling a mean prank on a very weary traveler. Several Greensboro buddies had needled me without mercy about the nice reviews *Final Rounds* had received in *USA Today* and other papers, after all, and I could picture them gathered around a table at Ham's Pub in Greensboro, our old watering hole, stifling guffaws as someone's wife or the barmaid pretended to be Winnie Palmer and wound me up like a top just to see me spin.

"In fact," she went on, "we think you're the perfect person to help Arnie write his autobiography. You two seem to have so much in common, and Arnie has so many connections to people from North Carolina. We think you two would make a good team. Would you be interested in meeting with us at the Francis Ouimet Banquet in Boston the week after next?"

I was indeed interested—except for one small thing. In my addled brain, I was suddenly convinced beyond any doubt that this nice person on the line was anyone *but* Winnie Palmer. I pictured my old goat-farm golf pal Patrick McDaid doubling over with laughter as his wife, Terri, spoke into a phone using a terrible Pennsylvania accent.

So I said the following:

"I'm deeply flattered, Mrs. Palmer, and I would certainly love to talk with you about the project. Unfortunately, Jack and Barbara Nicklaus are coming to Maine for Christmas. In fact, I'm on my way to Portland International Jetport this very minute to pick them up. I'm taking them to a holiday party down on Small Point, where I took them a couple of years ago. If things go tonight like they did that night, frankly, we're probably all going to get drunk as skunks. Last time, I'm embarrassed to say, Barbara Nicklaus and I wound up accidentally making out. So, if you don't mind, I'll have to call you back."

At which point I hung up on her and headed into the bookshop, where I found two live customers waiting to get a signed copy of my book, only one of whom was disappointed to learn I wasn't James Dobson. The other was my dear friend Bunny Dugan, who'd already purchased five copies of the book to give to his friends down in Florida, where he and Jane were headed for the new year. Tom invited me to stop by his house in Brunswick after the quickest book signing on record and poured me that much-needed bourbon by the fire.

By the time I plowed up my steep driveway into the snowy forest, the winter nor'easter was well into its fury, the snow already calf deep. I shoveled my way to the front steps, went in, and turned up the heat, and was warmly greeted by a pair of elderly golden retrievers named Amos and Bailey. I put on the teakettle for proper tea, the way the Queen Mum schooled me, and saw that the little red light on the answering machine was blinking. I fed the dogs their Christmas bones two days early, then pushed the machine's play button.

The first voice belonged to the Queen Mum, welcoming me home and inviting me to lunch the next day, weather permitting; she was eager to hear about my travels.

The second caller's voice was also familiar. She laughed almost girlishly.

"Hello, Jim, this really *is* Winnie Palmer calling. I decided to try your home phone this time. Doc Giffin [Arnold's longtime executive assistant] gave it to me. Arnold thought that was the funniest thing he's ever heard about Barbara and Jack, and now he wants you to do the book more than ever. Unfortunately, he's gone to bed. Would you mind giving us a call in the morning to discuss this? We're coming up for the Ouimet Banquet in Boston and would love to have you attend that with us. Arnie's being honored. He says we should have drinks before the dinner and get to know each other. Thank you—

and merry Christmas!" She provided the Palmer home number, and I heard her laugh again as she hung up.

My first thought was that Arnold and Winnie Palmer sure had a keen sense of humor. My second was that Christmas had come two days early.

=== • ===

A famous Roman philosopher once advised his pupils that one should never get to know their heroes too intimately—thus risk discovering they are all too human, and disappointing.

Arnold Palmer was the first name on my earliest list of "Things to Do in Golf." When I mentioned this fact in order to make a point during our conversation prior to the Ouimet Banquet three weeks later, adding my one tiny Roman apprehension, the King of Golf smiled. "I don't think you'll find many surprises with us. We're just ordinary people. Right, lover?"

He glanced over at Winnie, who was seated near us in the Sheraton penthouse suite overlooking Copley Square. She nodded. "Your dad sounds like such a wise man. Arnie's dad was, too. Something tells me you two would have very good chemistry."

I thanked her, but told them what the veteran journalist in me knew to be true—that the best biographies and autobiographies are the most candid about the people and forces that shaped the subject's life and worldview, willing, more often than not, to speak frankly about the painful and unhappy events and turning points that led to personal growth and eventual success through struggle, failure, and redemption. These were the core elements not only of great storytelling, I said, but of a meaningful life as well—the only route I knew to real happiness.

Arnold was sitting very still as I made this little speech, listening but giving me what I would come to think of as The Look, equal parts disapproving schoolmaster and constipated eagle. Winnie's expression betrayed no emotion whatsoever.

Just to make sure I *didn't* get this once-in-a-lifetime assignment, I plunged ahead. "If you read *Final Rounds*, you know it's full of some really terrible happenings—the murder of a girl I'd planned to marry, and a plane crash during the war that killed dozens of people, including dozens of schoolchildren, in an English village, reconfiguring my dad's worldview. These were events that shaped both our lives. At the heart of every great story are conflict, struggle, and resolution. Bobby Jones once said he never learned anything from a golf tournament he won."

"Actually," Arnold said, clearing his throat, "the idea of writing my autobiography has never really appealed to me. People have just been after me to do it forever." He gave a wintry little smile worthy of the light snow falling just outside the windows.

I assumed this might be his final word on the topic, so I took a moment to sip my expensive bourbon, if only to dampen my very dry mouth. Though he was arguably the most transparent sports superstar in history, Arnold Palmer wouldn't be the first icon to flatly resist going to the private places that hurt yet revealed all. The shelves were littered with celebrity autobiographies that were long on fluff and thin on substance.

"So how would you choose to write Arnie's book?" Winnie spoke up.

I looked at her and explained that Arnold was indisputably the most beloved sports figure of modern times—perhaps of all time. And yet he was also the most intimate sports star ever, someone every golfer felt a strong personal connection with. He was one of us, I said, someone we all felt that we knew like a hometown neighbor, a lifelong friend, the boy next door who happened to become the King of Golf. The King of Everymen. I glanced at Arnold.

"That *is* Arnie," Winnie said with feeling.

"I never really cared for that word," he put in, presumably meaning "king." He rattled the ice in his tumbler as if to remind us that he was still present. "To anyone who knows me, I'm just plain Arnie from Latrobe."

"And every golfer knows you," I said. "Or feels as if they do. That's the point. There have been dozens of books written about your amazing golf career and business acumen, but none that I know of that sound like your authentic voice or provide the intimacy your fans deserve."

Before I ran out of courage, and bourbon, I made my pitch: that we write an intimate memoir rather than an overly detailed autobiography, one that focused on a dozen or so major turning points in his amazing life, moments both good and bad that shaped the person he became. We would shy away from nothing; trials and triumphs alike, the things he most cared about and learned from—a book, if you please, that made his fans feel as though they were sitting with their good friend Arnold Palmer, having a Ketel One by the fire and listening to him tell the most revealing stories about his life and times, intimate things they'd never heard before but that, in the end, confirmed why they loved this man so much.

Finally, I told the Palmers the best advice I'd ever received from anyone about writing a book. It came, not surprisingly, from my own father, when I told him I'd stalled briefly on *Final Rounds* a week before he passed away.

"He told me, 'Write a book that you want to read—one that has a beating heart.' This book needs a beating heart."

"That's so nice," Winnie said. "I love that."

Arnold was now giving *her* The Look. "I'm guessing IMG won't like that very much. You know how they like to control everything. They won't want anything . . . well, negative."

"It's *your* life, Arnie," she returned with surprising vigor. "I think that sounds *great*, exactly the approach we should take. We'll do this book together, just the three of us and Doc, something your fans will love. A book with a beating heart."

Arnold glanced at me. "Well, I guess that's settled. Another drink before we go downstairs?"

I could have kissed Winnie Palmer—and indeed did so at the end of the evening, after Arnold gave his fine address about the fellowship of the game to the donors and guests at the sold-out Ouimet Scholarship Fund Banquet, before we parted company. We agreed to get down to work at Bay Hill when Arnold and Winnie returned from their annual winter trip to Palm Springs.

=== • ===

What followed were the two most challenging and enjoyable years of my book-writing life, and, better yet, the start of a friendship I could never have imagined as a kid.

No athlete in America has enjoyed a more successful public life than Arnold Palmer. During the course of his professional playing career, he collected ninety-two tournament titles, sixty-two of them on the PGA Tour, including seven major championships. But that was just the framework of his extraordinary impact on golf, and on American culture at large. Emerging at the dawn of a new decade, when a vigorous young president was talking of sending men to the moon and forty million color television sets were revolutionizing the way Americans viewed modern life, Palmer transformed the somnolent country-club game of golf into a national sports frenzy, becoming the first professional golfer to reach the million-dollar mark in Tour earnings, the first four-time winner of the Masters Tournament, and the first to purchase and fly his own jet airplane. Arnie's rugged good looks, earthy charisma, and go-for-broke playing style, which often found him playing from the kind of trouble any weekend hacker could relate to, made him the people's clear choice, a hero after their own hearts. Almost overnight, his quick and telegenic smile, visible passion, and genuine affection for fans transformed galleries into a vast mobile army on the march.

With the help of a Cleveland lawyer named Mark McCormack, Palmer transformed the way star athletes were marketed, licensed, and promoted, essentially reinventing the athlete-entrepreneur concept that made him wealthy beyond his own boyhood dreams and, for two decades, the most famous athlete in the world.

But as Winnie said to me one evening about a year into the research and writing of *A Golfer's Life*, as the three of us lingered at the Palmers' supper table well into a summer night in Latrobe, "Arnold really *does* think of himself as an ordinary guy to whom something extraordinary happened, the kind of thing that maybe only happens in America. He is exactly what he appears to be—a nice man who appreciates everything he's been given. Arnie loves people. The only time you'll ever really see him unhappy is when he's in a crowded place and people aren't all over him."

She glanced affectionately at her famous husband, who, predictably, had already dozed off in his kitchen chair, tilting slightly to starboard. It had been one of many long days of interviewing Arnold, beginning at dawn in his modest workshop next door and following him through a busy day that included jetting off to Maryland for a luncheon appearance at Bethesda Country Club and a quick flight home to Latrobe for afternoon golf with a couple of local buddies and his collaborator at Latrobe Country Club, the simple golf course where, as a kid, he'd earned nickels by knocking the tee shots of Latrobe lady golfers over the creek. That very afternoon, as we headed back to the private airport where his signature Citation X was parked, Arnold turned to me and asked, with a gently needling smile, "So, Shakespeare, you've been with me a lot of places since we started this project. Does anything surprise or even disappoint you?"

We both knew exactly what he was getting at—the Roman sage I'd quoted at our meeting in Boston about the danger of getting too close to your heroes and finding them too human and lacking in character.

Truthfully, Arnold Daniel Palmer was even more "human" than I'd expected, and was something of a literary collaborator's dream subject, so forthcoming with intimate details about his childhood, family, early Tour life and career, personal relationships, and business experiences both happy and disappointing was he that I was always surprised by the depth of his candor on any subject. A number of powerful, hitherto untold stories and observations found their way into our narrative, and there were other confidences he shared that I'll never write or even talk about—though they were nothing that wouldn't make you admire Arnold Palmer all the more. Maybe most extraordinary of all, he and Winnie and Doc Giffin simply trusted my judgment about what to use and what to leave out, an almost unheard-of circumstance in a literary collaboration involving a world-famous figure.

As a result of such uncommon trust, by my count, his memoir contains at least a dozen or more stories no one had ever read before, told in Arnold's inimitable small-town American voice—truly a book with a beating heart, and quite possibly the reason Arnold's memoirs camped on the *New York Times* bestseller list for months. Not long ago, nearly twenty years since the publication of what Arnie called his "last book," a Yale man working on his PhD about the collaborative process between writers and famous subjects asked to interview me about my work on *A Golfer's Life*. He'd heard from various industry sources that it was one of the most engaging books of its kind, and wondered what I'd done to make the book so intimate and appealing. I explained that I had told Arnold and Winnie that there wasn't anything he could tell his fans that wouldn't make them love him even more—proving he was one of their kind, just an ordinary guy to whom something extraordinary had happened. "After that," I added, "I just listened. The Palmers and their staff and friends were amazing."

Which explains why, in answer to Arnold's question as we were departing Bethesda Country Club for Latrobe, I confessed that something about him did greatly surprise me. "You don't travel anywhere with a bodyguard or even a PR person for your public appearances. I can't think of any star athlete or celebrity who doesn't travel with security or an entourage."

Arnold had a good chuckle at this, his big blacksmith's shoulders hopping merrily as we rode along.

"Let me tell you something, Shakespeare. The minute you think you need a bodyguard, you probably do. Know what I mean?"

I did indeed. And that essentially said everything one needed to know about "just plain Arnie," as Winnie liked to call him. Everywhere we went, I marveled at the way huge crowds surrounded the visiting King just to say hello, to share a family memory, to snap a photo, or to politely ask for an autograph. He never failed to oblige, and they, his adoring subjects, in turn never crossed the line in the way they treated the most beloved figure in golf history. Some visibly trembled with joy in his presence. Others beamed with pleasure as they posed with their hero. I probably took dozens of photographs for fans.

Since the start of our work together, however, Arnold's world had narrowed considerably. He was still recovering from recent successful prostate surgery at the Mayo Clinic, and not long after we got under way, Winnie had been diagnosed with a form of ovarian cancer, prompting us to accelerate production of the book. As the circle closed, I was fortunate to have dozens of evenings alone with Arnie and Winnie and their closest friends, to be welcomed into their most intimate family circle and to be included in so many occasions going forward.

One lazy spring afternoon, as we played Latrobe's leafy back nine together, Arnold led me off the fourteenth fairway to a handsome red barn standing nearby, explaining that his goal was to restore "Winnie's barn" in time for his seventieth-birthday party, which was going to be a small affair in early September. In the dim light he became unusually quiet, poking around in the barn. "This is where Pap used to keep his tractors," he explained, and then stood perfectly still, gazing out through the barn's open doors toward a distant hill where he and Winnie planned to plant a vineyard. Arnold sighed, his voice cracking. "I don't know what I'll do if I lose Winnie. She's the rudder on my ship."

I had no answer for him. So, as a friend, I simply nodded in agreement, my own eyes watering.

Later that afternoon, before the three of us went to supper at their favorite roadhouse on the Lincoln Highway, Winnie drove me west of town to see a tidy historic brick church called Unity Chapel, then on to check out the amazing summer garden of a friend. She and I shared a love of old churches and landscape gardens, and she had even urged me to consider writing about the horticultural world that fascinated us both. I eventually did, too, and dedicated the book to her.

"I think Arnie is very worried about me," she allowed on the drive back to town. "It's been good to have you around us at this time. Arnie and I have grown very fond of you. You two have such nice chemistry. You make him laugh. He loves to laugh. So thank you for that—and for the book. You made it sound just like Arnie's voice."

I thanked her for saying this, already fighting the sadness that comes with completing a project you know in your bones will never be rivaled.

"We'd better see you and Wendy often in Latrobe or down at Bay Hill," she playfully warned. "And I really want you to do that gardening book."

A few weeks later, we debuted *A Golfer's Life* at the Bay Hill Arnold Palmer Invitational. That same week, Winnie arranged to put my fiancée, Wendy Buynak, and our four kids up in the beautiful Lexington Cottage across from the Bay Hill Lodge, providing our gang with free VIP tickets to Disney World and Cirque du Soleil. My favorite moment of the week, however, was when Arnold invited my daughter, Maggie—the co-captain of her junior high field hockey team back home in Maine—to a golf lesson on the practice tee. He showed her the fundamentals and stepped back and watched as she drilled a ball two hundred yards straight at the target with a three-metal, whereupon he turned to me and boomed, "Shakespeare, this girl damn well *better* play golf!" Somewhere I have a picture of this moment, Arnold grinning with his arm around his blushing pupil, a photo forever in my head.

=== • ===

Whenever I give an evening talk, I'm always asked to tell stories about my time with Arnold and Winnie Palmer. Some people simply want to know what the King of Golf was *really* like.

"He's exactly like he appears," I like to say, channeling Winnie. "Only better."

That said, I have a few funny little stories about my time with Arnold and Winnie that I would like to share.

Here are three of my favorites:

Early one morning in Arnie's Latrobe workshop (where an entire wall was covered with racks of putters), I casually asked my subject a question almost every golfer wants to know the answer to: What did Arnold *really* think of Jack Nicklaus?

"Is he the man you feared most?" I asked.

Arnie was regripping a Callaway driver. He shook his head. "Nope. That distinction belonged to Harvie Ward."

"Really?" I was deeply surprised to hear this, and eager to know more. Harvie and Arnold were rivals during their college years at Carolina and Wake Forest, respectively, but Jack was the man who, in effect, dethroned Arnold on the Tour by beating him before a hometown crowd at the Open at Oakmont in 1962—not the first championship Arnold's short game allowed to slip through his fingers.

"That's right," Arnold said. "I could never seem to beat Harvie when it mattered in college. That, plus he was so good-looking and smooth with the ladies I always felt outgunned." He glanced at me and added, "Fortunately, I beat him when it counted the most—with Winnie."

Weeks after winning the National Amateur Championship at the Country Club of Detroit in 1954, Arnold was invited to Shawnee on Delaware to play in bandleader Fred Waring's popular Waite Memorial golf tournament. In the lobby of the rustic Shawnee Inn after his first practice round, he met pretty Winifred Walzer, who was working as a tournament hostess for the week. He invited her to come out and watch him play golf. She was so refined and polished that he assumed she must be a rich girl from Philadelphia's Main Line. In fact, she was the bright, levelheaded, no-nonsense daughter of a Bethlehem canned goods salesman named Shube Walzer. The next day Arnold spotted Winifred on the course and invited her to sit with him at that evening's dinner dance; she agreed. "I'd never met anyone like her. She was smart, beautiful, and independent, and studied interior design at Brown University. She was even something of a social rebel, who had no interest in being a debutante."

When he heard that she'd been out with his smooth-talking nemesis, Harvie Ward, once already that week, and that Harvie had asked for a second date, a bold plan formed in Arnold's mind.

"On Friday night, at our second dinner together, I reached under the table and found Winnie's hand and asked what she would say if I asked her to marry me. She looked startled and asked if she could have a day to think about it. I told her, 'Not too long. I've got places to go. We can use the Walker Cup for our honeymoon.'"

The next day, she agreed to marry him. Word quickly leaked out. Days later, Arnold won enough cash in a $20 Nassau money match at Pine Valley against four of his regular golf pals from Cleveland to purchase a proper engagement ring.

"And *that's* how I won Winnie's hand and finally beat Harvie Ward," Arnold declared.

"So what do you really feel about Jack Nicklaus?" I pressed him.

He thought for a moment, then set aside the club and picked up the morning edition of the Pittsburgh newspaper.

"Fair enough," he said, winking. "Let me go take my morning Nicklaus, and I'll come back and tell you exactly what I really think of Jack."

I was still smiling when he came back a few minutes later.

This time he wasn't joking. "Jack is, without doubt, the greatest player ever. His record stands alone and proves that. He's also a very good friend, and a great friend to golf in general. Winnie and Barbara Nicklaus, as you know, are almost best buddies. Jack and I share a passion for this game that goes way beyond our accomplishments. Beyond this, in a purely competitive sense, we needed each other. We made each other better players—and people. Jack is an outstanding man, and a great ambassador for the game."

With that, he winked impishly. "And I can tell you some pretty wild stories about Jack, if you're interested . . ."

═══ • ═══

One night shortly before my wife, Wendy, and I got engaged, we met Arnold and Winnie at Pebble Beach's Tap Room for a bite to eat. At one point, Arnold—a partner in a group that had recently acquired Pebble Beach from its previous Japanese owners—excused himself for the gents', and came back a few minutes later chuckling about a most unexpected encounter with an ardent fan that left his shirt soaked with water.

In the bathroom, he explained, he was standing at the urinal, minding his own business, when a short fellow who was obviously feeling no pain shuffled up to the porcelain beside him. He casually glanced over at Arnold once, twice, and then a third time, mouth open in pure astonishment. Next thing Arnold knew, the man was pawing with his free hand in his coat pocket, withdrawing a flip phone, and dialing with his thumb. Arnold picks up the story from there.

"He called his wife and said, 'Helen, you're not going to *believe* who I'm standing right beside at Pebble Beach. We're both taking a leak together. Just try and guess . . . Nope. In fact it's *Jack Nicklaus*! Can you believe it?' The next thing I knew, he handed me the phone over the divider, asking me to speak to his wife just to prove he wasn't joking."

We all laughed.

"What on earth did you do?" Winnie demanded to know.

"I took the phone and said hello, of course. I told Helen that I'd enjoyed meeting her husband here at Pebble Beach. His name turned out to be Phil. I informed her that Phil had been having a great time and had played so well that day that he'd won all the money in the company outing, and she could expect a *very* nice guilt gift when he got home."

"Oh, Arnie, you *didn't*!"

"I did. Phil was very happy. Unfortunately, I was laughing so hard as I washed my hands that I accidentally turned on the tap too hard and sprayed myself with water."

No story I can think of says more about Arnold Palmer, the gracious, fun-loving King of Everymen.

═══ ● ═══

One afternoon, after a long morning interview in the workshop followed by lunch, Arnold invited me to play a friendly match against

Rocco Mediate and Rick Smith, the well-known golf instructor. Arnold had known Rocco since he was a kid growing up in nearby Greensburg, Pennsylvania. When I expressed my hesitation about playing a match against a leading Tour player and his teacher, friendly as they were, Arnie waved it off with a laugh. "Don't worry. I've got you covered. You just have fun. I can handle those two."

My game at that moment was fairly respectable, a Maine State Golf Association six handicap, more or less, but my nerves were on edge during a shaky first nine in which I contributed absolutely nothing to our cause. I managed to halve a couple of holes on the back nine, however, and finally settled down enough to find my swing as we came to the fifteenth tee with several carryovers in the balance.

"This is where I hit the big mamoo," Arnold said to me with a reassuring smile.

We had the honors. I watched him make his famous corkscrew swing and send a blast to the top of the hill. Our opponents looked impressed. I teed up, took a breath, and finally made a full shoulder turn on the ball. Mine flew up the hill and rolled well past Arnold's. Moments later I reached the green in two and made a lengthy putt for eagle. Our opponents couldn't have been more gracious.

That evening at dinner, Arnold handed me $100. "What's this?" I asked.

"Our winnings—thanks to *your* big mamoo." He gave me a half-hearted version of The Look, and then smiled. "Just don't try that ever again unless you're my partner."

I used the money to buy a shirt from the Latrobe Country Club pro shop and a set of Arnold Palmer salt and pepper shakers we still use at our table today.

—— • ——

The last time I saw Winnie was at the party that September to celebrate Arnold's seventieth birthday and the opening of Winnie's barn. It was a small group that included family and friends, Winnie's wonderful brother Marty Walzer, Arnold's sisters Cheech and Sandy and their husbands, his brother Jerry, the Palmers' longtime neighbors Suzy and Ken Bowman, Carolyn and Howdy Giles, and other folks from town who had known Latrobe's first couple for nearly half a century.

The restored red barn resembled an Amish postcard. It was a wonderful evening of food and conversation and a birthday cake fit for a homegrown King. Winnie looked tired but was in great spirits throughout, telling me about her trip with Arnold earlier that summer to France with Arnold's longtime friend Russ Meyer—chairman of Cessna Aircraft—and his wife, Helen. "When we got to the Bayeaux Tapestry," Winnie told me, "Arnie said he'd had enough of museum-going. He went outside to wait for us. Russ and Helen and I took our sweet time looking at the tapestry. I was kind of worried about Arnie. But when we came out of the museum, there he sat on a nearby wall, drinking a beer and chatting away with a Frenchman like they were old friends. I don't think the man had any idea who Arnold was."

At this, Winnie laughed, just as Howdy Giles snapped a photograph of us standing by the barn's decorated front doors, near the spot where Arnold had shared his sadness the afternoon he showed me the barn. I still have that photograph on my office wall. She thanked me for coming but gently chided me for not bringing Wendy along. "I'll expect to see you both down at Bay Hill after Christmas, or even out West in January," she said, giving me a kiss for the road.

Winnie passed away eight weeks later, and I returned for her simple, beautiful memorial service at the tiny Unity Chapel, the little Presbyterian church she dearly loved. There was an overflow crowd. I sat next to Mark McCormack's wife, Nancy, feeling like I'd lost a family member.

We sang Winnie's favorite hymn, "Eternal Father, Strong to Save," the Navy hymn.

At the reception following the service, Barbara Nicklaus came over to me. She told me that Winnie had shared the funny story about the winter-night phone call in Maine, and smiled when I furiously blushed with embarrassment.

"Don't worry. Winnie and I were great friends. We shared lots of stories like that. She loved that story. And she loved you. You did such a nice job on Arnie's book. She was so proud of that."

The lump in my throat felt like a Titleist golf ball. But I somehow found the voice to properly thank her and collect a hug before I went to say good-bye to Arnold. He'd never looked sadder, I thought, as he managed to joke that I'd better not forget him now that Winnie was gone.

"Not possible," I said around the lump. We clasped arms like a couple of old Romans.

I drove out of town at sunset, headed for the interstate home to Maine, wondering when I might ever return to the home of Arnold Palmer.

Chapter Eight

The Perfect Mulligan

The summer I was finishing work on Arnold's book, a lawyer named Jonathan Sager phoned from Syracuse, New York, to invite me to be the keynote speaker at a fund-raiser for the Lung Association of New York, an October gala that included golf and dinner at the city's most famous golf club, the venerable Onondaga Golf & Country Club, where Walter Hagen played a lot of his golf.

I politely declined the invitation, explaining that I had a book to finish and wasn't traveling or speaking anywhere farther than my local golf club or my favorite pub in town.

But the lawyer wouldn't give up. He promptly dispatched a list of Ten Reasons to Visit Syracuse that included, among other key enticements, "the opportunity to see Richard Gere's childhood home in North Syracuse and maybe meet his father, Homer," and a chance to "see the world's first drive-in bank teller and the only traffic light in the United States with the green light on top." As an added bonus, he mentioned playing Oak Hill Country Club in Rochester (site of the 1995 Ryder Cup) and promised to show me "the only golf course Robert Trent Jones designed on a cocktail napkin." Finally, he wished to introduce me to his regular weekend playing pals, a group that called themselves the Dewsweepers. "Great bunch of guys. Totally nuts for golf. We're the first off the tee every Saturday morning, rain or shine," he said.

This last bit got my attention. My father had also been a Dewsweeper whose weekend group was first off the tee every Saturday morning. And unknown to my insistent host, I'd long wished to write a book about a group of ordinary guys for whom golf is both walking therapy and social glue, the tie that binds their friendship in an ever-changing world. Before I could mention this fact, however, the witty lawyer was already arranging my air travel.

"We'll make it easy for you to come. I have a buddy who has a plane. We'll fly over and pick you up."

To this day I don't know why I said yes. But several weeks later I watched a worryingly small airplane taxi to a stop at one end of the Portland International Jetport runway and three guys climb out wearing black Groucho Marx glasses with large rubber noses. They even had a pair for me, too.

One of them turned out to be Jon Sager. "You're younger than you look in your pictures," he said to me by way of introduction. "And bigger. You remind me of that guy Tim Herron on the Tour, the one they call 'Lumpy.'"

I replied that Sager reminded me of an old fraternity brother in college who went on to a distinguished career in state politics and was now in charge of running the laundry service at the state prison in Raleigh. Sager smiled as if I was his kind of guy.

I remember thinking, as we taxied to the end of the runway for takeoff and I put on my best Groucho face, how strange the newspaper account would be after searchers finally located our tiny plane somewhere deep in the White Mountains, bearing the earthly remains of four pasty white dudes wearing large eyeglasses and rubber noses—some kind of bizarre Groucho cult.

The weekend, in fact, was a blast. The Onondaga Club was

teeming with golf history, and the Dewsweepers—Lester, Tom, Tuck, Russ, Jon, Peter, and a dapper fellow named Zawadzki, whom everyone called "Z Man"—were everything I hoped they might be and more: seven diverse and classy fellows who played hard and constantly harassed each other with undying devotion, told great politically incorrect jokes, and clearly relished one another's company. As I chatted with all of them during and after our two rounds, my interest in writing about this everyman band of merrymaking golf buddies grew exponentially.

The only downside of the adventure was the blind date Jon had arranged for me—single again for going on a year—with a local poet named Mona, who'd written a best-selling memoir about her terrible childhood. Married guys can't stand the sight of an unattached friend, imagining all the illicit fun they must be having outside the binding ropes of matrimony. The lady in question showed up at the Onondaga Club looking sleek in a tiny sheath dress, but dropped so many deafening F-bombs in the crowded dining room that gasps could be heard, and more than one crystal goblet perished on the floor, falling from the startled fingers of an elderly Onondagan—a scene right out of P. G. Wodehouse come gloriously to life.

Just then, a pair of hands clapped me on the back, and I turned around to see my oldest pal, Patrick McDaid, standing there with a wide Irish grin.

"We convinced Patrick to come up for the roast," explained John Sager.

"This is a *roast*?" This was news to me.

Sager smiled. "Oh, *hell* yes. What did you expect—a Pulitzer Prize?"

Patrick and I had been inseparable buddies since the first day my family moved to the north side of Greensboro in 1966, the year I began making my "Things to Do in Golf" list. I'd gone for a spin on my bike around the new neighborhood and passed what looked like a leprechaun shooting hoops at the end of his driveway. He saw me and asked if I wanted to play a game of Horse. I parked, and we played. He beat me badly, so we played a second and then a third game, both of which he won. Then we went inside and played billiards in his basement. He won at billiards, too. His mother invited me to stay for supper, followed by more losses at billiards and a game of Chinese checkers, which I finally won. Somewhere late into the night I finally went home, only to have my mother threaten to ground me for life. Pat and I had been close ever since.

But Mona the poet clearly wasn't happy about being upstaged. She promptly unleashed a volley of blue words I sincerely doubt had ever been heard in the dining room of the stately Onondaga Club, save perhaps from one of the Haig's flapper girlfriends. A short time later, I walked Mona out to her equally tiny car.

"I have a confession to make," she said with a husky laugh. "I basically came to shake up a few rich Republicans."

"It's good to have a goal in life," I agreed.

"I probably won't buy your book," she said. "I hate golf."

"In that case, we'll have to stop meeting like this," I said.

The Lung Association gala was great fun, and only slightly mortifying. With assistance from the Irish Antichrist, as Sager quickly nicknamed Patrick McDaid, the event's host made good sport of my Lumpy-like demeanor and inability to beat my best friend at anything but Chinese checkers and golf. It's never easy when the guy doing the introductions is funnier than the speaker, but my golf tales seemed to be a hit with the crowd.

By the time he flew me back to Maine—sans Groucho glasses—my host and I had even made a plan for me to drive back to Syracuse for a long weekend in October to begin my research for what would become *The Dewsweepers* before the weather shut down the course.

"I know you're a lonely single guy again," Jon said. "We'll get you some really good blind dates this time."

"Thanks, but no thanks," I said. "Mona put me off blind dates forever."

"You don't have to marry them, for Christ's sake. Besides, I've already checked with a few gals, and they're up for spending an evening with you—most of them, anyway. For all they know, pal, you could be a serial killer who plays golf."

Over my objections, a week later he faxed me a sheet listing six eligible single women in the greater Syracuse metropolitan area with whom he thought I might enjoy spending an evening—a sort of Michelin Guide to the Onondagan divorced-mother set, a sorority of handpicked, Sager-approved potential dinner companions that included categorical ratings such as "Attractiveness Factor," "Interest in Golf Quotient," "Taste in Books," and "Ready to Date Index," plus Jon's own commentaries ("Ta-tas till Tuesday . . . Junoesque physique . . . My personal fantasy pick . . ." and so forth).

I phoned my host and told him this was completely juvenile.

"True enough," he conceded. "We all have to grow up sometime. But you can be immature forever. Just pick two and send back the list. Trust me, these gals you'll like. I'm personally vetting them."

I had no idea what *that* meant, but I reluctantly checked the two names that seemed safest. One was the director of the local historical society. We would at least have history to chat about over dinner. Chester A. Arthur, I knew, had been born and raised in Syracuse. The second sounded even better—a woman more reluctant than me. "A beautiful neighbor who just got divorced from a real estate lawyer. Everybody in the neighborhood loves Wendy. She has two little boys but isn't dating yet. Karen almost had to offer her an annuity to agree to come for dinner."

Frankly, I chose Wendy Buynak in the hope that she might get cold feet at the last minute and decide not to show. My kind of blind date.

═══ • ═══

Date number one that weekend was worse than Mona Crump. Hoping for a quiet dinner and a chance to learn about local history, I borrowed Jon Sager's car and drove us to a famous inn on Skaneateles Lake for conversation and an early supper.

Before we had even backed out of her driveway, however, she turned to me and sharply declared, "I hear you wrote a popular book about golf. Golf's a fascist game. Golfers are just a bunch of fascist doughboys."

"So, I guess hitting a bucket of balls before dinner is out of the question?" I innocently asked.

"Not a chance."

Truthfully, I don't remember much about the dinner. The attractive historian talked in a stream-of-consciousness flow about all the local people she detested and intended to somehow wreak vengeance upon for unspecified social wounds. I just pretended to listen, picturing myself teeing off with Arnold on a golden afternoon in Latrobe. We were back in her driveway before nine o'clock.

"Thanks," I said. "This was really interesting."

"Don't you want to hear me play my cello?" she asked.

I admitted that I was unaware that she played the cello; perhaps this was some kind of local divorcée code for consenting adults?

So I followed her inside. She vanished for ten minutes and returned with a large cello, sat down, and began to play. Whatever it was, it was unrecognizable. That's when I realized what was really going on. Jon Sager was secretly taping these disasters to show at the dinner scheduled for the next night, the ultimate golf-pal gag. His wife, Karen, had tipped me off that Jon loved to play practical jokes.

Eventually, the historian finished playing. "So what do you think?" she demanded.

I admitted that I'd never heard anything like the way she played, and politely said good night.

The next morning, I met the Dewsweepers on the first tee at the Onondaga Club. As we played, I pestered Jon repeatedly to provide me the phone number of that evening's victim so I could phone her and cancel the date. I was sure we would *both* be deeply relieved.

"No way. You can't cancel this one, Lumpy. If you do, I'll wind up divorced and as lonely as you." He mentioned that three Dewsweepers and their wives were going to be in attendance. "So how painful could it be?"

===== • =====

That question was answered a few hours later when a gorgeous auburn-haired woman wearing Scottish wool slacks—ideal for, say, a round at St Andrews—appeared at the Sagers' front door carrying a plate of fresh-baked oatmeal cookies.

We were introduced and sat down beside each other to begin chatting. Two hours later, the other guests went home. Wendy and I hardly noticed them leaving.

I walked Wendy Buynak home and invited her to lunch the next day. After lunch, we drove to Green Lakes State Park to have a look at what was supposedly the first golf course Robert Trent Jones built with WPA money during the Great Depression. Its clubhouse was a handsome stone affair, and the golf course looked almost as fetching as my date. That's when Wendy said something *truly* magical—that she really liked golf, and, in fact, had learned how to play after joining an evening league composed of her fellow employees at the bank where she'd worked.

"I wasn't very good at first, but I loved playing. I'd like to try it again."

Did I hear the angels singing? Fittingly, our first kiss occurred while we were parked beside Green Lake and Robert Trent Jones's first golf course. There should be a brass plaque marking the spot.

A week later I came back and we went on a tour of the Finger Lakes wine region, and wound up finding a roadside joint called the Glenwood Pines that had great sirloin steaks, skeeball, and longneck beers. Somewhere after midnight we ended up necking like teenagers by the lake until a cop knocked on the steamed windows of the car and wondered if we were okay.

I drove the seven hours home to Maine the next morning with my mind made up to soon propose to Wendy Buynak. It wasn't quite as fast as Arnold's courtship of Winnie Walzer, mind you, but it was in the same ballpark—or golf course, as it were. And just like Winnie, Wendy didn't hesitate to say yes.

"I was hoping you would ask," she said a few months into our courtship, not long after we introduced her two small lads to my daughter and son. They immediately bonded, and so did we, a golf version of the Brady Bunch.

══ • ══

Once upon a time, having a girlfriend who liked to play golf was a key item on my "Things to Do in Golf" list. Having a second chance at love and marriage with a woman who liked golf was almost too good to be true—the perfect matrimonial mulligan.

On our first golf trip together, I took Wendy to Pebble Beach and threw her to the wolves. Standing on the first tee, she explained that she'd never actually played a "full eighteen holes on such an important golf course." Her caddie's eyes resembled sunset over Monterey Bay due to an all-night bachelor party. He looked like a surfer dude who'd forgotten to go to bed.

Wendy teed up and swung her brand-new driver, one of the set of Lady Cobras I'd just given her. The ball trickled off the tee a few yards.

Her caddie rubbed his eyes and shook his head.

"No problem, honey," I spoke up loyally. "Everyone's nervous at Pebble Beach. Just relax and swing the club." I counted a dozen or so folks standing behind the wall by the tee, including a Japanese fellow taping the scene with a video camera.

She swung again, topping her ball a second time.

"Listen, let's just *put* it out in the fairway," suggested her hung-over surfer dude.

But Wendy would have none of it. She ignored him, picked up her ball, calmly teed it for a third time, took dead aim, and smacked it far down the fairway.

The crowd on the wall actually applauded. "Better be careful," I whispered in her caddie's ear. "She's liable to put that driver where the sun doesn't shine."

Wendy blushed adorably as we set off down the fairway. "Sorry about that. I was kind of nervous. What did you say to him?"

"Nothing much. I just told him you were Clint Eastwood's daughter," I joked. Eastwood and Arnold Palmer were part of a group that had just purchased Pebble Beach from its previous Japanese owners for a mind-boggling sum. Her caddy became amazingly attentive— or finally sobered up—after she just missed making a birdie on the famous par-three fifth hole.

═ ● ═

Ours was a match made in golf heaven. Wendy soon accompanied me on working golf trips to Arizona's Sonoran Desert and Hawaii's Big Island, where she took a golf lesson from Hall of Famer Jackie Pung, and we spent a charming evening with the First Lady of Hawaiian Golf at her home at Waikoloa Village, dining and listening to Pung's tales of life on the early Women's Tour, including the US Open she lost for signing an incorrect scorecard.

That happened at Winged Foot in 1957. "I was so excited at the possibility of winning a major championship that my mind went blank, and I mistakenly jotted down a par five on the fourth hole, where I'd actually made a bogey, and then foolishly signed the card. I came off the course believing I'd won." Her true total of 70 would have been good enough to beat both the designated winner, Betsy Rawls, by a stroke, and the runner-up, Patty Berg. Jackie Pung displayed uncommon graciousness and agreed to disqualification, and went from first to also-ran with the signing of her name.

"Needless to say, I was completely crushed. I couldn't believe my stupid mistake. My daughter Barnette was with me. We were staying at a member's house at Winged Foot. Everyone was so kind. The members even passed around the hat and presented me a check for $3,000. That was $1,200 more than the check for winning. Isn't that amazing? The money was nice, but nothing would take away the sting. Everyone was sympathetic, even Patty Berg and Betsy Rawls. But rules are rules, and I had broken one." And so, instead of finding a place in the record books, Jackie Pung wound up an unfortunate footnote in the sport's history, known for the ultimate golf disaster. Everywhere she went for the next decade, people asked her about the mistake.

"I won't kid you, the years afterward were an ordeal at times," she said. "But I learned that there are major trials in everyone's life. It's not always how you react when you make a big mistake, but what you learn from it."

Hawaii's First Lady of Golf went on to have a distinguished eleven-year career in the LPGA, famous for her colorful Aloha shirts and the sweet hula dance she often performed on the final greens of her rounds, utterly captivating galleries. "It was important to me to be a role model," she explained. "Golf is far more than a score on a card. It's a soulful game that reveals what you're made of and who you really are inside—far more than any other game."

Jackie Pung logged five wins and fourteen runner-up finishes on the LPGA Tour before hanging up her spikes in 1964 and returning home to Hawaii for good, where she coached golf at the University of Hawaii, became the state's first female director of golf at Laurance Rockefeller's Mauna Kea Resort, and later ran her home club at Waikoloa Village, teaching golf primarily to women. In 1967, the LPGA named her Teaching Professional of the Year.

═══ • ═══

The next morning, Jackie gave Wendy her first golf lesson on the range at Waikoloa Village. I lingered close enough to eavesdrop on their ninety-minute tutorial, hoping to pick up a few tips. I heard Jackie speak about the importance of "flowing hands" and "shifting your hips like you're doing the hula." I also heard her explain to Wendy how a woman needed to "flatten your boobs by placing them beneath your arms" and tried to picture myself doing the hula (minus the flattened boobs), but it didn't really work for me. By the hour's end, however, Wendy was making very fine shots, beaming with a spirited joy all her own.

On the way home from Hawaii, we stopped off for a weekend of golf with Arnold and Winnie Palmer at their Palm Springs home at the Tradition Golf Club. One evening before heading out to Arnold's new restaurant, Wendy and I slipped off to a large rock outcropping overlooking the seventh hole, wineglasses in hand. It was supposedly a spot sacred to the area's original Native American peoples. We watched the sunset, and I used a piece of a flowering mesquite plant to fashion a crude engagement ring, which I placed on her finger. Later that evening, after toasting us with fine French champagne, Arnold leaned over and told me that having a beautiful wife who played golf was every true golfer's dream. I couldn't disagree. "You're playing *way* under par there," he added with a wink.

We got married in the backyard of my house in Maine in June 2001, on my parents' sixtieth wedding anniversary, postponing the reception to the second week of September, when, we assumed, a number of our friends from all over could come to Maine for a genuine lobster bake and Irish fiddle dance.

The unspeakable events of 9/11 derailed the party, though only briefly. Owing to grounded airplanes and our collective shock over the events in New York, Washington, and Pennsylvania, we canceled the reception the Wednesday of that week. By that next weekend, however, guests began calling up to ask if the party might still be on. Many said they needed to get away from their TV sets and would find a way to get to Maine, whatever it took.

Arnold and his staff sent a huge bouquet of flowers and more champagne. Barney Adams and his bride, Jackie, sent a beautifully framed copy of our wedding invitation. Old friends like Bill Fields from *Golf World* magazine and Rees Jones drove up, as did Carolyn and Howdy Giles, him snapping photos with his famous camera every other minute that evening. Jon Sager and the Irish Antichrist and their wives showed up, too, along with 150 or so locals who pocketed more than ten dozen brand-new Titleist Pro-V golf balls that my friend George Sine sent as a gift. I missed getting a taste of the wedding cake Wendy made or getting to use any of the wedding golf balls the guests took away. But the dancing went on until way after midnight beneath a full harvest moon, a welcome break from our national nightmare.

My new golfwife, as I took to calling her, a gifted special-ed teacher, traveled to many places with me over the next three years, including to the newly opened Lodge at Sea Island Golf Club, where I'd officially placed an engagement ring on her finger on our first visit (and shot two over par), and then to Pinehurst, where she went to have a one-hour tune-up golf lesson with Bonnie McGowan (Peggy Kirk Bell's daughter) at Pine Needles and wound up having a three-hour playing lesson. On the drive home, she confided that John Derr and Tom Stewart had both lobbied for us to move home to North Carolina.

"They've been saying that for years," I pointed out. "What did you tell them?"

"All things are possible. But the timing has to be right."

Dame Wendy seemed to know my thoughts—and my heart's desire—even before I did.

A year later, she accompanied me to France for my final story for *Departures* magazine—a tour of great clubs around Paris. Our favorite day came at Chantilly, home to a spectacular Tom Simpson course at the club of the same name. A bored office girl filing her nails and about to close up shop collected one hundred euros and sent us out with a Gallic shrug. The course was empty and spectacular beyond belief, a joy to play, with only the serene sound of cuckoos calling from the surrounding forest.

Wendy broke 95 for the first time, and I shot 76. We finished in a blue twilight and saw six fellows playing dominoes on the club terrace. We asked them about a good place for supper, and the one who spoke English directed us to a bistro off the main drag in Chantilly center. "Ask for Naba. Big Egyptian," he said. He was wearing a Golden Bear polo shirt.

We found the bistro and Naba the big Egyptian, who led us to a large table at the rear of the restaurant and made us sit, promptly placing chilled Sancerre red wine and delicious *asperge blanche* in front of us. "You eat," he commanded. We looked at each other, shrugged, and did as instructed. A few moments later, a large party of people streamed into the bistro and headed for our table, smiling and waving. It was the six fellows from Chantilly Golf Club and their wives. My French was terrible, and their English was almost nonexistent, save for a few notable celebrity names.

"Do you know Air-*nold* Pall-*mare*?" the lone English speaker inquired when I mentioned we were there to research a golf story for my magazine.

He nearly fainted when I explained that I'd actually helped Arnold write his memoir. For an instant I thought he might try to kiss me on both cheeks. The others were so impressed that they bobbed and smiled and ordered half a dozen more bottles of chilled wine to mark the moment.

Four or five hours later, well after midnight, the party broke up. We hugged and kissed one another's wives and fondly bid *bonsoir, mes amis!* and promised to meet again someday, and finally went our separate ways through the darkened streets of Chantilly.

I have no idea how we found our way back to the beautiful country estate somewhere north of town where we were staying. But sometime later that same morning, we both woke with smiles on our faces and only slightly blinding hangovers.

"That was one of the most magical days and nights of my life," said my wife, the perfect mulligan, over breakfast, suggesting a farewell toast with freshly squeezed OJ before we set off to try to find a certain yellow beech tree by an arched stone bridge in the Forêt de Compiègne.

"To an unforgettable day of golf and night with new friends," I proposed, massaging my throbbing temples.

"Even if we remember only half of it."

CHAPTER NINE

FARAWAY PLACES

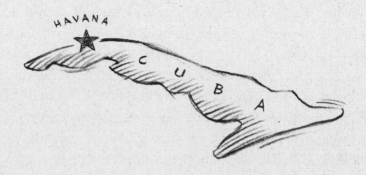

O ut of the blue in late 1997 a man named Bob Walz from a Colorado-based company called Last Frontier Expeditions got in touch to ask if I had any interest in sneaking into Cuba in order to play the sole golf course that survived Fidel Castro's takeover of the Caribbean island in 1959.

What true-blue history-loving golfer doesn't dream of playing in some exotic, faraway place, especially a tropical paradise held captive by a banana-republic revolutionary who nearly caused World War Three and forced millions of ordinary schoolkids to practice crawling beneath their desks?

Walz had just read my column in *Departures* about the colorful veteran PGA Tour pro named Tommy Bolt, whose sweet swing and foul temper helped him claim the 1958 US Open at Southern Hills, plus fifteen other Tour events and a pair of Ryder Cup appearances. Bolt was known for his volcanic outbursts and a tendency to toss uncooperative golf clubs during competition, earning him the nicknames "Thunder Bolt" and "Terrible Tommy." Among other things, Bolt and his wife, Mary Lou, traveled with newlyweds Arnold and

Winnie Palmer during Arnold's first full year on Tour in 1956, a friendly foursome that broke up one evening at a lakeside cottage in Canada when the Bolts got into a fiery domestic spat that resulted, according to Winnie, in steak knives being thrown with near-lethal accuracy. "We literally fled into the night," added Arnold with a chuckle. "Fortunately, we were hauling a little trailer with us. So we had a place to stay."

As a result of Bolt's antics, the PGA Tour adopted a rule prohibiting players from throwing their golf clubs during tournaments. Bolt only threatened to hurl clubs after that, often cracking up his galleries and playing the Thunder Bolt to the hilt. In 2002, he was inducted into the World Golf Hall of Fame.

Though I made only passing reference to Bolt's particular affection for the late Havana Open that ended just days before the rebel forces of Fidel Castro overran the "Crown Jewel of the Caribbean" in late 1959, Bolt made it clear why he loved going to Havana in his early Tour days—and how he nearly got caught in a revolution.

"The women were gorgeous, the food was wonderful, and the old Country Club of Havana was one of the best tropical courses you've ever seen, a really fine Donald Ross layout," he explained. "So was the Biltmore Havana course, where the LPGA played for a couple of years. Everyone loved going down there at the end of the long season, because most of us had a few bucks in our pockets and the Cubans treated us like goddamn kings. Booze, gambling, women—you name it, they had it. Of course, the mob totally ran the place—the entire island, in fact," he added with a sly grin. "Hated to see it all come to an end the way it did."

Following the '59 Havana Open, Bolt told me he decided to stay on to do a little tarpon fishing and enjoy "some more Cuban hospitality. That's when all hell suddenly broke loose. A guy I knew at the Hotel Nacional—the night manager, I think—informed me that the communist rebels were about to overrun the city, and I'd better get the hell out in a hurry. He had a speedboat somewhere across the bay and said he'd take a few of us over to Miami for a couple hundred bucks. The airport, see, was already shut down. So, brother, we grabbed whatever we could and ran. I actually left behind a new set of clubs and the most comfortable custom-made golf shoes I ever owned. What a damn shame."

"When Castro took over," Bob Walz explained to me, "the first thing he did was plow up the Country Club golf course, and the Biltmore course as well, insisting they were symbols of capitalist greed and corruption. But he left a modest nine-hole course that belonged to the former British Embassy. It was called the Rovers Athletic Club in those days. It's still there, now called the Diplo Club—used primarily for visiting Soviet-bloc types who want to try their hands at golf. Nobody from America has been there in fifty years. But I can get you into the country, and you can be the first American golf editor to play it."

Walz sweetened the deal by explaining that "certain key elements within the Castro government" were "greatly interested" in discreetly courting American investment in Cuba's recreational future. "The Spanish are about to complete a new golf resort course at Varadero on the eastern end of the island," Walz said. "It's just a matter of time until Castro dies and the whole place breaks open for golf development. But you can see it and play the Rovers course before the *second* Cuban Revolution takes place. Bring a photographer, too."

"Is it legal for us to go there?" I asked.

Walz chuckled. "Not really. But nobody in Cuba will hassle you. I'll arrange everything. You can get in through Canada, or, better yet, just pop down to Cancun and take a half-hour flight over on Havana Air." He mentioned that a group of folks from the Marriott hotel organization were scheduled to do just that in order to see a property west of Havana where one of the commandants of the Cuban Revolution maintained a horse farm and banana plantation and hoped to soon build a world-class golf resort.

Walz didn't have to wait for my answer. And I knew exactly the photographer to invite along for the adventure. Macduff Everton was one of the world's most acclaimed photographers, a man whose photographic landscapes hang in the British Museum and the Museum of Modern Art in New York. The *New York Times* once called Macduff the Ansel Adams of travel photography. More important to me, though he'd never played a full round of golf in his life, he and I had traveled extensively around Ireland, Scotland, and New Zealand for my golf column in *Departures*. Macduff was also fluent in Spanish and had recently completed work on a beautiful book about living with the Mayans of Central America. His wife, Mary Heebner, a distinguished lecturer and artist in her own right, enthusiastically agreed to join us, arranging to give a lecture at the Havana Institute of Art while we were there over two weeks the following March.

As Walz suggested, we met in Cancun and took a brief flight over to Cuba, during which—and I'm not making this up—a dusty fellow in the seat beside me held a caged rooster on his lap, smiling toothlessly. At the arrivals hall, a sallow, pock-faced man in a green military uniform who reminded me of Captain Segura in Graham Greene's classic spy novel *Our Man in Havana* eyed my passport and calmly asked the nature of my visit.

"To play golf," I replied, pointing to my golf carryall lying all by itself on the cement floor directly behind him. He turned and stared at it as if it might contain a human body or a bazooka.

"Just a moment, *señor*," said Captain Segura. He walked slowly across the room, disappearing into a smoked-glass office.

Mary and Macduff had already cleared customs by mentioning Mary's scheduled visit to the country's leading art school. The captain was gone for an unnerving amount of time, but finally wandered back, handed me my passport, and said with a cold little smile, *"Bienvenido a la Habana, señor,"* while waving me on. At which point I started breathing again.

My assigned driver was a fellow named Manuel Rivera, a trim, muscular sixty-year-old with roughly barbered white hair and a quick smile. His car was an immaculate Lada, circa 1965, a relic of the Soviet years of influence, when America's complete trade embargo turned Cuba into the world's largest antique auto show. Havana itself was a beautiful ruin, like a wedding cake left out in the rain. We were driven to the historic Hotel Nacional and put up in beautiful rooms overlooking the city's famous Malecón waterfront. According to a plaque on the wall above my bed, my guest room had been the one preferred by Lana Turner, which made me think of Tommy Thunder Bolt, who'd told me he'd once dined with the Hollywood starlet and her entourage in Havana.

On our second day there, Manuel drove me to the Diplo Golf Club, where I found a modest white clubhouse with a palm-filled bar and a tiny pro shop manned by a delightful young man named Jorge Duque, the club's youthful professional. Jorge was only too happy to grab his clubs and play the nine-hole course with me, explaining how he'd learned English and fallen in love with golf by watching the PGA Tour on his family's snowy TV screen. The original Rovers course, he believed, might once have been a full eighteen holes and possibly was also designed by Donald Ross, though there was no documentation to support this notion.

The fairways were spotty and the greens were poor even by American goat-farm standards, but the bones of a decent course were clearly visible in the form of holes that roamed naturally up and down small hillocks, which offered some nice strategic shots. Jorge explained that after the Soviets had vacated the island, the Diplo's rate of play dwindled to a trickle—mostly Spaniards and Canadians who somehow heard about it through word of mouth. The greens fee was just five dollars. As we played along, Jorge drew a hilarious picture in my head of sunburned Soviet bureaucrats wearing Speedos, sandals, and black socks as they violently hacked beaver pelts out of the springy turf of the former Rovers Club. The fairways and greens were mowed only once a week, and Jorge often did the mowing himself.

We developed, in fact, an instantaneous friendship and played the course twice that day before retiring to the bar for mojitos. There, Jorge told me about his dream to someday be a "real professional in America" and introduced me to another character straight out of Graham Greene, a mysterious American who dropped in almost every afternoon around quitting time for drinks. We shook hands. The American's name was Dan. I never caught a last name.

"So, how'd you like the course?" Dan asked, joining me at a table on the terrace. He was wearing a heavily wrinkled summer-weight suit, sans necktie.

I replied that I liked it very much, given the obvious limitations.

Dan didn't look particularly impressed. I asked where he came from. Dan shrugged, sipping his vodka on the rocks. "Kansas. More or less."

He reminded me of the bland American spy in *Our Man in Havana* whose cover is selling vacuum cleaners. "So, what do you do here in Havana?" I asked.

A shrug. "This and that. I run an agency of sorts that unofficially operates between government agencies."

"Which agencies?" I asked.

He smiled. "Whichever ones need me."

Dan, I later learned, worked for the American diplomatic section that represented America's "interests" in the captive island, the unofficial link between our government and whoever in Cuba was willing to talk to godless capitalist Americans.

"Do you play golf?" I wondered.

Dan shook his head, waving for a fresh drink. Drinking mojitos with a shadowy figure on the shady terrace of the old British Embassy was better than being in a Graham Greene novel. It was a true RBL moment.

"Nah. Detest the bloody game, actually. But I like this place. They say it was once the happening spot in Havana."

He asked why I was there, and didn't appear to believe that I'd come all the way to Cuba simply to play a modest, poorly maintained nine-hole golf course.

I pointlessly mentioned my high affection for glorious goat farms and hidden gems, and said that the opportunity to be the first American golf hack to play the sole surviving golf course in Cuba was one I simply couldn't pass up.

Dan rubbed his bristly chin. "Well, good thing you're seeing it now before the fucking place blows wide open. In twenty years, there will be a McDonald's on every corner in Havana—and fucking golf courses all over the island. The big money is already here. The Spanish are building a course out in Varadero. Everyone's quietly scurrying after the all-holy American buck."

The next day, Macduff and I accompanied Mary to give her lecture at the art school and then hoofed all over Old Havana, dropping in on the bar where the mojito was supposedly invented (Papa Hemingway's photo was on the wall, as this was a beloved former hangout of his), which lay in the shadow of the oldest cathedral in the New World. During a walking tour there, we became friendly with a docent whose daughter—a pediatrician named Maria—had recently set off on one of the illegal boat flotillas that took off almost every day from the Malecón for Florida. At about this time, a six-year-old boy named Elián González would be found clinging to an inner tube in the Florida Straits, becoming a symbol of the plight of the Cuban "boat people" and the central figure in an intense international custody battle.

Understandably, the gray-haired docent was deeply anxious about his daughter's fate, praying that he would soon hear that she was safely ensconced with relatives in Florida. Before setting off on her perilous journey, he explained, she'd been working nights at the famous Tropicana ballroom, regretfully selling her body to European tourists, earning more money in one evening than she could make working for six months as a physician.

"She is divorced with a small son," he explained. "She is desperate for a better life for him. This is the great paradox of Mr. Castro's revolution," he said with an air of emotional exhaustion. "Medical services are free, but he's reduced our daughters to whoring." I gave him my card and offered to help any way I could. He accepted it and thanked me, gently patting my arm.

=== • ===

That evening, Bob Walz took us to a luxurious private mansion called the Hacienda in the city's old quarter, not far from where the Country Club once existed. Beautiful young women circulated around a seductively lit courtyard pool, offering the well-dressed male guests Cuban cigars, premium cocktails, or whatever else they had in mind.

Macduff asked Walz how Fidel Castro happened to miss this place when he plowed up the fairways of the golf club a few blocks away.

Walz smiled, tugging on his white beard in a way that made us think of Papa Hemingway. "Castro knows all about this place. He even comes here from time to time."

On the ride back to the Nacional, I asked Manuel about the Hacienda.

He explained that it was created to entertain wealthy foreign visitors and potential investors in Cuba's shadow economy, a safe house filled with the pleasures of Old Havana. On the streets of the city, in fact, the American dollar was already the currency of demand, openly transacted with by street vendors in the largest market stalls along the Malecón. Many government stores, on the other hand, were shockingly bereft of life's basic staples.

"Cuba is opening up like a piece of ripe fruit," Manuel observed, sounding more like the philosophical grandfather he was than the "special emissary" to the KGB deputation we eventually discovered he'd been during the Cold War years.

I asked if he would like to see American tourists and others allowed to come to Cuba.

He smiled. His teeth were as immaculate as his Lada. "Oh, yes, of course. The Cuban people are so eager to meet Americans. We're neighbors, and we have so much in common. I'm a grandfather, after all. I want to see this in my lifetime." He added, "Best of all, my friend, the Russians are gone."

═ • ═

The next day, we took a long drive into the hills west of the city to a beautiful banana and horse plantation, where we met an elderly gentleman clad in khaki on horseback, who turned out to be one of Castro's key military leaders the night they overthrew Batista's regime. They called him simply "the Commandant." He spoke no English but couldn't have been more charming, driving us around beautiful groomed meadows where he hoped to build the government's first golf course and create a world-class resort. Through his attractive female interpreter, the Commandant explained that Davis Love III and several executives from the Marriott chain of hotels were scheduled to tour the property soon. Discussions, he said, were under way for my old friend Davis Love to design and build a championship golf course. I never learned the fate of this development.

We also drove down to Varadero to see the new luxury hotel and view the golf course there, which was designed by Canadian architect Les Furber and featured an elegant white clubhouse that had formerly belonged to the Du Pont family before the Communists overran the island. The beach was spectacular, with pure white sand and aquamarine-blue water. A sleek hotel was being completed just down the beach, racing to make a deadline for the island's first golf tournament since the late, great Havana Open of 1959. As we toured the handsome course with one of the club's new managers, a loud explosion occurred over by the hotel. Our host calmly explained that every now and then a speedboat, driven by "crazies from Miami" (i.e., Cuban expats), sped by the property and lobbed some kind of explosive onto the shore, hoping to cause havoc. "They've only killed a poor dog so far," he explained with a shrug.

"That gives new meaning to the term 'hazard' on a golf course," Macduff piped up, right on cue.

On the way back to Havana, we stopped off in a tiny fishing village to tour a local cigar factory and visit with an ancient blue-eyed man named Gregorio Fuentes, Ernest Hemingway's longtime fishing buddy and the inspiration for *The Old Man and the Sea*. His granddaughter sat by his side as Macduff and Mary chatted pleasantly with him for twenty minutes or so. He agreed to pose for a photograph and directed us around the block to a private residence, where the three of us paid about ten dollars to eat one of the best suppers I've ever had.

On my last morning in Cuba, I went back to play the Rovers course a final time and to say good-bye to Jorge Duque, half tempted to try to smuggle him home in my big golf carryall. Macduff came along to photograph our final round together. At one point, a man in ragged pants, leading a cow and carrying what looked like a dirty pillowcase, came up and gave us a toothless smile, speaking in Spanish.

"He collects golf balls, and wonders if you would like to buy some of his," Jorge explained. "Don't feel obligated."

The man opened his sack. It was full of vintage golf balls, relics from another time, including some real gems like Spalding Kro-Flights and ancient Top Flights, Dunlop 65s, and even a few well-scrubbed original Titleist balata balls from the early days of Arnie and Jack.

I gave him ten dollars for an old Wilson Staff and a MacGregor ball with Byron Nelson's name on it and thanked him. The man bowed and thanked me and said, *"Dios te bendiga, amigo."*

Back at the bar, I congratulated Jorge on his incredible determination to keep golf alive in Cuba, joking that Mr. Castro should give him a medal, or at least an all-access gold card to the Hacienda. I also promised to help him if or when he ever managed to get to America.

We exchanged addresses and promised to stay in touch. My heart belonged to Scotland, I admitted, but I confided that playing the Rovers with him was one of the biggest thrills I'd had in golf, an unforgettable experience. He smiled, and we shook hands.

═══ • ═══

Several years later, Jorge phoned to let me know he'd reached Miami Beach and was staying with relatives, hoping to find a job working for a local golf course. I made a few calls and wrote a letter or two in his behalf, but a short time later he found a job working for a golf club in Spain, at which point we lost touch.

═══ • ═══

Golf in faraway places is a beguiling business. A few years ago, I was invited to make a speaking tour of the famed Sandbelt golf clubs in Melbourne, Australia, and fell hard for the charms of classic Sandbelt layouts like Metropolitan Golf Club, Kingston Heath, and Royal Melbourne Golf Club, places where the members were as welcoming and fun to be around as their golf courses were to play.

For good reason, many call the area Melbourne's golfing heaven. I happily concur—and have considered emigrating more than once.

Not long ago, purely for fun, I even counted up how many of the world's current top one hundred golf courses I managed to visit and play over three decades of travel for work and pleasure.

The number, a bit surprisingly, came to seventy-one courses.

Some of those courses I can recall in vivid detail, my personal litmus test of greatness. Others I can barely remember at all.

Why is this?

My best guess is because tastes vary, and golf courses are some of the most subjective works of art on earth—far more inclined to start a lively argument among friends than religion, politics, or modern art.

Not long ago, I also had the unique opportunity to work on a privately commissioned book about the creation of Tara Iti Golf Club in New Zealand, watching Tom Doak and his celebrated Renaissance Golf Design team transform a dense commercial pine forest on traditional Maori lands on the North Island's pristine northeast coast into one of the most breathtaking links-style courses ever built. The owner and visionary behind the project is a laid-back Los Angeles–based private investment legend named Ric Kayne, who set out to build his dream course in a mythic and faraway place with the stated aim to achieve a top-fifty-in-the-world designation.

Kayne's lofty ambition may soon pay dividends. Already, Tara Iti—named for a nearly extinct little shorebird that has been granted a nice reprieve thanks to extensive dune reconstruction and a protective wildlife preserve that has essentially doubled the population of nesting Tara Iti birds since the club's creation—has earned a coveted spot as New Zealand's top-ranked golf course.

That said, as one glance at my own highly eccentric and ever-changing personal list of Top Twenty Favorite Golf Courses might reveal, I've never been terribly keen on the idea of rating golf courses

in any way. You love Augusta National, with its meticulous groom-
ing and blazing green perfection, while I live for windblown links
courses full of rabbit scrapes and stinging sea wind.

The one faraway tropical course I dream of someday returning
to is probably still something of a Glorious Goat Farm—or so I
hope.

=== • ===

With the process of normalization of relations with Cuba that began
under President (and golfer) Barack Obama in 2016 well under way,
it didn't surprise me at all when my old travel pal Macduff Everton
recently got in touch to suggest we make a twentieth anniversary
return trip to Cuba to check out the Old Rovers Club, as I prefer to
think of it, and to verify reports of several ambitious golf resort proj-
ects in various stages of development. I couldn't disagree with him
that our secret Cuban Golf Ball Diplomacy provided a unique perspective that would make for a fine follow-up investigation. Hopefully this will happen in the not-too-distant future.

The nicest surprise, however, came when I found an old email
from Jorge Duque on an out-of-date computer and wrote him an
email just for the heck of it, fully expecting to hear nothing in return. Almost two decades, after all, had passed.

But then came a wonderful return email from my best Cuban
golf buddy, explaining that he and one of his two children were now
legal residents of Florida, where Jorge works as a senior instructor
for GolfTEC. He had immigrated nine years ago and was now living
his American dream.

"When we met in Havana," he said at one point during the ensuing hour-long phone conversation, "my dream of coming to America
was just a crazy dream. But life can be so amazing. I'm sometimes
moved beyond speech when I think how far my dreams have taken
me and my family thanks to golf." He mentioned that he'd been mar-

ried and divorced but had two grown children he was very proud of—a daughter named Claudia (residing in Cuba) and a son named Dario. In this way, we had yet another "life" thing in common.

I told him he needed to plan a road trip from Florida to Pinehurst soon so I could introduce him to my own favorite Donald Ross golf course.

"Nothing," he replied, "would give me more pleasure."

He seemed touched when I told him that I still had dreams about the Old Rovers Club, my favorite faraway golf course, and wondered if he might be willing to return there someday with Macduff and me to update the dream and check out the changes.

"Of course I would," he answered excitedly. "I'll introduce you to my many uncles and aunts and little cousins. They'll feed you like you cannot believe."

"It's a date," I said, always up for a good meal and an unforgettable golf adventure.

CHAPTER TEN

LIFE BEHIND THE
PINE CURTAIN

Two days before the start of the US Open of 2005, I showed up in Pinehurst to work for the *Pilot* newspaper's award-winning *Open Daily* tabloid, and to have a chance to check off one of the earliest items—"Live in Pinehurst"—from my truant teenage "Things to Do in Golf" list.

The timing seemed ideal. My children had grown up ridiculously fast and were now on the threshold of heading off to college, and the two magazines that had been my happy working home for more than two decades, *Golf* and *Departures*, had undergone major changes. *Golf* had recently been taken over by a multimedia colossus that forced out its legendary editor and fired most of my colleagues and the magazine's support staff. I'd been invited to stay on by the new regime, presumably because of my books, but felt that was a sign from the gods that it was time to move along.

Simultaneously, a different circumstance ended my rewarding run at *Departures* when the magazine's editor in chief resigned to become the editor of a new start-up magazine called *Expedia Travels* and invited me to jump ship and follow as a contributing editor for golf and the outdoors; I did so, picturing a welcome new adventure. The new publication lasted only a handful of issues before the owners pulled the plug.

Suddenly, like millions of middle-aged Americans, I was out of *two* regular, well-paying jobs that had taken me everywhere I had ever dreamed of going in the world of golf for decades, though I was far luckier than most, because I'd just published an ambitious authorized biography of Ben Hogan and had agreed to serve as writer in residence for a small, distinguished college in western Virginia for the winter of 2006.

Truthfully, after decades away from the South, I wanted to go home again—which every southern son eventually yearns to do, as Truman Capote supposedly said, if only in a box.

My opportunity to go home to Carolina unexpectedly came about as the result of a speech I gave to the North Carolina sponsors of the approaching US Open at the Pinehurst Resort in the spring of 2004, after which I went with a heavy heart to say good-bye to Harvie Ward.

Harvie's liver cancer had come back with a vengeance, and my Hogan biography had taken a year longer than planned to complete. We'd simply run out of time to collaborate on the *Last Amateur* project. The last afternoon I saw him, a very frail Harvie walked me to the door of his pretty house on Blue Road in Pinehurst, handed me one of his old Callaway putters, and asked that I give it to my teenage son, Jack, who'd just started playing on his high school golf team back in Maine. The next morning, a Sunday, Tom Stewart took me to play the Old North State Club in the nearby Uwharrie Mountains, and we had a wonderful day playing golf and talking about Harvie and how in the middle of his life Tom left a prestigious club job in Florida in order to "reinvent" himself by opening an outstanding golf collectibles shop in the heart of Pinehurst—a place he, too, had always dreamed of living.

My late southern grandmother loved to say that when the Good Lord closes a door, He opens a window. Maybe that is true.

When I returned to the Pine Crest Inn after golf with Tom, I was handed a note from someone named David Woronoff inviting me to lunch the next day. David, I knew, was the young publisher of the local *Pilot* newspaper, a fine little community paper that enjoyed a distinguished history. So, just for fun and a chance to linger a day longer in a place I'd loved as a kid, I added an extra day to my trip and went to hear what the young publisher had in mind.

David turned out to be collegial and upbeat, qualities I had admired in my late papa. Moreover, in a newspaper world that was reportedly withering on the vine, the *Pilot* was enjoying apparent prosperity, having recently been named the top community newspaper in the nation for a second time. Over lunch at a crowded café on Southern Pines' busy East Broad Street, he complimented me on my remarks to the Open sponsors and invited me to come work for the *Pilot*'s team covering the 2005 US Open.

"I can't pay you what you earn from your magazines, but I can promise you all the genuine North Carolina–style barbecue you can eat—and lots of fun," he said.

We shook hands, and I promised him I would think over his offer. That afternoon I struck out for Maine feeling a good bit more optimistic about the future, taking a different, slower road up through the Blue Ridge Mountains toward home, having made up my mind—like a true son of Opti—that the answer would come if I simply let the universe do its work.

═══ • ═══

A funny thing happened on my first day at the 2005 Open. As I was passing through the cavernous media center, I bumped into a group of longtime colleagues from the golf trail and paused to chat just as the new publisher of one of my old magazines strolled up. The collar of his hot-pink polo shirt was turned up jauntily.

My friends were congratulating me on the fact that earlier that week, *Ben Hogan: An American Life* had been named the USGA Book of the Year, now called the Herbert Warren Wind Award. Sadly, Herb Wind had passed away shortly before the start of this Open. He'd helped me immeasurably with the Hogan project. Not long after the publication of *A Golfer's Life*, the dean of America's golf writers called to invite me to lunch at his assisted-living community north of Boston. Our first lunch took place on Patriots' Day of 2000. As we sat alone in a sunny dining room, Herb told me wonderful little details about Ben Hogan's life and their collaboration on the bestselling golf instruction book of all time, *Five Lessons*. Mr. Wind—as I called him—was a dapper little gent in a beautiful tweed sports jacket, with an almost formal air about him. At one point he mentioned how much he'd enjoyed reading *Final Rounds* and my Golf Life columns about ordinary people who loved the game with uncommon fervor, and observed, "I hope you won't be offended if I say that I think you are a genuine voice of the everyman." On the contrary—I was deeply touched by his comment, and I thanked him. For the next two years in a row, as my research and writing on Hogan was completed and went to press, we met for lunch on Patriots' Day until Herb's dementia finally ended our wonderful solarium luncheons.

"So," said the publisher in the sporty pink shirt, inserting himself into my circle of friends, "what's this I hear about you going to work for a small-town weekly newspaper? What a comedown after winning Book of the Year," he added, not quite sympathetically.

My friends all shuffled their feet, more embarrassed for him than for me. Just then, young David Woronoff sidled up, smiling as always. David liked to say that the *Pilot* was "small-town but not small-time," a line I wish I'd had the presence of mind to use at that moment. I introduced him to the group as the publisher of the *Pilot* and the *Open Daily*. They were pleased to shake his hand.

"Listen," I said to Pink Shirt, "I love being back here in North Carolina. My dad was a newspaper man, and this is where my journalism career began." I was half tempted to tick off the list of famous golf journalists who'd finished their illustrious careers living and working in the Sandhills, but decided that would be pointless. Besides, my former colleagues all knew what I was up to, because their publications were also threatened by the same rapidly changing circumstances, and many were shedding staff because of dudes exactly like Pink Shirt.

Summoning my inner Herb Wind, I simply excused myself and bid them all farewell, because I had my first deadline story to write in more than two decades. Though I didn't say so, I figured I might be working my final golf tournament as a journalist. But what a fitting way—and place—to say good-bye.

Just outside the media center, however, I stopped, turned around, and walked back inside to where my friends were still shooting the breeze.

"Oh, by the way," I said to Pink Shirt, "let me make something clear. The *Pilot* isn't just a small-town weekly newspaper. I want you to know that sucker comes out *three* days a week!"

My friends erupted with laughter, and Pink Shirt turned even pinker.

═══ ● ═══

On the Thursday night of that week, I went out for a stroll around the pretty Weymouth Hills neighborhood in Southern Pines, where I was living in a rented cabin for the week, and bumped into an elegant older lady walking a small white dog. The dog, a Jack Russell, growled at me.

"Hush now, Rex," she said, quieting her bossy little beast. She told me her name was Myrtis Boone Morrison and that she and her husband, Max, the town's longtime eye doctor, now retired, resided just around the corner. She wondered if I might wish to come by for a home-cooked supper the next evening. Something about her serene, steel-magnolia bearing reminded me of my own southern mother. So I said yes.

"Don't mind Max," she warned me with a trilling laugh, heading off into the twilight. "His bark is worse than Rex's. But he's really an old sweetie."

I met Max the next evening. He'd been playing golf with his regular group at nearby Southern Pines Golf Club—a Ross course owned by the local Elks Club—and was in high spirits because he'd broken 90 using a new driver he'd purchased online from some knockoff equipment firm.

"I saw a great bumper sticker in the parking lot at the golf course today," he announced, placing an iced tumbler of bourbon in front of me at their kitchen's big round table. "It read: 'Sometimes I wake up grumpy. And sometimes I let her sleep.' I have to get myself one of those!" he chortled, glancing at Miss Myrtis Boone. Their grown daughter, Jean, a physical therapist, was also at the table.

"Daddy, *you're* the one who wakes up grumpy," Jean said sweetly, smiling at me. Jean was the youngest of the three Morrison daughters. Her older sister Marianne was married to a doctor and lived with their two sons in Columbia, South Carolina. Middle daughter Elizabeth, I was saddened to learn, was a talented, free-spirited artist who had recently passed away from cancer, which had quietly devastated the Morrison household and Elizabeth's many friends in town. It was quickly obvious to me that she had been the apple of her daddy's eye.

"Maybe I should call *you* Grumpy," I proposed to Max, which tickled Myrtis Boone to no end and prompted her to ask whether I had plans for supper the next night. In fact, I wound up eating supper five of the next seven nights at the home of Myrtis and Grumpy Morrison.

After the Open circus left town, David Woronoff wondered if I might wish to stick around to write a Sunday essay for the *Pilot* before I geared up to teach biography and memoir-writing at Hollins University in Virginia.

"No newspaper in America has a writer in residence," he pointed out. "You could be a first."

I liked the idea. I also confided to him that I was toying with writing my next golf book about the Home of American Golf, since I had such a meaningful relationship with the place that dated from my earliest teenage years. I told him about Mid Pines being my first true championship course and about the fateful afternoon with Opti on No. 2 in 1983. "Arnold Palmer once told me that anyone who loves Pinehurst and Southern Pines is a true son or daughter of the game," I said, floating the idea of sticking around until my teaching duties at Hollins started that winter.

"Great idea," he said. "You can write about my lifeguard good looks and Tigeresque golf swing." David was, in fact, a highly ranked tennis player who looked more like an athletic version of Where's Waldo. Even so, he reminded me of the little brother I'd always wanted.

The locals seemed to appreciate my silly Sunday essays about anything that caught my fancy, and I was soon playing golf with Grumpy Morrison and deep into the writing of a book called *A Son of the Game* about the place where my "higher" golf education began.

That October I gave a speech at a local festival and found a skinny black puppy running wild and untethered along US Highway 1. I took her home to my rented cabin and tentatively named her Mulligan, in honor of the third phase of my journalism career in the Home of American Golf.

By winter I was bouncing among Maine, the Sandhills, and Hollins University every fortnight, joking to friends in all three places that I was merely performing a larger version of what my great-great-grandfather—an itinerate Methodist preacher and surveyor who established the modern boundaries of the state's central counties following the Civil War—did when he roamed the Old North State preaching and surveying land.

=== • ===

One evening the next spring, as Wendy, Mulligan, and I were walking home under a tranquil half-moon from Easter supper at the Morrisons', my wife pointed out the handsome old manor house that I often walked past on my way to work at the *Pilot*. That afternoon she'd played Mid Pines Golf Club for the first time and had been thoroughly charmed by the course and the old hotel, not to mention the thousands of dogwoods and azaleas then in riotous bloom.

"That looks like such a happy house," she said, pausing in the fragrant night. "I understand it's empty and up for rent. Maybe we should rent it."

This, I confess, took me by surprise, though it probably shouldn't have. My teaching gig in Virginia was drawing to a close, and my book about life behind the Pine Curtain, as Grumpy Morrison once colorfully described Pinehurst and Southern Pines, was nearly finished. I'd had casual discussions with a board member at Hollins and another small college in Greensboro about full-time teaching— another little dream—but I wasn't quite ready to take the plunge into academia.

To fully own the truth, now that I'd checked "Live in Pinehurst" off my RBL, I was secretly wondering how I might engineer a return all the way home to Greensboro, just seventy-five miles up the road. In my mind, I'd long pictured myself circling back home to where I began in the historic Piedmont city, the place where I struck my first golf ball and where my family went back generations. But that was yet to come.

"Let's rent it and see what happens—a true *Maison du Golf*," I agreed. The historic manor house actually reminded me of "an old house in Paris that was covered with vines" from Ludwig Bemelmans's famous Madeleine series, my daughter, Maggie's, favorite picture books when she was young. But Pinehurst and Southern Pines were America's horse and golf capital, and that romantic old manor house sure looked like a happy place to put down roots for a while until I could figure out a way to make it all the way home to Greensboro. In fact, as I learned soon afterward, that house and an identical one sitting just next door, linked by a driveway, were originally built by a wealthy New York industrialist for his twin spinster daughters—one of whom loved horses, the other of whom was mad for golf. When I looked into the matter, I was pleased to learn that our charming Madeleine house had indeed been the home of the golfing sister, and was thus a true *Maison du Golf*.

=== • ===

In many ways, Wendy and I were like generations of New England and upper midwestern refugees who'd found their way to a fabled pine wilderness that offered foxhunting, golf, and splendid isolation from the broader world, hoping to make some kind of new start on the next phase of life.

The rambling old house we soon occupied with two golden retrievers and a foundling named Mulligan dated from 1911, not long after wealthy Boston do-gooder James Walker Tufts heard that the dry winters and the mysterious "ozone" emitted by the mythical longleaf pines of the remote Carolina Sandhills were good for healing congested northern lungs. Tufts arrived in Southern Pines to see for himself one afternoon in 1892, hired a carriage to drive him five miles due west to view a moonscape where turpentine crews had leveled the pine forest, and agreed to buy more than six thousand acres of the ruined wasteland for about six grand from a local family named Page, prompting jokes that "another rich Yankee" had been politely "separated from his money."

Within a year, though, Tufts had laid out an entire New England village, complete with a proper village common, handsome Victorian public buildings, and a fancy white hotel named the Holly Inn, choosing to call his recuperative spa town "Pinehurst" over other choices like "Sunalia" and "Tuftstown." Soon afterward he began construction of an even grander hotel called the Carolina, driven by an ambition to create a winter retreat where all classes of people, rich and poor alike, could escape the ravages of the northern winter. In theory, they would take hikes in nature, play badminton, attend mind-enriching lectures, and eat healthy, home-cooked meals. As the first "cottages" were being built on Pinehurst's curvilinear lanes—intentionally designed to confuse unwelcome strangers, the spiritual antecedent of gated communities—Tufts hired the design firm of the ailing Frederick Law Olmsted to beautify the barren, sandy landscape with vibrant hollies and stately water oaks, azaleas, rhododendron, and camellias imported from Florida and Europe.

For the first few years, Tufts—a man who had made his fortune by inventing the first automated soda fountain—heavily advertised his visionary health spa in the major newspapers of the Northeast, emphasizing a newly built rail line that brought travelers from the coast directly to the town of Southern Pines, where the streets were artfully named for northern and midwestern states and lots were being sold to attract wealthy cottagers and fox-hunting enthusiasts. Regardless of class or income, anyone who wished to take the cure—even "consumptives," the common name given to suffers of tuberculosis—was initially welcome in Pinehurst.

The scheme worked promisingly at first, until medical authorities determined that tuberculosis was, contrary to early widespread belief, dangerously contagious in all stages of its development. This prompted Tufts's customer traffic to drop off like a stone, causing him to starkly reverse course and begin advertising that "No Consumptives" would be allowed in his visionary spa town. A dedicated teetotaler, he also forbade the consumption of alcohol, and—quietly—discouraged Jewish customers from visiting his pine-girdled haven. So much for Utopia in the Pines.

At about the time his grand Carolina hotel was nearing completion, and eager to find a new attraction to revive his flagging trade, Tufts heard rumors that several of his northern guests were playing a newfangled game involving "sticks and small balls" in one of his town's dairy meadows. He went out to investigate and was introduced to a recently imported Scottish game called "golf," which was reportedly growing in popularity back home in the suburbs of Boston. A visiting physician who had some familiarity with the game agreed to lay out Pinehurst's first crude sand-green nine-hole golf course, which was by all accounts a big hit with Tufts's paying guests. A short time later, through friends from up North, Tufts met a solemn young man named Donald James Ross, not long off the boat from Scotland with just six bucks in his pocket, who was serving as a teaching professional and rebuilding the rudimentary Waverly Oaks Golf Club in Cambridge, Massachusetts. Tufts hired young Ross to come to the Sandhills and do the same with his modest nine-hole course.

The industrious Ross expanded the first course over an ancient sandy seabed that reminded him of his native Dornoch, and soon began work on a championship golf course called No. 2 that, in due course, attracted the attention of British champion golfer Harry Vardon when he made a celebrated exhibition tour of the United States in 1900. An estimated two thousand spectators somehow managed to watch Vardon's exhibition round at Pinehurst No. 2, which was covered widely and with much vigor by newspapers across America, setting off the first public golf boom in this country. Four new Ross-designed courses soon followed, and America's first golf resort was born.

== • ==

On a cold February night that next winter, David Woronoff and I were chatting at Tom Stewart's surprise sixtieth-birthday party at the Fair Barn near the Pinehurst racetrack. David, the newly installed president of the North Carolina Press Association, made a joke about trying to figure out a way to keep me in the Sandhills short of bribing me with barbeque for life.

I half joked that he should consider purchasing the handsome little monthly arts tabloid called *PineStraw Magazine* that circulated around the town and village and agree to let me "turn it into a real magazine."

He smiled. "Actually, I've been speaking with one of the owners of *PineStraw.* Her name is Andie Rose. She's the art director, a very talented lady. If we buy it," he added, "would you agree to stay and become its editor?"

Without thinking it over, I said yes, wondering how much it would take to acquire the handsome tabloid. He seemed very pleased with himself.

"We'll only have to pay off her partner."

"So how much?"

"A new set of golf clubs."

It was the perfect deal. I still kid David about making the largest media acquisition in Sandhills history with a new set of Titleists.

== • ==

When I look back on more than a decade living in the *Maison du Golf,* a place where I managed to write five books in a quiet upstairs bedroom and doze away countless blazing Sandhills summer after-noons in a comfortable wooden Adirondack chair on a terrace out back with Mulligan by my side, shaded by a pair of ancient trained Savannah holly trees, I sometimes feel a little like the dinner guest who never bothered to go home.

A few months after we occupied the *Maison*, the Women's 2007 US Open came to Peggy Bell's Pine Needles Resort for the third time, and I had the opportunity to watch my son, Jack, work the tournament as an assistant to acclaimed Pebble Beach photographer Joann Dost, part of our *Open Daily* coverage team. On the eve of college, Jack's summer internship at the *Pilot* would help seal his own budding passion for journalism and film.

By that point I was fully into my third career in journalism. Work-ing with David Woronoff and Andie Stewart Rose, we transformed *PineStraw* into a full-fledged arts and culture magazine—an over-sized, handsomely illustrated monthly, unapologetically done in the style of long-gone magazines like *Collier's* and the *Saturday Evening Post*, with a pinch of *Yankee* magazine for proper seasoning—that told the stories of the Sandhills through the eyes and words of the state's finest photographers and writers. It was enthusiastically em-braced by the region's residents.

Three years later, we successfully introduced an ambitious sister magazine called *O.Henry* in Greensboro, the birthplace of William Sydney Porter, and followed that up two years later with a third sister publication called *Salt Magazine* in the historic port city of Wilmington. In time, we would even acquire the state's venerable business magazine and create a beautiful home design magazine for the Piedmont Triad, becoming one of the region's most diverse and successful media companies in the process.

It's worth clarifying that my original ambition from my "Things to Do in Golf" list had been to "Live in Pinehurst" for an unspec-ified amount of time—probably a month would have satisfied the

146 • THE RANGE BUCKET LIST

requirement nicely. But all it took was a walk with my wife in the spring moonlight to alter that scenario rather significantly. By my math, this was the third time in half a century that golf and Pinehurst had changed the direction of my life. Suddenly, living there took on an entirely different meaning.

And make no mistake, this place is all about golf.

Outside of St Andrews, the original Home of Golf, there is no place more fully dedicated to the game's perpetuation and fellowship than the Village of Pinehurst and its prosperous neighbor, Southern Pines.

The late golf writer Charles Price understood this life-affirming power when, following his own return to the place where his career began, he wrote: "If golf can be mentioned as some kind of religion among people, then Ross regarded Pinehurst as his Vatican City. There was and is something venerable about the place, something almost holy about its atmosphere that you can't find in the newness of Palm Springs or the clutter of Palm Beach. While Pinehurst is nowhere as graybeard as St Andrews, it still has a church quiet you won't find even there. While St Andrews has its magnificent old university, its coastline and sliver of beach, its history that predates the entire United States, Pinehurst has nothing but golf. . . . After sundown and the day's golf is over with, nobody talks about anything but golf—not politics, not religion, not even sex. Pinehurst is the total golf community, and the only one I can think of that you won't be disappointed with after many years. I know I wasn't."

That sums up the unchanging charms of Pinehurst and its environs pretty nicely, I think. Suffice it to say, my life behind the Pine Curtain has been enriched incalculably by the friendships I've established and the fascinating people I've met as they passed through village and town pursuing their own golf dreams and Range Bucket

Lists, including dozens of evening talks I'm always happy to put on for visiting groups of golfers.

That said, a trio of small and private moments best summarizes the qualities I most admire about the St Andrews of America and the kind of memories that are made every day in the Home of American Golf.

═══ • ═══

Late one August afternoon, not long before Jack went off to school at Elon University (where he chose journalism over the golf team—smart lad), Tom Stewart and I invited our sons to play a father-son match on Pinehurst No. 2. Bryan and Jack had something very different in mind, however.

"We want to play you two straight up," Jack announced on the first tee. "Sons against fathers."

Tom looked surprised, then delighted. "Are you *sure*?" Bryan had never beaten Tom, after all, and Jack—fresh from his high school golf team in Maine, where he briefly held the nine-hole record on a course I helped design—also had yet to beat his old man.

"Absolutely," said Bryan, a rising star on the local Pinehurst golf team.

Tom glanced at me. I shrugged. He grinned.

"Well, okay, then—if you boys think you're up to the challenge, let's do it. Hope you guys know how to say ten and eight."

Tom and I played pretty well. I think he shot his customary 75, and I at least managed to break 80.

But our sons won the match with back-to-back birdies on the two closing holes, first by Jack, who holed a long putt on seventeen, followed by a birdie Bryan calmly rolled home from roughly the same spot where Payne Stewart made his dramatic twelve-footer to win the US Open on Father's Day in 1999.

"The torch has been passed," Tom declared as we removed our caps and shook hands.

The boys were beaming. The fathers were laughing, though also in danger of shedding a small tear or two.

═══ • ═══

That next winter, an old friend from Greensboro phoned to say I needed to meet a remarkable man he called Ace Borel.

"His real name is Paul," said my friend, Jimmy Alley. "He's ninety-four and is the most amazing golfer in the Sandhills, a guy who literally lives for golf. He just made his second ace, and sounds like he could be your father's twin brother. Paul is the sweetest guy you've ever met, a total charmer. But you better hurry. He collapsed on the fourteenth hole a couple of weeks ago, and they thought they'd lost him. He told the EMS crew to send out a pretty blonde next time so she could give him mouth-to-mouth resuscitation. He's back playing, though, and wants to meet you."

Paul Borel's adorable wife, Miriam, met me at the door of their Longleaf home a few days later. She was nearly blind from macular degeneration, but you wouldn't have known it by the way she swept me into the house and led me back to Paul's study, where a regal, white-haired gent rose from a chair to offer his hand. He pointed me to a seat and handed me a neatly typed piece of paper.

"Thought you might want to read my obituary before lunch and golf," he said, with a roguish twinkle in his eye. "I know all about you from your book about your father. It's my favorite book, by the way. You never know when either of us might be summoned to a higher tee."

I sat with the morning sun shining over my shoulder and read about Paul Borel's amazing life. Born in Zurich, Switzerland, he'd emigrated with his family to Kansas City just before World War One, and graduated from the University of Kansas with an engineering degree before earning an MBA at Harvard and an MA in international relations from Columbia. During the Second World War, he served for six years as a Navy intelligence officer and followed Roosevelt to the Potsdam and Paris peace conferences. After the war he joined the fledgling Central Intelligence Agency and directed its Foreign Broadcast Monitoring Services, retiring as one of the agency's most honored employees in 1972. He'd also helped write a book called *Secrets, Spies and Scholars* and was a published poet. Weirdly enough, despite his full head of white hair, Ace Borel even looked like Opti the Mystic.

Like lots of Americans, Paul Borel discovered golf after retirement. In the early 1990s, the Borels moved to Pinehurst to be closer to their six children and twenty-two grandchildren. "I heard there was pretty good golf in the area," he told me over lunch. "The first thing I did was join the men's golf association, and I once managed to win the club's Last Man Standing tournament over thirty-seven other guys. Can you believe it? I think I was eighty then." He laughed and poured me a glass of very good wine. "That's what a thirty handicap will do for you."

I was surprised to learn that Paul had collapsed twice on the golf course. The first time was on Longleaf's eighteenth green, when he lost consciousness and toppled over. A cardiac surgeon taking a lesson nearby rushed over but found no pulse or breathing and administered CPR. Ace was diagnosed with a faulty aortic valve that sometimes stuck, owing to calcium buildup in his heart. The doctor recommended surgery.

"How much time can you buy me if I have surgery?" Paul asked him.

The surgeon said at least two or three years. Ace Borel laughed. "In that case, go fly a kite. I'll just play golf until I really am the last man *not* standing."

"Are you sure we should play?" I asked him cautiously over Miriam's lovely lunch.

"Don't worry," he quipped, "if you collapse, I'll have them send the blonde back out to give you mouth-to-mouth, too."

The golf course was empty that mild January afternoon. Before teeing off, we sat for a few minutes in his riding cart, enjoying the warm winter sun and talking about his long life and love of the game. "I was struck by something in your book that your father told you early in life—that there's plenty of sorrow in this world and it's up to us, you and me, *anyone*, to add the joy." He paused and smiled. "If love is the most powerful force in the universe, joy is certainly its progeny. Einstein said that, I think. In any case, people who accomplish great things almost always understand this principle. That's why I play golf, by the way. I'm terrible at golf, but it gives me such absurd hope and simple *joy*. And as I've proved, all it takes is one great shot to make the angels sing."

Right on cue, he proposed that I give him two strokes a hole and that we play for a quarter a hole. "You can even play from the old-man tees," he quipped. "Since you're headed that way anyway." Ace had a smooth swing, pegging his opening tee shot well down Longleaf's first fairway with his forty-six-inch Killer Bee driver. His six beat my bogey five and put the first quarter in his pocket.

Longleaf's second hole is a par-three that borders historic Midland Road and the entrance to the golf course, which is built on the remains of the famous Starland horse track. The hole measures about 125 yards from the forward tee. I watched Paul swat his ball smartly onto the putting surface, and then I wedged mine to within half a foot of the flag. "Whoa!" cried my delighted host. "I thought for sure you had one there!"

He asked how many aces I'd bagged—plenty, he surmised, given my long love affair with golf. I admitted that I'd never had a true hole in one, only an unofficial ace that wound up in the Queen Mum's teacup one springtime Sunday long ago, a tale that seemed to delight Ace Borel; he demanded to know more about Kathleen Sinclair Bennie. So I gave him a brief description of our family's extraordinary matriarch. After thirty years in her ancient farmhouse above Moose Pond, she'd recently moved to a shingled cottage by a blackwater cove near the Bowdoin College campus, enabling my former wife, Alison, to better look after her ailing mom and our children to see their beloved Mum more often when they were home from college. Kate and I stayed in touch via notes and occasional phone chats, but I owed her a visit and made a mental note to accomplish this task sooner rather than later, given time's penchant for scampering down the rabbit hole before you notice it.

On the green, I held the flag for Paul as he lined up his lengthy putt for birdie. He gave his bright optic-yellow ball a solid rap. It was dead on line, but I failed to see where it stopped, because Paul suddenly slumped to the ground. By the time I reached his side, he was ashen gray, and there was no pulse.

Suddenly I was the last man standing. I rolled him over onto his back and pulled out my cell phone but discovered it was out of juice. A van was just turning into Longleaf's entrance, so I jumped the fence and tried to cut it off, waving my arms like a crazy man. The van swerved and sped on. I looked around and saw a woman a few hundred yards away unloading her groceries from her trunk, and bolted that way. While she phoned the EMTs, I sprinted back to the green, trying to remember how to administer CPR.

Paul hadn't moved. He was even paler, had remained deathly still, and had no pulse that I could find. I stretched out his legs and tilted his head back and lifted his chin to begin CPR.

At that instant, color suddenly returned to his cheeks, and his blue eyes popped open. He smiled up at me.

"Did I make the putt?" he asked.

In fact, his ball had stopped one full revolution from dropping into the hole. But I never thought to retrieve our balls.

Ace Borel waved off the EMS crew, and we rode home together

in his cart. "If you'd been that blonde I requested," he joked, "I'd have let you do CPR."

We spent another couple of hours sitting in his study and talking about his Kansas childhood as he rested and put down some fluids.

Miriam came in to check on us. "Now, Paul, I hate to say this, but I think it's time for you to give up golf forever. I know how that hurts. We'll just have to find something else for you to do."

Paul thought about this for a moment. The day every golfer dreads had finally arrived. But the roguish twinkle returned to his eye.

"Okay," he said. "Want to make out?"

Miriam shook her head, smiling, and left us.

He walked me to the front door.

"Thanks for coming," he said. "I really enjoyed being with you. Sorry I gave you such a scare. Wish you'd made that ace."

"I still heard the angels sing," I assured him.

"One more thing," said Ace Borel, growing serious. "I think you owe me a quarter."

According to his daughter, Nancy, this was indeed the last time Paul Borel played golf. He moved to a hospice home a short time later, and quietly passed away within a few months. This time he didn't come back. His big family honors him every time they get together.

"He was so full of joy," Nancy reports, "to the very end."

Miriam Borel, on the other hand, is still going strong. She recently turned 101.

$$=== \bullet ===$$

One more for the road: the first—and last—Ross Country Invitational.

One day at lunch, as another year drew to a close, David Woronoff and I were chatting about Donald Ross's fancy for wacky, made-up golf events such as moonlight golf and playing courses in reverse just for fun.

"We should do something like that here to keep the tradition alive," David proposed.

"I've always been curious to see whether you could play from the first tee of No. 2 to the eighteenth green of Mid Pines," I tossed out, pointing out that there were no less than seven golf courses linking the two most famous layouts in the area, a distance of about five miles, or, roughly, the length of a championship golf course.

"You mean go across country?" he asked. I said yes—though it would mean crossing at least one major highway and two other roads, and negotiating a large patch of woods and several residential neighborhoods.

Within days, he'd organized and named the First Donald Ross Country Invitational Team Championship, an alternate-shot affair that took place on the crisp and clear New Year's Eve of 2007.

Off went four teams composed of two players each on a frosty morning, fueled by simple curiosity and no shortage of good Scotch whiskey, each pathfinding their own way across golf courses and sleepy lawns. Had Ladbrokes been handicapping the field, Tom Stewart and a local sawbones named Walter Morris would undoubtedly have been among the favorites, followed by Mid Pines owner (and simultaneous Pine Valley and Seminole club champion) Kelly Miller and Dr. John Dempsey, the golf-mad president of Sandhills Community College. Pinehurst CEO Pat Corso and his head professional, Matt Massey, also figured to challenge for the title, while bringing up the rear of the field were David Woronoff, my cousin Bobby Tracy, and yours truly, the only three-member team in the field. We were allowed three players because, as I say, Woronoff was really a non-golfer, a fine tennis player but possibly the "best worst golfer" I'd ever seen, whereas Cousin Bobby (who was visiting with wife Claire for the New Year weekend) was a heck of a stick. Somehow this balanced out the field. Naturally there were wails of protest, but the event's governing body—David and I—ignored them.

In any case, every team chose a slightly different route, though we inevitably came together at a spot on Pinehurst Course No. 7, where we faced four lanes of traffic on a federal highway. An ad hoc committee decided that each team would play into the back of a *Pilot* van heavily stocked with munchies and adult beverages, then be required to pitch out of the vehicle on the opposite side of the highway. Much merriment and body-specific name-calling ensued. The real challenge to shot-making turned out to be the patch of woods where Team Stewart-Morris found itself stymied by a young sapling, prompting Doc Morris to whip a handsaw out of his golf bag and remove the offending tree to howls of environmental protest from their fellow competitors.

A little while later, we played over the heads of an oncoming elderly couple out for a quiet New Year's Eve round on a popular executive course called Pine Knoll, prompting the woman to shake a fist and holler at us, "You *idiots* are playing the wrong way! Are you people *drunk*?"

By the time Team Dodson-Wornoff-Bobby reached the fairway of Mid Pines' beautiful eighteenth hole, the other teams had already placed their approach shots on the green, two of them facing short putts for a total of forty-four strokes. The others, including us, already lay at forty-five.

Unfortunately, Team Dodson-Woronoff-Bobby wasn't there yet.

"David," I said quietly, "all you have to do is hit a simple wedge shot onto the green. It's less than one hundred yards, the easiest shot in golf. Give me a chance to get home with one putt. We'll need it to catch the others, I'm afraid."

"Easy," he replied, and promptly buried our ball deep into the face of the bunker in front of the green.

As we walked that way, much to the delight of our competitors,

I called David every outrageous name I could think of in faux disgust, theatrically whipping out my sand wedge and marching into the bunker, making a big show of wiggling my feet into the sand and taking dead aim at the flag eighty feet away, declaring, for dramatic effect, "Thank you *very* much, pal! Now *I'm* going to have to make the most incredible bunker shot ever played on this hole!"

Our opponents were howling with laughter.

I swung hard, and the ball popped up, bounced once on the green, and dropped into the cup. I looked up in time to see it fall into the hole—and to see David leap into the air.

Three sets of jaws dropped in unison. There was a moment of disbelieving silence, followed by even more intense howls of protest as David and I replicated Hale Irwin's famous victory gallop around the final hole of the 1990 US Open at Medinah, slapping hands as we passed each other. I think David did the Macarena as well, just to rub salt into the wound.

The two teams who had short downhill putts to win both lipped out, and the first-ever Donald Ross Country Invitational ended in a highly controversial three-way tie between Miller-Dempsey, Stewart-Morris (the tree killers), and Dodson-Woronoff-Bobby.

Inside the pub at Mid Pines, we ate delicious homemade chili and toasted the success of the inaugural Ross Country Invitational, which everyone agreed was the most fun one could have on New Year's Eve and still remember in the morning.

"We should do this next year," Tom Stewart insisted. "We need revenge."

"Maybe every year," added Doc Morris.

For a few years after that, in fact, we tried several variations on the Ross Country—playing with hickories or left-handed, even cold sober—but nothing quite matched the fun and wacky fellowship of that first made-up holiday classic. This is the only known account of a Pinehurst event that's already the stuff of legend in our own minds. But that's life behind the Pine Curtain, where golf dreams of one kind or another come true every day.

Step into Tom Stewart's golf shop on the square and look above the front door, and you'll see a special plaque commemorating the co-winners of the first—and last—Donald Ross Country Invitational. The plaque holds the infamous hacksaw but, sadly, mentions only the name of *one* team that tied for first: Team Stewart-Morris.

"Revenge is sweet," Tom likes to tell the customers who ask about it. "Besides, it's my shop."

CHAPTER ELEVEN

ROAD TRIP

From their earliest days, the Village of Pinehurst and Town of Southern Pines were meant to be places of escape for Americans who could afford time away from the quotidian demands of life and work, places of pilgrimage in a formerly remote pine wilderness, where—as old man Tufts and others envisioned—the fortunate few could recreate among their own kind, riding horses and playing golf in a place that seemed blissfully frozen in time. Indeed, as the resort's phone operators are trained to answer all calls, rain or shine, it's always "a beautiful day in Pinehurst."

But after ten years of living and working in the Home of American Golf, a place I'd originally intended to "live in" for only a few weeks, I suddenly felt out of touch with the outside world; maybe it was even a kind of nostalgia for my former life roaming the diverse golf and social landscape of the planet. Regardless, I was hit by a powerful hankering to hit the road with my golf bag in order to see what was really happening outside the "Pinehurst Bubble," as some longtime residents of the Sandhills refer to it.

A solo road trip to places I had yet to visit in American golf had long been an entry on my ever-expanding Range Bucket List, but the desire took on fresh urgency on the warm summer evening I was asked to give the keynote celebrating the reopening of the Member's Club at Pinehurst Resort, a gala marking a recent four-million-dollar renovation of the clubhouse in preparation for hosting the historic dual men's and women's US Open Championships in 2014.

Coming on the heels of the comprehensive restoration of Pinehurst No. 2 by design partners Ben Crenshaw and Bill Coore, which removed traditional rough, restored sandy waste areas, and effectively took Donald Ross's masterpiece back to its minimalist roots, in theory all lay in readiness to host the twin Opens, a novel undertaking most veteran Open watchers believed could only realistically be staged at Pinehurst, with its wide-open countryside and easy access—not to mention its heritage of hosting important championships dating back to the game's early days on American shores. It was, without question, a night to celebrate.

But there was an unvoiced issue weighing on my mind that night, one I felt obliged to somehow address as a native son and a golf historian.

A disturbing headline in the *Washington Post* summed it up: WHY AMERICA FELL OUT OF LOVE WITH GOLF. In brief, the story outlined how the combination of the Great Recession and America's shifting social demographics had dealt a major blow to the once-thriving golf industry and ended the biggest golf boom in American history—six decades of unprecedented growth that saw the formal creation of six professional golf tours, the restoration of the Ryder Cup, the rise of the Europeans, seven of the ten top players in history, and nothing short of complete revolutions in equipment technology and golf-course design.

Over the previous decade, according to the *Post*, the number of Americans playing golf had dropped precipitously, particularly among millennials, the rising force in the economy. Despite rosy industry projections around the start of the new millennium that a new course would need to open every day in order to accommodate the public's insatiable demand for golf, there was now, according to those same industry sources, a golf course that closed its doors every day in America.

What went wrong? Nobody could say for sure. But the short explanation seemed to be that golf had become too hard, too expensive, and too time-consuming to suit the modern family lifestyle. With the collapse of Wall Street in late 2008 and the resulting Great Recession that burst the nation's real estate bubble, gutted pensions, and put millions of middle-class Americans out of work, golf had suddenly fallen on hard times. By one industry estimate, more than eight million people had abandoned the game since the year 2001. A similar article in the *Wall Street Journal* wondered, HOW DID GOLF LOSE ITS WAY? and seemed to suggest that golf might even be retreating into its sleepy country-club past, becoming once again a game played only by the wealthy on the gilded margins of American society.

═══ • ═══

Whatever else might be true, despite its relatively short life span of 125 years in America, the game of golf has proved a surprisingly reliable snapshot of our national economic health and social ambitions. In simplest terms, whenever times are good, golf participation tends to flourish, as evidenced by the game's robust growth during the so-called Golden Age of Golf, the nation's first golf boom, which lasted from roughly 1900 to 1930 and produced more than two thousand outstanding golf clubs and public courses designed by the evangelical talents of people like Donald Ross, Arthur Tillinghast, Seth Raynor, Alister MacKenzie, and others of their ilk who were determined to help the ancient game take root in a new world.

During this span of years, as the First World War receded from view and broader economic prosperity touched millions of ordinary lives, America's so-called leisure class first emerged—middle-class working people with disposable income and weekends off—and participation in golf grew dramatically. At this time the nation found its first authentic stars in the amateur Bobby Jones and professionals Walter Hagen and Gene Sarazen.

All of this came to an abrupt end with the crash of the stock market in 1929, the retirement of Jones from competitive golf less than a year later, and the pulverizing economic depression that wiped out half of America's Jazz Age wealth, shuttering at least a third of the nation's golf clubs and public courses in the process. It wasn't until a trio of former caddies, all born in the same year of 1912, rose from the dusty anonymity of the American heartland to find stardom on the eve of the Second World War that golf regained its popular footing in America. In the wake of the American triumvirate of Sam Snead, Ben Hogan, and Byron Nelson, who rewrote the record books and returned coverage of golf tournaments to the front of the nation's sports pages, the stage was set for the emergence of a new generation of college-bred stars, led by a charismatic greenskeeper's son named Arnold Palmer, whose corkscrew swing and yeoman smile symbolized a rebirth of an even broader democratization of the game, a perfect conjunction of stars just as televised sports arrived.

Thanks to Arnie and his passionate army, an even larger golf boom took place in America, producing an unprecedented era of growth, a Second Golden Age of Golf that attracted upward of ten million newcomers to the game.

As I took the lectern that warm, celebratory evening in Pinehurst, it was my job to offer some kind of historical perspective on Pinehurst's forthcoming Opens and, if possible, to reassure my anxious fellow members—many of whom were retirees who'd watched their pensions and life savings go up in smoke as a result of the worst global economic crisis since the Great Depression—that the ancient game of golf was here to stay. On the bright side, some industry types openly expressed optimism that the novelty of dueling Opens might, in fact, rekindle public interest in the game, and possibly even inspire a surge of new growth similar to the one unleashed in the wake of Harry Vardon's visit to Pinehurst in 1900, an exhibition that effectively introduced Pinehurst's name to the world and laid the foundation for the first golden age.

I personally had my doubts about such a grassroots rebirth happening anytime soon, having watched the explosion of overpriced, overbuilt golf developments through the 1990s and early 2000s and often wondering who the heck was going to be joining all the absurdly expensive private clubs with Taj Mahal–sized clubhouses or playing the Myrtle Beach resorts that were charging upward of three hundred dollars per round. In those not-so-faraway days, everyone who claimed to know the difference between Arnie and Jack seemed to be cashing in on golf's gold rush, determined to make a financial killing and a personal statement about the game. In our own backyard, there was a perfect symbol of golf's boom-gone-bust called the Dormie Club, built by a pleasant fellow who'd purchased Donald Ross's house on Midland Road and hoped to create the next Pine Valley, an elite club for "golf purists" who could afford the lofty price of membership. The club's outstanding Coore-Crenshaw layout was now being played for a modest daily greens fee by visiting golf groups and was, like many fine courses across America, engaged in a fight for its survival. Down in Myrtle Beach, meanwhile, a dozen different "signature" golf courses had been sold off and plowed up for housing developments to accommodate the exploding population of the Grand Strand area.

Without question, this was discouraging news. Moreover, at least three popular monthly golf magazines had either folded or fled to the Internet, and most major daily newspapers had cut loose their longtime golf writers in an effort to streamline their reporting staffs.

Several of my friends and former colleagues were either out of jobs or scrambling to latch on to anything that could allow them to make it to retirement age.

I'd been luckier than most, returning to my old stomping grounds at about the time the boom began to go bust, able to use my years working for several outstanding magazines to help create several regional publications that were, knock wood, doing well— an achievement that maybe constituted the most rewarding years of my working life. Somewhere, both my parents had to be smiling.

But for all that good fortune, thanks to the "Pinehurst Bubble," I lacked real perspective on what was happening in the world beyond Moore County and felt a powerful desire to grab my golf bag, fire up my new Outback, and go see for myself what was really happening *out there.*

In the end, lacking the gift of prophecy, all I could really do that evening was spin a few amusing stories from Pinehurst's rich lore and remind my friends and neighbors that golf is a five-hundred-year-old game that has survived at least two world wars and a Great Depression, not to mention countless civil wars, European plagues, and innumerable economic upheavals reaching back to late Medieval times, remaining pretty much the same maddeningly elusive sport that we know and love today through the rise and fall of nations and cultural revolutions of every variety—"even the disturbing birth of high-yellow-optic golf balls," I added, drawing my final good laugh of the evening.

Determined to wind up on a positive note, I suggested that there was actually nothing wrong with the game of golf—only an industry that got too far out over its skis, so to speak. Golf would recover its balance and eventually reemerge from this fallow period for the same reason it has been part of Western life since Shakespeare's day: it's a game that challenges both body and soul with its elusive charms, provides a healthy walk through nature, and gives one a genuine opportunity for friendship and exercise in a world moving faster and faster by the day.

"So here's how I plan to get ready for these historic twin US Opens," I said, concluding my remarks. "Tomorrow morning, I'm going to load my golf clubs in the back of my car and honor a great American tradition called the road trip in order to get back in touch with America's golf roots by going to see a few people and places I've always meant to see. A golfing road trip may not do wonders for the ailing golf world," I said, "but hopefully it will do wonders for *me*."

As Wendy and I walked out to our car under a serene August moon, she took my hand and gave it a loyal squeeze. "Nice talk. I think they appreciated your perspective. Are you really going to take off on a solo golf trip?"

"Yes, ma'am." I admitted this urge had been brewing in me for months, if not years, and I was eager to break out of the Pinehurst Bubble and just *drive*.

She seemed amused. "Where do you want to go?"

"Not sure yet. That's part of the fun. I'm open to persuasion and best offers."

My first thought, I said, was to drop in on my favorite golf teacher for a quick tune-up and his thoughts on golf's reported identity crisis, then drive all the way to northern Michigan in order to play a match against my major golf nemesis, Tom Stewart, who was running a shop in his old stomping grounds of Harbor Springs for the summer. I'd never managed to beat the Lord Mayor of Pinehurst, but something said my time might be at hand. On the way there, I thought I might stop off at Scioto Golf Club in Columbus to investigate the life of young Jack Nicklaus and learn more about his teacher, Jack Grout, and check out a beloved Donald Ross golf course. I also had a golf writer buddy who lived in Toledo and wanted to show me how the key to golf's future was its golden past.

"I also need to go see Bill Campbell. I hear he's not doing well."

Bill Campbell, the celebrated amateur champion, former USGA president, and only the second American to serve as captain of the Royal and Ancient Golf Club, was a close friend of many years who—along with the Queen Mum—had kindly read all my golf books save for *Final Rounds* in their early stages, offering valuable insight and advice. I owed him more than I could possibly repay, along with, without question, a proper visit that might be our last.

"In that case, you definitely *should* go," Wendy agreed. "You need to see Bill and have some fun with Tom. Too much work and not enough play is making Jimmy feel old and cranky—not to mention this Sandhills heat."

She was right about the heat. Historically the Tufts closed down their hotels and headed for the coast of Maine when the furnace blast of Sandhills summer struck, rendering the Home of American Golf a gilded ghost town until October. Perhaps because my own thermostat was stuck on cool Maine summer, I rarely played golf during the long dog days. Also encouraging my own northern flight, the US Kids International Golf Championship was in full swing across the county, an annual occupation force of more than five hundred kids from around the world (and their doting parents) that occupied most of the golf courses of Pinehurst and Southern Pines for a full fortnight—perhaps one indicator that the game of golf wasn't quite as moribund as some insisted. In any case, it was an ideal time to run away and chase my Range Bucket List.

I pointed out to my wife, however, that she sounded rather pleased to see me go.

She patted my hand. "I am. While you're off getting in touch with your inner teenage golfer and chasing your bucket list, I'll hold a huge garage sale and get rid of a lot of stuff we no longer need.

Who knows, I might even get into that foyer closet where you've stuffed a few hundred golf caps you never actually wear."

"Please don't do anything rash," I said anxiously. "Those caps tell the story of my long journey through golf. Besides, there's really only a couple dozen of them."

But she seemed to feel her time of liberation was at hand, too, and blithely ignored my protest.

"After that, I might even get to all those clubs collecting dust in the basement that you've been promising forever to thin out . . ."

"Maybe I shouldn't go," I said.

"Nonsense. It will do us both a world of good. I'll help you pack your bag tonight," she volunteered cheerfully.

═══ • ═══

It was high noon the next day when I pulled into a popular golf learning center called the Eagle Zone, perched just off an interstate exit in Greenville, South Carolina, in search of Dr. Hook.

John Gerring and I met in 1986 when I was researching my first Tour profile for *Golf* magazine. The subject was appealing Tour rookie Davis Love III. John was running *Golf Digest*'s Sea Island Golf Learning Center, which Davis called home and where his father served as the club's head professional. A disciple of traditional golf methodology, eschewing video and computer-analyzed golf-swing technology in favor of traditional teaching techniques, Gerring had shaped the games of Open winners Larry Nelson and Betsy King, among other notables, and had earned the sobriquet "Dr. Hook" for his belief that a manageable draw is the most useful shot in golf.

After visiting with Dr. Hook at Sea Island before he left for posts running the Atlanta Country Club and Bloomfield Hills in Detroit (and later returning home to finish his career at redoubtable Biltmore Forest in Asheville—the club where Bobby Jones honeymooned and Hogan won his third professional tournament in a row in 1940, after Pinehurst and Greensboro), my game achieved its scoring peak, producing a Maine State Golf Association handicap index of 5.2 that I more or less carried back to the Home of American Golf in 2005—and have ironically watched ascend toward true duffer status ever since.

Having set my mind to venture all the way to northern Michigan in hopes of vanquishing the Lord Mayor of Pinehurst in his own ancestral backyard, I thought a few minutes with the one teacher who had significantly improved my game during that first visit might be both informative and useful on several fronts—including insights on the golf world's current problems.

I was correct on both counts. After we watched one of his teen protégés, wearing unlaced, muddy FootJoys, hammer spectacular three-iron shots to the back of the Eagle Zone's crowded driving range with near-perfect draws, Dr. Hook watched me hit balls for less than five minutes before diagnosing the problem. My elbow was flying, and my setup was off target. He adjusted my stance to aim slightly right of the target, lowered my right shoulder a touch, and reminded me that a good swing begins with a smooth, one-piece shoulder turn and full finish. Soon he had me making the sweet little draws that make Dr. Hook a happy fellow—though that may not be apparent from his normal blank expression.

After retiring from Biltmore Forest in 2013, Gerring and his wife, Jo, moved home to Greenville, where John was invited to head up the teaching staff at the Eagle Zone, which featured a beautifully maintained range, chipping and putting greens, and a small executive practice course. On the hot summer afternoon when I rolled up unannounced, the range was teeming with teenagers and middle-aged dudes like me with their shirtsleeves rolled up, pounding golf balls into the summer sky.

Over a ginger ale after my lesson, I asked John what was ailing golf—and, moreover, if there was a cure.

"Soccer is a big problem," he said.

"You mean playing golf with soccer balls?" Somewhere I'd recently read about a club out West that was hoping to make golf more appealing to a generation of soccer kids by creating a course where players booted soccer balls into oversized holes.

"No. I mean the game of soccer—what the Europeans call football. It's killing golf, and is a perfect metaphor for how America has culturally changed since you were a kid in Greensboro. The middle class is vanishing, and both parents are working to make ends meet and shuttling the kids to soccer games on weekends. Family life is very different than it was just a generation ago. Dropping off a kid to play golf all day at the club is a thing of the past. Soccer is far more affordable and doable."

"Maybe golf is just too slow for a fast-paced world," I prompted.

"Golf is a slow game," he continued. "That's part of its charm. You don't learn to do it well overnight. Kicking a soccer ball seems pretty easy by comparison. But nobody picks up golf that quickly—even the great ones. Look at Hogan and Nelson and Palmer. They worked their rear ends off, practicing till their hands bled. They figured it out on their own. Golf takes time, dedication, and practice. The problem is, as you say, we live in a fast world of instant gratification that's getting faster by the year. And when you combine how expensive golf has become over the past decade with the game's natural difficulty, not to mention the shorter attention spans in a world where time and money are more precious than ever—well, you have a formula for a declining game."

"What could bring it back?" I asked.

Dr. Hook sighed. "That's the big question. Society has changed. The middle class that always served to grow the game in America from the ground up is shrinking. We're also living in such an anxious time. Everyone I know senses this, young and old alike; there's a feeling that nothing is working the way it ought to anymore. Our institutions are failing, and the old values don't relate anymore, so we're rushing even faster to try to find an answer to our collective anxiety."

Before I could probe this idea deeper, Dr. Hook softened and added, "You and I both know that no game on earth can slow you down and make you stay in the moment quite like a round of golf. It can give you great perspective and even make you count your blessings as you walk the earth and play the game. Unfortunately, the only way I see golf growing significantly again, in both our lifetimes, at least, is by going small."

Dr. Hook suddenly sounded like a Buddhist holy man offering a zen koan for an ancient game. I'd come seeking a swing guru and found a grassroots philosopher parked on an interstate golf range.

"How is that, exactly?"

"We need to quit worrying about trying to create another golf boom and focus instead on taking care of the people who *already* love the game. There's absolutely nothing wrong with the game of golf. The real problem lies with the golf industry, the people who see golf as a splendid merchandising opportunity. Golf is the most personal game on earth, something you do alone or with friends, a walk through nature. We've spent the past ten years building high-priced golf courses that nobody can afford to play and selling equipment that gets more expensive every year. We overbuilt and overcharged for the game. And, like the big real estate bubble, it was an illusion. The bubble was destined to break.

"My other firm belief is that we need to make the game more welcoming and much easier to play—and far less expensive, so *anyone* can take up the game. The key to golf's future lies with its past. In Scotland, every town or village has a wee course where it costs basically peanuts to play for men, women, and children, old and young folks alike. Golf is part of the cultural fabric. That's *small*. We need to go small like that, and quit building clubhouses that appeal to personal vanity."

He explained that right at this moment across America there were twenty-nine thousand certified PGA professionals, most of whom were doing little more than selling overpriced golf attire in their shops instead of teaching ordinary people how to play a game they can enjoy at every stage of life. "Thanks to the Ryder Cup and its huge TV revenues, the PGA of America is a very wealthy organization. What if the PGA used its money to purchase hundreds of these reportedly troubled golf courses and invited folks from the inner cities and suburbs and anywhere else to come out and play the game for a low cost, or, my goodness, even for free, with lunch and instructions included? School groups, retired folks, anyone! Can you imagine what that would do for golf?"

Dr. Hook looked as if he expected an answer from me. So I told him I'd recently read that there were roughly sixteen thousand golf courses in America, the vast majority of them—at least 90 percent—public-access layouts. The Great Recession had wiped out hundreds of high-priced courses, but thousands of inexpensive and unfussy public courses like the ones my buddy Patrick McDaid and I wore out around Greensboro in the late 1960s and early '70s were still hanging in there—many of them doing pretty well, in fact, because they had little or no debt.

"That's exactly what I'm talking about—growing small in order to grow large again." Then he told me something I'd never known about him: his father was the head professional of a popular public course in High Point where I played a lot of my early golf with my own father, reminding me once again how only a degree or two of separation exists between true sons and daughters of the game. As he related this surprising fact, I realized that tough old Dr. Hook was giving me something dangerously close to an actual smile.

"And now I have a favor to ask of you."

He handed me a folder containing the pages of an instruction book he'd been working on for years, the accumulation of six decades' worth of his teaching wisdom, an instruction bible containing the Gospel According to Dr. Hook and the Power of the Draw. It contained elegant stick drawings that explained his famously basic teaching methods. The book was aptly titled *Simple Enough*.

He wondered if I would consider reading it on my travels and giving him my opinion, adding that Larry Nelson and Betsy King had agreed to do the same.

Naturally, I told him I would be pleased to have his book to read on my road trip.

"Good," he grumbled. "Just remember what I told you about your setup and you'll be fine."

"Think small," I said, offering him my hand. "That's simple enough."

"Exactly," said Dr. Hook.

CHAPTER TWELVE

THE HOUSE THAT JACKS BUILT

SCIOTO

The next eight days were exactly what the good doctor ordered and what I needed most at that moment—a road trip into the heart of American golf.

At rush hour the next afternoon, I rolled into Columbus, Ohio, barely in time to take an absurdly quick walking tour of the Jack Nicklaus Museum twenty minutes before it closed—just enough time to speed-walk through Nicklaus's extraordinary career. After that, I found my way to a famous German restaurant in the city's historic Germantown district, where, in honor of the museum's star, I ate my approximate body weight in schnitzel, brats, and excellent German beer, passing a mostly pleasant hour with a computer-software salesman from Cincinnati who deduced from my faded Seminole golf cap that I was a fellow hacker off his lead. He filled me in on roughly every detail of his first, second, and third trips to the Masters—all company expensed, he noted—and wondered if I'd ever been to Augusta. "A few times," I admitted, and left it at that, diving safely into a cream puff the size of a radial tire. A short time later, I bid my dinnermate a cheerful adieu and found my way to an early motel bed in preparation for a 9:00 a.m. appointment with the club historian at Scioto Country Club, the house that two Jacks built.

The first Jack I was eager to learn more about was one John Frederick Grout, who came to the club as head professional following a journeyman's career on the early professional golf circuit that eventually evolved into the modern PGA Tour. The other was his star pupil, Jackie William Nicklaus.

But more on them in a roaring Buckeye moment.

Named for the river (and the Indian tribe that originally inhabited its banks) that meanders through the bustling, leafy northern suburbs of Columbus, Scioto was born in the grip of a national fervor unleashed by Francis Ouimet's US Open heroics at Brookline in 1913. Cofounded by Samuel P. Bush (GHW's grandfather) and designed by Donald Ross not long after he created Pinehurst No. 2, it was little-known outside Ohio and something of a surprise choice to host the thirtieth United States Open in 1926 when Bobby Jones showed up just two weeks after claiming the first of his three British Open titles at Royal Lytham. Jones was weary from weeks of foreign travel and press interviews, not to mention troubled by the ailing stomach that often bedeviled him before and during major championships.

On the eve of the final Saturday double round—Scioto, by the way, was the first place the Open was extended to three full days of competition—a local doctor prescribed Jones a digestive for his stomach. He started the final round three back of Joe Turnesa (of the vaunted Pennsylvania golfing clan that spawned seven professionals) and reached the final hole needing only a birdie to win. He accordingly unleashed a 310-yard drive that he later described as the finest shot of his career. A four-iron to the green left him twelve feet for eagle, and a careful two-putt for birdie gave Jones the edge over Turnesa and the second of his record four US Open wins—making him the first player in history to claim both the British and US Open in the same year.

Beneath its drowsy vaulted oaks, beautiful Scioto suddenly grabbed the world's attention, going on to host the Ryder Cup of 1931, the PGA Championship of 1950, a US Amateur in 1968, and the US Senior Open Championship of 1986. In 2010, aforementioned native son Jack Nicklaus and designer Michael Hurdzan updated Scioto's spectacular parkland course in preparation for the 2015 US Senior Open, which returned in honor of Scioto's centennial.

I'd first met Jack Grout and his good friend Henry Picard through my research on Ben Hogan's life and times. Both men were products of the caddie yard who made it onto the nascent tournament circuit of the 1930s playing more for glory than dollars, doubling as club pros who made their primary livelihoods by giving lessons and serving members at private clubs during a time when there was no formal PGA Tour. The two men bumped along the circuit at a crucial crossroads of the game's evolution, with America struggling to emerge from the devastation of the Great Depression and steel replacing hickory shafts in golf equipment, a major technological advance that would alter everything from ideas about golf swings to the composition of golf balls.

More importantly, traveling pals Picard and Grout exchanged and refined pioneering ideas about the evolving swing Henry Picard had picked up directly from Alex Morrison, the innovative and flamboyant teacher who maintained that golf was 90 percent mental, 8 percent physical, and only 2 percent technical.

Though Grout collected only seven titles in a modestly successful tournament career that stretched from 1931 to 1953, he forged close friendships with every great player of his day, swapping ideas and formulating his own fundamentals based on concepts learned from Picard and Morrison, all of which came to spectacular flowering during his Scioto years. Between the two of them, Picard and

Grout shaped the swings and philosophies of no less than a dozen top players of the modern era, and half that many future Hall of Famers.

I've long thought of them both as the founding fathers of modern American golf.

Early in Grout's career, while working as a shop assistant to his older brother Dick at Glen Garden Golf Club in Fort Worth, the younger Grout agreed to look at the golf swing of a runtish loner from the caddie yard named Bennie Hogan. Grout, in fact, may have been the one who fixed the young Hogan's "hog-killer" grip and smoothed out his flat, hooking swing, and quite possibly introduced him to a beloved local businessman who took up golf on his doctor's orders not long after Hogan showed up to caddie. Marvin Leonard was a Fort Worth retailing legend who in time became young Hogan's surrogate father, the guiding influence of his life. Grout also became friendly with the club's most popular caddie, a sunny farm boy named Byron Nelson. In December 1931, twenty-two-year-old Jack Grout invited twenty-year-old Ben Hogan to join him and another aspiring pro named Ralph Hutchinson for the West Coast tournament season. The trio headed for California in Hogan's secondhand Hudson roadster. After two months on tour, they returned to Fort Worth with little to show but lint-filled pockets. These were Ben Hogan's darkest years, when he worked as a stickman in a jackleg casino and did odd jobs around the oil fields and local hotels of Cowtown to supplement his meager pay at a local nine-hole golf course near the bottom of the Great Depression. Three years later, Grout headed for the West Coast circuit again, this time with newlyweds Byron and Louise Nelson in Byron's unheated 1932 Ford Roadster. Grout's long and languid golf swing didn't produce tangible results, but that didn't stop him from trying for a third time with a colorful young pro named Jimmy Demaret for a traveling companion. Years later, Grout would say that the real value of his struggling years on the pro circuit was the chance to share ideas with the finest players of the day, many of whom became his closest friends—future legends Hogan, Nelson, and Demaret, but also short-game wizards Paul Runyan and Jack Burke Sr., and, most influential of all, a suave and polished son of Massachusetts named Henry Picard.

Having racked up seven titles by 1935, Picard was the hottest player in the game when he invited Grout to travel with him beginning in late 1936. The tandem shared a love of family and a powerful interest in what made a golf swing tick. On New Year's Eve the next year, Picard and Grout bumped into Ben and Valerie Hogan quietly arguing in a corner of the dining room of the Blackstone Hotel in Fort Worth. Valerie Hogan was trying to convince her new husband that he needed to take another stab at the West Coast circuit before giving up, but Hogan would have none of it. Picard and Grout politely intervened, agreeing with Hogan's bride and offering to cover Hogan's expenses if he came up lint-pockets again. Hogan reluctantly agreed—and later cited this as the turning point of his life. That same year, Hogan's friend and caddie-yard rival Byron Nelson won the Masters, making a strong and positive impression on founders Cliff Roberts and Bobby Jones.

Henry Picard won the Masters the following year, and saw his faith rewarded when Hogan captured the first of his sixty-four Tour titles at the Hershey Four-Ball Invitational, held at the famous Pennsylvania club owned by chocolate baron Milton Hershey where none other than Henry Picard served as head professional with Jack Grout as his assistant, running the well-stocked pro shop and giving lessons in Picard's absence.

A year later, at the 1939 PGA Championship in New York, Picard showed Hogan how to weaken his grip and achieve a reliable fade that led to a breakthrough at Pinehurst in the spring of 1940, when the solemn, moody, and not particularly popular Hogan surprised the world by running away with the prestigious North and South Open, the Greater Greensboro Open, and Asheville's Land of the Sky Open, all within the same twenty-day period.

I heard these evolutionary tales for the first time in the late 1980s when I called on Henry Picard at the Country Club of Charleston, where he served for many years as winter head professional and pro emeritus. During our friendly chat on a sunlit terrace, Henry referred to his old friend and traveling pal Jack Grout as "the most underappreciated man in American golf—the greatest club pro in history. Every golfer in America needs to personally thank him." Though I knew Grout principally as Jack Nicklaus's longtime mentor, I didn't fully grasp the broader implications of this comment until a decade later when Arnold Palmer, of all people, told me pretty much the same thing.

Few remember that Arnold showed up for a charity match at Scioto in 1962 with his new young rival only days after "Fat Jack" had beaten the new "King of Golf," as he was suddenly being hailed, in front of rowdy partisan fans at the US Open at Oakmont. Years later, Arnold told me the opportunity to get to know the *other* Jack was one of his prime motivations for going to Scioto. "Frankly, I'd never seen anyone who had the ability to concentrate the way Jack Nicklaus did, given the crazy atmosphere at Oakmont. I wanted to see who taught him that—where that incredible concentration came from."

In a nutshell, that was exactly why I was dropping into Scioto on a perfect summer morning—to see a golf course that shaped the character of American golf, and to learn more about the greatest player in golf history.

═══ • ═══

The club's youthful historian, Scott Kelly, and head professional, Bill Stines, a fellow Carolinian, met me at the front door and gave me a guided walking tour of the beautiful clubhouse, explaining how Scioto—like its close Ross relation, Pinehurst—had recently undergone a complete renovation as part of a $6 million improvement scheme to prepare the club for hosting the US Senior Open. Equally impressive, Kelly spearheaded a team of amateur archivists that gathered all sorts of memorabilia and vintage photos from its illustrious championships that make a visit to the club, dare I say (with no slight to the Golden Bear intended), even more exciting to a golf history buff like me than a power walk through the handsome Nicklaus Museum.

Photos from Jones's Open triumph in 1926 merit a hallway of their own, showing Scioto in her wonderfully primitive state, with midsummer rough that looked like hayfields and a fancy Victorian clubhouse that later burned to the ground, as every early clubhouse in America seems to have done. For his part, Jones was so relieved and exhausted by his final-hole heroics that he could only respond "Thank you, sir," when USGA president and seasonal Pinehurst resident W. C. Fownes—the 1910 US Amateur champ—presented him the winning trophy. One story holds that a grateful Bobby Jones gave his winning ball to the doctor who calmed his dodgy stomach.

My favorite gallery of photos and stories, however, concerned the 1931 Ryder Cup, the second to be played on US soil, in which a weakened British team, still smarting from its own PGA's refusal to allow three of its best players to participate (owing to a residency rule that would soon be abandoned, Percy Alliss, Aubrey Boomer, and the great Henry Cotton were excluded from the squad), resorted to other means to try to rattle a formidable American team. They made gentle mockery of the larger ball used by their American hosts and cheekily illustrated their protest with a gigantic driver created by a local craftsman—the kind of casual, good-humored theater early Ryder Cup matches were known for.

Alas, the playful stunt did them little good as the Americans, led by plucky Gene Sarazen and hard-drinking captain Walter Hagen, crushed their largely unknown visitors 9–3 in the wilting Ohio heat. As Scioto's photo documentation reveals, the Brits, ill equipped for summer in America's heartland, wore insanely heavy wool clothing throughout the proceedings. Not long afterward, the Ryder Cup competition committee voted to move the gathering permanently to the autumn—yet another way Scioto shaped the game we know today.

The highlight of the walking tour for me, however, came when Scott Kelly led me into the beautiful Nicklaus parlor room, where small mementos from Jack's early life at Scioto and his many amateur trophies are handsomely displayed, a tribute room inspired by a similar one now honoring the young Bobby Jones at East Lake. My host pointed to a great photograph of Jack Grout standing with a row of seven boys, most wearing the standard striped T-shirt of the Ozzie and Harriet years, watching as one of their own awkwardly strikes a golf ball.

"Do you see him?" Scott asked quietly, almost reverently.

I stepped closer. You couldn't miss it—the round face, the Germanic scowl. The kid standing immediately to Grout's right, tilting to his left with an impatient thumb jammed in his hip pocket, looking intently on, was Jackie Nicklaus. The photo was taken early in the Ohio summer of 1950, the summer Grout arrived as the new head man at Scioto and started the club's first junior teaching program. Big Charlie Nicklaus, who owned the local pharmacy, was one of the first to ask about the junior clinic.

"How old was he there?" I asked Kelly.

"Almost eleven."

"Seems to be the age we all began," I found myself mumbling, more to myself than my host.

After lunch in the crowded grillroom, Bill Stines grabbed a golf cart and drove me around the course, explaining the recent renovations that had significantly lengthened the Donald Ross gem, including a full rebuild of all green and bunker complexes. It was easy to see why Scioto makes every top one hundred list of courses in America, typically ranking somewhere in the low fifties, for it is a masterpiece of economical routing and strategic shot-making challenges, all contained within a modest 110 acres surrounded by a stone wall in the middle of a handsome old neighborhood almost in sight of downtown Columbus. On this perfect summer day, with the faintest hint of early autumn in the air just to make things all the more painfully alluring, the course was in immaculate condition, owing to the club championship having been played there the weekend before.

"It's hard to believe that we took down more than fifteen hundred trees," Stines said. "But, frankly, the course and membership were tired. This is a shrine of the game that was really in need of a facelift." Before the restoration, Stines pointed out, Scioto, like many old-line memberships, especially in the wake of the Great Recession, was really suffering. But thanks to the restoration, Scioto had come full circle, with a waiting list that now included a lot of young families. As we sat by the fourth green watching a foursome putt out beneath a canopy of ancient oaks, Stines quietly added, "I have come to believe, rather passionately, that what golf needs to grow again is to rediscover its past the way we have here at Scioto, to remind people that golf is a true family affair. Tradition has value in people's lives. Our members live and breathe it every day here— and so do the guests and visitors. This game is all about the human connections we make, the friendships and relationships we create over time. I'm always amused but never surprised at how close we really are to people like Bobby Jones and Donald Ross, Jack Nicklaus and Arnold Palmer—no more than two or three degrees of separation. We're like one big family. No other game I can think of has this quality quite so powerfully."

To his point, Stines told me about another unsung hero of the game, his grandfather Pug Allen, a super athlete and baseball star who played for the Canton (North Carolina) Bulldogs with Jim Thorpe before becoming a golf pro. While attending the Georgia Institute of Technology in 1919, Pug Allen played halfback on the school football team that beat Cumberland College 222–0 in a famously lopsided game and was befriended by a polite but hotheaded young Tech student named Bobby Jones, the Southern Amateur champion of 1917 who would soon qualify for his first US Open in 1920.

The pair played a number of golf matches at Druid Hills Golf Club in Atlanta, including one in 1923 after which Jones was so upset over missing a short putt in a money match against Allen that he hurled his clubs through a plate-glass window into the club swimming pool. Several years later, an African-American steward at the club came up to Bill's grandfather and told him that he remembered him from that match, because he'd been the one who went into the pool after Mr. Jones's clubs, including his famous putter, Calamity Jane.

Pug Allen later served as head professional at the Fort Wayne Country Club and became a close friend of Walter Hagen, "bailing him out of jail a number of times after his famous nights out," Bill noted wryly. In 1944, Allen purchased a golf course in Deland, Florida, and ran it until his death.

But the small-worldliness of golf didn't end there. As we shared traveling notes while driving around beautiful Scioto, I learned that Bill's parents both attended Wake Forest with Arnold Palmer, and that his grandfather had given early golf lessons to both Pete and Alice Dye and none other than Arnold's old Wake Forest teammate, John Gerring—Dr. Hook himself. The point was driven home further when Stines cordially invited me to stick around another day and play Scioto, prompting me to ask for a rain check because I planned to drop in and pay my respects to my Sandhills neighbor Peggy Kirk Bell's childhood course just up the road in Findlay, per her firm instructions, before I moseyed up to see friends in Toledo and northern Michigan. Bill smiled and explained that he'd known the Bell family for years and that his daughter, Ginny, was in fact attending lacrosse camp that very week in Findlay. One big family, indeed.

Somehow this all made perfect sense—and brought us neatly back to a historic spot on the golf course at the house that two Jacks built, the wee and treacherous sixth green, where Gene Sarazen made an extraordinary recovery shot from inside a concession tent in 1931 that sealed his singles match against the sweltering Brits. Bill reminded me that Sarazen later told *Sports Illustrated* that his shot at Scioto might have actually been better than his albatross at the 1935 Masters, the so-called shot heard round the world.

"Just about every hole here has a great story," Stines said, "though most of them involve a guy named Nicklaus as a kid."

Jackie at Scioto is indeed a wonderful story, as all-American in its own way as Arnie at Latrobe, two boys from very different circumstances—rural working-class hill town versus country-club midwestern city, a scrappy self-taught greenskeeper's kid who was never allowed in the clubhouse versus a brainy son of the new American upper-middle class who learned at the feet of a true Jedi golfmaster yet dreamed of growing up to become a pharmacist just like his daddy. Together, their exploits and rivalry would rewrite the ancient game's modern record books and ignite the sporting imagination of the nation, fueling the biggest golf boom in history. At eleven years old, Arnie Palmer was strictly forbidden to practice near his papa's greens but was allowed to hit balls anywhere else on the course as long as members weren't playing, teaching himself the game. A decade later, "the first little boy to come into the pro shop and register for Scioto's first junior clinic was Jackie Nicklaus," Dick Grout recalls his father saying. "And the day we started, the first little boy on the tee was Jackie Nicklaus." Folded into the yeoman hills of Pennsylvania, young Arnie dreamed of being a gridiron star, whereas young Jackie grew up believing he might play baseball for Ohio State. Together, they rewrote the script of American golf.

Arnie had no formal teachers. Like Hogan and others before him, he learned principally from watching older players and adapting whatever worked for them. From the beginning with his eager young pupil, Jack Grout stressed the fundamentals and believed in keeping things simple. He illustrated the importance of holding one's head as still as possible in his very first lesson with Nicklaus by having one of his assistants stand in front of Jackie and grasp a tuft of the youngster's thick blond hair. "Okay, Jackie boy. Let's see you take a swing." Years later, Nicklaus noted in his autobiography that he learned the hard way to keep a steady head over the ball, lest he lose a handful of hair.

Grout's second cardinal rule was proper footwork, a "rolling" effect of the feet he picked up directly from Alex Morrison and Henry Picard. His six primary basics—good grip, proper setup, steady head, proper footwork, quiet hands, and full extension at the start of the downswing—were a distillation of everything he'd learned from decades on the tournament trail. These refined ideas were destined to make him arguably the greatest teacher ever, which is why after Jackie Nicklaus began winning every city, state, and national amateur title in sight from the midfifties onward, beginning with the Ohio State Open at age sixteen and the first of his two US Amateurs just three years later, a stream of top players began showing up at Grout's office door seeking help.

In time the list would include the likes of Raymond Floyd, David

Graham, Lanny Wadkins, Olin Browne, and many more. What separated young Jack Nicklaus from every other prodigy who came through the door seeking his help, Grout later said, was that nobody ever practiced the basics of the game longer and harder than young Nicklaus, including his friend Ben Hogan.

Perhaps the most distinguishing feature of Grout's tutelage, however, was to give Nicklaus the invaluable skill of self-correction under fire. "I taught Jack the fundamentals of the game," Grout once explained to a reporter. "But there came a time when he had to go figure out his own problems and their cures." Many modern swing gurus teach systems that aggressively reject this notion, but almost every great champion, from Bobby Jones to Tiger Woods, has possessed this ability.

"That was Jack Grout's true genius," Nicklaus writes in his introduction to Dick Grout's delightful recent book about his father. "He knew the golf swing probably as well as any instructor ever has. But I think his greatest gift to his students was his belief in them and his ability to get them to believe in themselves. He wanted you not only to be skilled technically but also to be so confident of your skills that you could identify and fix your own swing flaws even in the heat of battle, even without him there by your side. In other words, Jack Grout worked to be *dispensable*. He wanted his students to be able to function at the highest level without him."

From his own years of closely observing the likes of Hagen, Hogan, and Henry Picard on the early Tour, Grout gave one final gift to his Scioto prodigy: the power of absolute concentration—the very thing Arnold Palmer spotted instantly in his young Ohio rival at Oakmont in 1962 and came to get a closer look at a fortnight later at the Scioto exhibition. "I had never seen anyone who could stay focused the way he did," Arnold relates in *A Golfer's Life*. "And I've never seen anyone with the same ability since. In my view, that's why he became the most accomplished player in the history of the game. You just couldn't crack his concentration."

When Charlie Nicklaus succumbed to pancreatic cancer in 1970, Jack Grout became even more important to the thirty-year-old superstar, now the dominant player of the age. Charlie Nicklaus had been his son's idol, and Grout filled an unfillable void as a surrogate father, not unlike the stabilizing role Marvin Leonard served to a fatherless Ben Hogan well into stardom. By then, Jack Grout was running a popular club in Miami, Florida, and closing in on official retirement, though the relationship between teacher and student continued for another two decades.

My favorite story of the Jacks not only beautifully illustrates the point but places a poignant coda on their extraordinary relationship. In March 1986, Nicklaus was in the middle of the longest major championship drought of his illustrious career. After finishing somewhere in the middle of the field at Doral, he sent his son, Jackie, to fetch his mentor from his home in Tequesta, Florida, just north of Palm Beach. Grout watched his longtime pupil on the range for a few minutes and quickly identified the problem. "Too handsy." The key to Jack's power had always been his efficient use of large muscles, but with age he'd begun to rely upon manipulation of his swing by his hands and wrists, robbing him of the power and accuracy he once enjoyed. A few weeks later, at forty-six years old, a revived Nicklaus went to Augusta. Spurred on by an *Atlanta Journal-Constitution* sports writer's comment that he was "washed-up, *through*," he did the almost unthinkable: shot 30 on the final nine and rallied to beat Tom Kite and Greg Norman by a margin of four strokes to claim his sixth and final Masters victory and eighteenth major championship title.

This was to be the capstone of the most successful professional tournament career in golf history, though I've long thought his record of eighteen major runners-up is maybe even more telling of Nicklaus's golfing genius—an opinion shared by his leading rival, Arnold Palmer, I might add. Nevertheless, an admiring Herb Wind was moved to write that Jack's feat was "nothing less than the most important accomplishment since Bobby Jones's Grand Slam in 1930."

True to form, Jack Grout watched it all unfold on TV from his favorite chair back in Tequesta.

As we finished our tour of the golf course, Bill Stines gave me one final, lovely Jackie Nicklaus story for the road, further proof of golf's remarkable connective tissue, linking us all to our boyhood heroes. One afternoon when Jack was about thirteen, already one of the club's longest hitters, he attempted to drive the dogleg of the fifteenth hole and wound up in the rough near a deep fairway bunker. After making a poor shot, he tossed his club in disgust—only to have his father grab him by the ear and walk him off the golf course. "Charlie told his son that if he ever did anything like that again, he wouldn't play golf," explained Bill. "As far as I know, Jack never threw a club again."

"I know the feeling," I admitted to Bill, telling him about my own painful coming-of-age and Opti's clever ruse at Mid Pines in 1966.

"We *all* have a version of that family story," Bill said with a laugh.

CHAPTER THIRTEEN

HOLY TOLEDO

As a perfect Ohio afternoon flared around us, Fred Altvater turned to me and said, "This may be the best-kept secret in golf. Could be the answer to the game's future, too."

We were standing together on the first tee of the Ottawa Park Golf Course, a public facility near the campus of the University of Toledo. I'd been in town for just two hours, hoping to play the mighty Inverness Golf Club, where Byron Nelson served his final stint as a head professional and a half dozen major national championships had been contested. But Fred, a fellow golf writer and popular Ohio golf radio show host, had pulled a fast one and brought me here instead.

"You need to see this place first," he'd said. "Without Ottawa Park, there would be no Inverness. The man who built it had as much to do with Inverness as Donald Ross did. His name was Sylvanus P. Jermain. Even here in his hometown, I'm afraid he's not really appreciated. But Jermain is a true hero of America golf, a lost founding father—some say the father of public golf in America."

A handsome bronze statue of old Sylvanus presided over the first tee at Ottawa Park, looking very much the nineteenth-century man, a wiry gent wearing a tight Norfolk jacket and a traditional flat wool cap, addressing his ball like an elderly Pinehurst Putter Boy.

The first tee stood invitingly open—a rarity, I would learn—and the first hole was a beauty, a classic par-five framed by mature hardwoods arching over a broad fairway that swept uphill to an elevated green. Blue-winged swallows were zooming across the fairways at great speed, shoulder high, dining on afternoon bugs.

"Shall we get our clubs?" Fred teased.

"Absolutely. You had me at 'lost founding father.' "

As I'd been reminded at Scioto the morning before, American golf had many founding fathers and mothers, notably beginning with crusty Charles Blair Macdonald, who built the first eighteen-hole course in America in 1893, the Chicago Golf Club, and became the driving force behind the creation of the United States Golf Association. Macdonald was an inspiration to Donald Ross and the generation of golf-course architects who quickly followed. For his later work on the National Golf Links of America—a visit to which had long been on my RBL—Macdonald rightly earned the sobriquet Father of American Golf Course Architecture.

But as my buddy Fred Altvater knows, I've always had a special thing for the lesser-known designers (most of whom called themselves "builders") who are all but forgotten today, denied their proper recognition in the evolution of the game on American shores.

Guys like pleasant Scotsman Tom Bendelow.

Just two years after Macdonald opened the Chicago Golf Club, the same year James Walker Tufts went down to Carolina to investigate a site for his utopian health spa in the pines, a group of Manhattan businessmen calling themselves the Riverdell Group petitioned New York Parks commissioner James Roosevelt for permission to construct a private golf club, which they planned to call Mosholu Golf Club, on some wildflower-covered hills in the sprawling and

newly opened Van Cortlandt Park in the Bronx. Roosevelt provision-
ally granted permission on the condition that the public be allowed
to play the course five days a week. The Riverdell Group agreed to
the terms, and members laid out nine rudimentary holes at a cost of
$624. The first eight holes were relatively easy affairs, with no hole
more than two hundred yards in length. The concluding ninth, on
the other hand, was a seven-hundred-yard brute that crossed two
stone walls and a pair of small brooks, the longest golf hole ever
created in the United States.

The public's response was frenzied—overwhelming, in fact.
During the course's first year of operation, as many as seven hundred people showed up to play on weekends. There were no greens
fees or rules of order in place, which led to bloody brawls and even a
fatal stabbing, prompting the *New York Times* to blast the poor con-
ditions of the course and the absence of public manners. The paper
of record even went so far as to question the wisdom of allowing the
club to remain open.

As a result, in 1899, the city imposed new rules of order and a
modest greens fee of twenty-five cents, hiring a Scottish-born former newspaper linotype operator turned self-declared golf-course
architect named Tom Bendelow to revise and expand the course
into a full eighteen holes on 120 acres, renaming America's first
eighteen-hole municipal links the Van Cortlandt Park Golf Course.
In addition, this likeable son of a village pie-shop merchant, who
grew up playing at Aberdeen Golf Club on Scotland's east coast,
supervised the course's maintenance and daily shop operations, sold
golf equipment, organized the first players' associations, gave lessons, and staged America's first public tournaments—a true one-
Scot operation.

Bendelow's crucial role in spurring the development of American golf was almost identical to that of Donald Ross down in

Pinehurst—yet he, like S. P. Jermain of Toledo, as I would learn that day at Ottawa Park, remains a largely forgotten pioneer of the American game.

At the time he revised Van Cortlandt Park, Tom Bendelow was working for sporting-goods manufacturer A. G. Spalding—the same Spalding company that sponsored Harry Vardon on a barnstorming exhibition tour of America in 1900, highlighted by his well-publicized stop in Pinehurst. For his part, Bendelow went on to have an extraordinary career designing more than five hundred golf courses across the Midwest and selected places in the South, many of which he built as part of Spalding's ambitious scheme to grow the game among working- and middle-class Americans. Bendelow's layouts were typically simple affairs routed over natural land, cheap to build and economical to maintain, with small, flat greens that were often simply extensions of the fairway, able to tolerate heavy foot traffic from players who wore workboots and meant to be within reach of every citizen golfer's budget. If Bendelow is remembered at all, it's for the three outstanding championship courses he created that feature significantly in the American story: Chicago's Medinah Country Club and Olympic Fields' South Course, both created at the summit of his design career in the 1920s, and the golf course where Bobby Jones learned the game—and where I rediscovered mine—East Lake Country Club in Atlanta.

By the early summer of 1920, there were an estimated six hundred players a week teeing off at Van Cortlandt Park Golf Course, whose popularity within a decade led to half a dozen more public courses being hastily constructed in the New York City park system under legendary parks administrator Robert Moses. Among other things, Bendelow is also credited with opening America's first school of golf instruction in the Berkley Gymnasium of the Carnegie Building in New York City. He has rightly been called the Johnny Appleseed of American Golf.

Though there's no direct evidence to show the two men ever met, Bendelow's early success at Van Cortlandt Park—widely heralded in the national press as a breakthrough in a new concept called "public recreation"—clearly inspired the highly civic-minded S. P. Jermain to follow suit at Toledo's beautiful Ottawa Park in 1899, initially fashioning a nine-hole layout he threaded through an ancient hardwood forest that took advantage of the park's ample meadows and rolling landscapes. By late 1902, Ottawa Park was so overrun by novice golfers that several regulars began looking around suburban Toledo for suitable land on which to build a private club, logically enlisting the help of Jermain.

In February 1903, news broke in the *Toledo Blade* that six original stockholders planned to build a golf club worthy of hosting state and national championships on eighty acres of farmland near the end of the new trolley line west of town. The next evening, thirty-eight additional investors signed up for membership in the new club. A local man named Bernard Nichols was hired to create a nine-hole layout with "significant input" from the organization's newly elected president, one S. P. Jermain, whose mother suggested the name for the new club—Inverness.

Jermain promptly wrote to the Scottish village council of the same name asking permission to use their town name and distinctive club crest, which featured a camel and an elephant, symbols of harmony and faithfulness, for the new private golf club, which was to be built in the best Scottish tradition—that's to say, true to Jermain's conviction that the new club should be "within the means of any working citizen of Toledo," not merely a gathering place for the privileged few. An eight-handicapper from Ottawa Park named Bill Rockefeller was named the course's first superintendent.

In 1907, at age forty-eight, Jermain also published one of the earliest rule books of American golf, *The American Code of Golf*, which was widely distributed and clearly influenced the first official

USGA rule book, prompting a syndicated sports columnist to declare him the Father of Public Golf in America. Though there is no known direct link between Jermain and Pinehurst's Richard Tufts, the title, language, content, and intent of Tuft's elegant *Code of the Amateur*, published in 1951, clearly drew inspiration—and even elegant snippets of language—from S. P. Jermain's literary contribution to the evolving American game.

A fire in November 1911 destroyed Inverness's original wooden clubhouse. A second clubhouse burned to the ground during the same month in 1918, destroying whatever early records remained. Exactly when Donald Ross made his first appearance in Toledo to suggest improvements to the existing Inverness course remains a bit unclear, though surviving club minutes indicate that he appeared at a board meeting in 1916 and was hired to undertake expansion and improvement of the original nine holes of the course between early 1917 and late 1919. The Donald Ross Society officially lists 1920 as the debut year of Ross's redesign and expansion of Inverness, boasting an enlarged clubhouse completed just in time to host the Ohio Open in 1919. USGA members on hand for this event were suitably impressed by what they saw, granting Inverness the right to host the US Open Championship of 1920, yet another pivotal moment in the history of American golf.

Sporting his flapping linen campaign coat, drooping mustache, and signature pipe, Englishman Edward "Ted" Ray nipped Jack Burke Sr. for the title and the $500 prize, besting an Open field that included the flamboyant Walter Hagen, the aging Harry Vardon, Ohio Open winner Jock Hutchison, "Long Jim" Barnes, who was fresh off a win at the Shawnee Invitational, and a brassy newcomer named Gene Sarazen. Before the championship began, the Toledo papers had established "Sir Walter" as the Open's odds-on favorite, many taking note of his remarkable stunt just one month before at the British Open at Deal that brought about a sea change in the culture of tournament golf.

Resuming after six long years of suspension during the Great War, the 1920 British Open would be best remembered as the championship where Hagen created a stir on Fleet Street by hiring a Daimler limousine and a footman to serve himself and other "professional" competitors lunch just outside the members' clubhouse in quiet protest of a practice common to British clubs that prohibited golf professionals from entering. The resulting public outcry drowned out the grumbles from traditionalists, who deemed the Haig's orchestrations simply a vulgar grab for headlines, and served to end the policy of excluding professionals from the clubhouse, sending a revolutionary wind through all of golf.

That same wind of change blew open the doors for the first time on American turf just one month later at Inverness, where a membership shaped by the egalitarian values of Sylvanus P. Jermain and other like-minded Toledoans enthusiastically voted to allow professionals complete access to their handsome new clubhouse, treating them like members—a first in all of golf.

The sentimental favorite in Toledo was Harry Vardon, still a greyhound at the advanced age of fifty, making a final bid to add a second US Open title to his record six British Open championships. Inverness was the finale of a second and final exhibition tour of the States Vardon had made with his good friend Ted Ray to say thank you to an American public that had lavished him with affection and gratitude. For his two opening rounds at Inverness, the greyhound was paired with an appealing young amateur from Georgia who was making his national debut at the Open, Bobby Jones, then eighteen and studying mechanical engineering at the Georgia Institute of Technology. They were the oldest and youngest players in the field, respectively. Not until a gray and preternaturally solemn Ben Hogan was paired with a roughly barbered amateur from the American heartland named Jack Nicklaus at Cherry Hills in 1960 would the golf world see a pairing as historic as Harry and Bobby.

For his part, trailed by a number of attractive young females who didn't go unnoticed by the event's most flamboyant star, the Haig put forth a gallant effort before fading away in the final round. As if to punctuate the end of an era, though, it was Vardon, the aging greyhound, who won the hearts of the record-breaking Toledo crowds that flooded Inverness that week—producing the first recorded traffic jam in golf tournament history.

Leading by four with seven holes to play, the game's greatest player's right forearm began twitching so violently that he was forced to lurch at several short putts, missing them all by a surprising margin. Over the three previous days, Vardon had produced the peerless golf of a man half his age. But when his fabled putting stroke yielded to nerves, so did his confidence. With the championship his to claim, he lost seven strokes over the final seven holes of play and finished in a tie for second with Burke, Hutchison, and Leo Diegel. A promising young Chicago-area amateur named Charles "Chick" Evans finished a respectable four strokes off the lead, one stroke ahead of newcomer Bobby Jones.

If there was any consolation for Harry Vardon, it was that his good friend and traveling mate Ted Ray slipped past Hutchison and Diegel at the wire to become the oldest man to win a US Open. Afterward, the greyhound quipped philosophically, "I could have kicked my ball around in fewer strokes than that." But he graciously tipped his hat to the nine thousand spectators who mobbed Inverness's lethally bunkered eighteenth green and disappeared into the clubhouse. Soon he sailed home to England, never to return.

Not surprisingly, S. P. Jermain was the man most responsible for bringing the US Open to handsome Inverness. Golf was the principal love of his bachelor's life, especially amateur golf—which explains why when Bobby Jones blew up and stormed into the club-house following a poor opening 78, threatening to withdraw from the championship, the avuncular Jermain calmed down the sulking youth and convinced him to stay the course. Jones posed for a photograph with the club's dapper president, and later wrote a letter thanking Jermain for reminding him of the importance of self-control and sportsmanship in golf.

The pros were also grateful for the warm welcome they received at Inverness. At Walter Hagen's suggestion, they even took up a collection to pay for a beautiful, handmade chiming cathedral clock that was presented to the members of the club. The clock still stands in the entry foyer of the Inverness Golf Club today.

A far lesser-known nugget of American golf lore relates to the "Inverness Oath" many of the American players took immediately following the awards ceremony, vowing to win back their national honor from the British invaders. Naturally, it was S. P. Jermain who envisioned a positive way to channel such intense national pride into something more enduring than a onetime championship. He proposed a "friendly team competition" between the leading players of Great Britain and America, the seeds of which grew into the biennial Ryder Cup matches just five years later.

The next year, in a project that was nearer to his heart, Sylvanus P. Jermain undertook the expansion and rebuilding of Ottawa Park's public golf course, which reopened to outstanding reviews in 1922 and served as host site for the nation's first public-links national championship. He also became the driving force behind a second eighteen-hole golf course at Toledo's popular Bayview Park, founded two additional clubs in the city's growing suburbs, and supervised the building of a children's golf course at Jermain Park, which was named in his honor.

Golf's most humble Founding Father was still active in Inverness affairs when the US Open returned in 1931, the first Open to be broadcast on national radio. It was won in a historic marathon by Billy Burke, a twenty-eight-year-old pro fresh from the sweltering Ryder Cup at Scioto who beat long-hitting George Von Elm, an amateur and self-described "businessman golfer" who had yet to be officially declared a professional. The two played a pair of exhausting thirty-six-hole playoffs, 144 total holes in the oppressive July heat—the equivalent of two tournaments—before Burke managed to eke out a one-stroke victory of 589 strokes to 590 in the longest national championship in US history. A newly retired Bobby Jones tagged along in the galleries with his movie camera. "I'm sorry it had to end this way," Burke reportedly apologized to the crowd at his award ceremony.

Despite the looming threat of the Great Depression, the game of golf that Jermain evangelized and made accessible to all classes in Toledo and America at large would be this visionary pioneer's greatest legacy. Sylvanus P. Jermain was not a wealthy man, and in fact worked most of his life as a moderately compensated treasurer for a Toledo woolen-manufacturing firm. True to his modest lifestyle and core principles, he quietly passed away at the city's Mercy Hospital on April 21, 1935, widely reported to be penniless at the time of his death.

One of the largest wreaths at his funeral days later bore a condolence card signed "In deepest gratitude, Robert Tyre Jones, Jr."

═══ • ═══

Accompanied by iridescent green dragonflies and the aforementioned swallows, bumping gently over Ottawa Park's undulating terrain in a puttering gas cart, I felt completely under the spell of Sylvanus P. Jermain's tale and Ottawa Park's brilliantly economical design. As a result, I wasn't the least bit surprised to learn from Fred that the centennial edition of the National Publinx Championship was scheduled to return to Ottawa Park in 2020. Hometown architect Arthur Hills was reportedly scheduled to restore the golf course before the Championship comes to town.

Truthfully, if my big day in Holy Toledo had ended right there, I would have been amply pleased with my discoveries. But once upon a time, as we sat by his crackling fire in Roanoke, Texas, I'd promised Byron Nelson that I would someday drop in on the club where he served his last stint as a club professional, if only to finally see that beautiful cathedral clock that symbolized golf's coming-of-age in America.

It turned out to be as magnificent as advertised, ticking serenely away in Inverness's quiet entrance foyer. Time and history were still good companions there.

The Ohio State Junior Amateur, it emerged, had just completed play the day before our arrival, and the course was officially closed for the balance of the year in order to undergo a restoration à la Pinehurst No. 2 by the same Arthur Hills, all in hopes of eventually luring a fifth US Open championship back to Toledo.

Missing a chance to play the course was disappointing, but new head professional Derek Warren—fresh from an assistant's post at Augusta National—received our unannounced visit graciously, with the timely news that Sylvanus P. Jermain was going to be posthumously inducted into the Ohio State Golf Hall of Fame in early September, just a few weeks hence. He also invited us to explore the property and even to walk the golf course, if that was our pleasure. I asked for a rain check to play the revised Inverness, and he warmly extended the courtesy.

During his five happy years at Inverness, Byron Nelson made some of the closest friends of his life in Toledo, gave lessons to a hot-headed local kid named Frank Stranahan (Champion Spark Plugs heir and future National Amateur champion), started a successful golf umbrella company, and elevated his game to the peak of its performance, capped off by the most sensational year anyone has ever had in professional golf in 1945, during which he won eighteen Tour events, including an unprecedented eleven in a row, and finishing second sixteen times. The press took to calling him "Mr. Golf."

"I don't believe any of that could have happened the way it did if Louise and I hadn't had those final nice years in Toledo," Nelson told me by the fire on that cold winter's day in Texas. "She and I made a lot of friends for life there, and my game was never better. It was terribly difficult to leave Toledo behind, quite honestly—especially for Louise—but I've happily gone back any time they've invited me, and I always will. That city is like sacred ground to me. It made our dreams come true and brought us home to Texas."

The third US Open hosted by Inverness happened in 1957 and was won by Dick Mayer in a playoff over Cary Middlecoff (in a bid for back-to-back Open titles), the first US Open in which a promising if scarcely noticed Ohio youngster named Jackie Nicklaus competed, and in which a forty-five-year-old legend named Hogan claimed the biggest headlines by suddenly withdrawing due to severe chest pains that turned out to be a nasty case of pleurisy rather than the initially feared heart issue.

The club's fourth US Open, in 1979, featured four new holes created by Tom Fazio and his uncle George and was captured by Hale Irwin in uncharacteristically undramatic fashion. The biggest drama, in fact, revolved around Tour journeyman Lon Hinkle, who spotted a gap in the trees off the par-five eighth tee and took a shortcut to the hole through an adjacent fairway, making birdie and prompting several other players to follow suit. A hastily assembled panel of USGA and club officials decided to plant a twenty-five-foot Blue Hills spruce in the gap overnight rather than move the tee. To this day, the tree is called the Hinkle Tree.

The 1986 PGA Championship, extended an extra day owing to violent storms that ravaged Toledo, provided mighty Inverness— and tournament golf—one of its most enduring images, that of Bob

Tway holing his bunker shot on the seventy-second hole to win, setting off a wild celebration among the estimated fifteen thousand fans cinched around the green. As Tway hopped up and down and broke into tears, stoic Greg Norman, fresh off his first British Open victory and the first player in history to lead after three rounds in all four majors, crouched to size up his own chip for a birdie that would force a playoff. He narrowly missed, and the likeable Tway hoisted the Wanamaker Trophy.

Seven years later, a record fifty-seven players broke par in the first round of the 1993 PGA Championship, causing consternation among some members who valued Inverness's reputation of never having yielded a subpar aggregate score in four Opens. To add insult to injury, in the second round, Vijay Singh shot 63 to tie Byron Nelson's course record and set a new tournament course mark. But the real magic—and disappointment—once again belonged to golf's greatest major bridesmaid, Greg Norman, who once more came to Toledo from a victory at the British Open, having edged out Nick Faldo at Royal St Georges to claim his second Claret Jug. The final round in Toledo saw a host of major championship winners within range of the lead, including Lanny Wadkins, Hale Irwin, and the forty-four-year-old Tom Watson, in quest of his career Grand Slam. On the seventy-second hole, however, Norman lipped out an eighteen-footer for birdie that left him in a tie with Paul Azinger, who'd played remarkably steady golf despite a Friday-night phone call from a famed orthopedic surgeon, Dr. Frank Jobe, asking the Zinger to come in for tests after spotting some bone abnormalities in a recent X-ray of his shoulder.

On the second hole of their sudden-death playoff, in the humid and lengthening shadows of a late August afternoon, a visibly spent Norman missed a four-footer to tie that allowed Azinger to win his first and only major championship. Days later, Zinger was diagnosed with lymphoma and underwent treatment. One of the game's most promising young stars, he never quite recovered his major championship form, going nearly seven years and 120 tournaments before he won again, but earning the respect of his peers and, in time, ably following his hero Byron Nelson into the broadcast booth.

Not long before he started his comeback, I had dinner with Paul and his father in Tampa. "Whatever happens in the rest of my career," he told me quietly at one point, "given what it means in the world of golf, I'll always look at Inverness and the people of Toledo as the highlight of my career."

═══ • ═══

The next morning before I left town, Fred had one more thing to show me.

"You've seen Toledo's glorious past," he said. "Now I want you to see what could be American golf's promising future—or at least this city's."

The Golf Performance Institute of Toledo, or the Golf Pit for short, turned out to be John Gerring's Eagle Zone on steroids, a comprehensive learning facility situated behind an upscale shopping center at the confluence of the Ohio Turnpike and State Highway 93. For an all-day pass of $25 or an April-to-October subscription of $500, players have unlimited access to a twenty-acre driving range with fifty-two hitting stations, twenty-three heated all-weather stalls, a beautifully groomed short-game practice area with bunkers, a putting green, and a six-hole executive practice course. Services include custom club fitting and repair and all levels of group and individual instruction, including state-of-the-art computer swing analysis, fitness training with certified Titleist Performance Institute instructors, guidance on nutrition, and even a resident sports psychologist. The Pit's "pro shop" was like a mini Golf Galaxy, staffed with cheerful folks in red polo shirts that made you feel like you ought to buy something just to prove you'd been there. I purchased a new knitted Titleist head cover for my driver.

Fred, I also discovered, was even more of a golf Renaissance man than I knew—he was a certified instructor who taught anywhere from six to ten private students at this Cadillac of learning centers each year. He walked me through the impressive facility, explaining that it was the brainchild of former Inverness head professional and master PGA professional David Graf, recognized by *Golf Digest* as the fourth-ranked teacher in Ohio, who believed, as Fred did, that these kinds of golf learning centers are the wave of the future—exactly what the game needs to attract more time-strapped working folks and families.

"We have a very strong First Tee and junior program in Toledo," he told me. "They're supported by seven private clubs and a number of fine semiprivate and public courses. This place has become a feeder for many of those clubs, running year-round clinics, summer golf camps for kids, individual lessons for men and women—you name it, it's here. The idea is to provide a Tour-quality experience for people at a very reasonable cost." He nodded toward the pretty six-hole golf course, where several groups of kids were out playing in the deepening summer dusk. The course was framed by a pair of major highways already congested with evening commuter traffic.

"This place has become like a crossroads of golf for northern Ohio. I know guys who drop in here on their way home just to hit a bucket of balls or take a spin around the course. You'll see everybody out here—kids, seniors, men and women, young and old, all races and religions, complete beginners and some of the city's top amateurs. It's a working golf democracy—really grassroots stuff."

It was easy to see why this Disneyland approach to golf might be one way to stimulate the roots of the game at a time when attention spans and lifestyles were so limited. I asked Fred what he thought the Father of Public Golf in America would make of this wondrous Golf Pit.

Fred smiled. "Honestly? I think he'd absolutely love it. He'd probably be out here every afternoon hitting a small bucket of balls and greeting folks—especially the kids."

CHAPTER FOURTEEN

SAINT BILLY

"I hear you've been on quite an adventure. Tell me about that."

Bill Campbell was sitting in his favorite reading chair by the window of his handsome, log-walled den. Through the window behind him, a golden August afternoon was fading into the rolling West Virginia hills, bathing the beautiful hilltop meadow above the Greenbrier River northeast of Lewisburg, where Bill and Joan Campbell lived in a stately brick house called Three Valleys, in a stream of light. Joan's perennial beds were at their summer peak.

He motioned to a chair near to him. I sat down and pulled it close.

"It was just a road trip up to northern Michigan to play a match against my Pinehurst golf pal Tom Stewart. He spends his summers up there. I've been trying to beat him for more than fifteen years."

"Do I know him?"

"He runs the village golf shop."

"Oh, right. Lovely fellow."

"Except when he beats you."

I told him about a marathon thirty-six-hole match in which Tom took me to play a beautiful semiprivate club called Belve-

dere near the resort town of Charlevoix that leapt instantly into
my ever-changing Top Twenty, a Willie Watson gem on the shores
of Lake Michigan that was about to host its fortieth state amateur
championship—where Tom's papa, a mailman from Petoskey, caddied in the Great Lakes Open of 1939. As courses I fall in love with
often do, Belvedere brought out the best game in me. Unfortunately
it did Tom as well, which is why Tom finished three holes up in our
match.

We raced to Walloon Lake, where Tom had worked his first job
in golf as the club's night waterman. It was a beautiful parkland
course, where a young Tom Watson played golf when his family visited from Kansas every summer. The magic continued, and I made
up two holes to draw within one by the thirty-fifth hole—at which
point Tom made birdie and I wound up losing 2 and 1.

He consoled me by suggesting we catch the last ferry to Mack-
inac Island to try to beat the sunset and play the Wawashkamo
Golf Club, Michigan's oldest active nine-hole golf course, laid out
by Open winner Alex Smith in 1898. This required a mad dash to
Mackinaw City, where we made the day's last departing ferry with
minutes to spare.

Unfortunately the sun was gone by the time we reached Wawashkamo's tidy gingerbread clubhouse, and pro Chuck Olsen was just
locking the front door. He was delighted to see Tom, an old friend
from Stewart's days running the northern Michigan section of the
PGA, and as the pair sat on the porch catching up, I hiked over a
good bit of the course in the blue dusk and felt the gravitational pull
of a sweet handmade layout, savoring the familiar smells of cool
northern summer. To tell the truth, it all made me suddenly miss my
old life in Maine, and even my hometown of Greensboro, which had
the same kinds of ancient hardwoods and earthy scents of leaves
already turning in late August, not to mention the fragrant fescue

and silky bent grass underfoot. For a few crazy moments in the half-light of a rising Michigan moon, I felt almost like a kid again, remembering what it was like to play barefoot into the darkness at long-gone Green Valley Golf Club, as I sometimes did when playing alone, a nostalgia that prompted me to remove my sweaty golf shoes and walk back to meet Tom and Chuck in my bare feet.

"We thought you might have gotten lost," Tom said when I appeared out of the dusk.

"I did," I said. "It was great."

An unforgettable day of golf, boat rides, and laughs ended back on the mainland with us dining on the porch of the famous Dam Site Inn, the last customers served before the kitchen staff went home.

I thanked Bill for allowing me to drop in so suddenly. An hour before, approaching the highway exit that went over the mountain from Charleston to Lewisburg, I'd phoned just to check up on Bill's condition. His wife, Joan, mentioned that Bill's adult children, Vicky and Colin, had arrived to be with their father, and I was pleased to hear that he was resting comfortably, and only partly surprised when she insisted that I come by for a brief visit, if possible. "It would do Billy good to see you," she said.

"I'd be hurt if I learned you were in the area and didn't come to see me," he said now, demanding to hear where else I'd been on my golfing busman's holiday. "I'll live vicariously through your road trip."

Bill's visible frailty made me hesitate. But I knew he was genuinely interested, so I gave him an abbreviated version of the trip's highlights, mentioning a stop to play Crystal Downs (long on my RBL) with its popular head pro Fred Muller, and a nine-hole public course called Lincoln Hills in rural Sandusky, Ohio, run by former mini-tour player Dave Bastel and his charming wife, Debbie. There, a trio of Lincoln Hills regulars named Mark, Al, and Jim invited me to join them for a chilly Sunday morning round in which, teamed with Al, who was tuning up for the local Elks Club championship, I won seventy-five cents, just enough for a hot dog for the long road home. It was a five-star, Glorious Goat Farm experience, I added.

"That sounds wonderful," Bill said, visibly pleased. "That's what golf is supposed to be. The soul of the game."

Bill Campbell, one might argue, was also the soul of the game—or at least a true keeper of golf's best traditions. Our mutual friend Sandy Tatum, who had preceded Bill as president of the USGA, once told me that he believed Bill to be "the conscience of golf, almost a saint" owing to his deep love of the amateur game and determination to keep golf true to its everyman roots and accessible to all regardless of creed, color, or place of origin, unspoiled by the outside influences of corporate power and money. Perhaps only Bobby Jones had enjoyed a more accomplished and uncompromised playing life in the game.

Though this rangy (6'4") and humble insurance man from Huntington, West Virginia, was far too modest to ever talk in depth about his own competitive accomplishments, Campbell's amateur playing career was the stuff of American legend. Between 1938 and 1981, he'd played in thirty-seven US Amateur Championships, taking his lone title in 1964, and qualified for fifteen US Opens and eighteen Masters Tournaments. He'd won dozens of local, state, and national amateur titles, including fifteen West Virginia Amateurs and four North and South Amateur titles. He also anchored eight Walker Cup teams, serving as playing captain in 1955, and amassed a nearly flawless 7–0–1 record in singles competition.

His impact on the broader game was even more impressive. As the only man in history to serve as the head of golf's two rules-making bodies—president of the USGA and captain of the Royal and Ancient Golf Club of St Andrews—Bill Campbell championed diversity and helped bring the two organizations together on the rules of the game and other matters at a time when the golf industry was booming and technology was rapidly altering every aspect of golf.

I first met Bill by phone in 1983 when, embarking on my story about the quest of Barnes and Yates to save East Lake Golf Club from the bulldozer, I tracked him down to his Huntington insurance office to ask him what he thought of the grassroots effort being put forth by Jones's friends. Bill was president of the USGA that year and, I knew, also a close friend of the late Bobby Jones.

"I think that's a very good thing and it must be saved," he stated with lawyerlike conviction, launching into a sweet tirade about the importance of preserving the game's past in order to inspire its future. "From a modern player's perspective, I suppose the golf course is something of an anachronism—too short and easy by today's standards. But what it symbolizes is incalculable, and far more important than how it stands up to modern players. It's an important place to every American golfer, because it's where Bobby Jones fell in love with the game. We're all connected to him—and that course."

He also politely asked me where I came from.

I explained that I was calling from the *Atlanta Journal-Constitution Sunday Magazine*. But mentioned that I hailed from Greensboro, North Carolina.

"How about that?" he said cheerfully. "I'll bet you know my good friend Sam Snead. He won the Greater Greensboro Open eight times. But I'm sure you know that."

I did know this. I had actually been on hand to see Sam win the last of his record-setting eighty-two Tour victories there in 1965, the year I turned twelve. My aunt Polly, who lived off the sixteenth hole at Sedgefield, introduced me to Snead, and he signed my copy of *Education of a Golfer*, the first golf book I ever owned.

"Good for you," said Bill. "Sam and I are old friends. I'm sure you've been down to Pinehurst."

Way back then, Bill Campbell was suddenly interviewing me—something, I would learn in time, he commonly did when meeting people in golf: politely turning the tables, aiming to peek into *their* souls.

I told him about my father driving me to the Sandhills to introduce me to the "higher game" when I was thirteen, careful to skip the part about my banishment from Green Valley. He seemed pleased by this mutual connection and said that if I ever got anywhere near White Sulphur Springs, I should call him up and he would take me to the Greenbrier to meet Sam.

Two years later, I took Bill Campbell up on his offer. I showed up to play golf with Sam Snead for a story about his return to the Greenbrier as the pro emeritus and then went to dinner with Snead, Bill, and Bill's wife, Joan. Over the next decade, as my golf writing life took root and grew, I returned to visit Sam and Bill and their friend Paul Moran, who ran the West Virginia Golf Association, probably half a dozen times, at least twice staying at the rambling old house the Campbells then owned on a mountainside five miles north of the Greenbrier. When they moved to the beautiful brick federal house called Three Valleys sometime in the late 1990s, Wendy joined me there for dinner the night Bill and Joan hosted Sandy Tatum and his wife. The conversation went late into the spring night. In 2009, I was honored when Saint Billy invited me to attend the inaugural gala for the new West Virginia Golf Hall of Fame, at which he and his best buddy Sam Snead were the first honorees.

Over the years since, we'd spoken many times by phone whenever I needed a thoughtful quote on a current issue or was working on a historical piece for one of my magazines. Saint Billy, as I'd fondly come to think of him, read early manuscripts of my golf books and offered invaluable insights and suggestions.

Over the course of many years I also paid him a number of visits at Three Valleys just to sit at his elbow in his cluttered barn office and chat—and listen. Bill was always gracious with his time and was refreshingly candid about the rapidly escalating costs of the game and the way new technology was altering the golf ball (in particular) and could compromise the rules of fair play and hurt the game's broader popularity down the road. Like Cliff Roberts and Bobby Jones before him, at a time when golf was booming, Bill Campbell worried about the rampant commercialization of the game, making tournaments more about revenue than promoting the intrinsic values of golf. In this respect, Bill Campbell really was the game's greatest guardian, a Cicero in golf spikes, a steady voice of reason as the good times rolled.

Back home in my files I kept a dozen or so handwritten letters from Saint Billy, who typically followed up our in-person conversations with points he wished to clarify, always written in a hand so blessedly illegible that it was always fun to try to decipher his missives.

In terms of our relationship, the only regret I had was that I'd been unable to prod Bill Campbell along with his own memoirs. Few this side of Bobby Jones or Harvie Ward had enjoyed a more diverse and far-reaching life in amateur golf, or played a more influential role in shaping and preserving golf's highest standards as the modern game evolved, rubbing elbows with just about every great player from Francis Ouimet to Tiger Woods. He'd also been involved with some of the most important decisions the USGA and R&A ever rendered, and for a while I'd made a genuine pest of myself by gently urging him to provide the golf world a full account of his amazing life and times and essential beliefs, as well as his hopes and concerns about its future. True to form, he sent me several promising pages, but the book never quite materialized. For me, it was like saying good-bye to Harvie Ward all over again.

"Will you see Paul while you're here?" Bill asked. His voice had settled to a husky whisper. I could see him losing energy.

I explained that we planned to play Greenbrier's Old White in the morning.

"I wish I could play with you boys."

"Come join us," I said. "We can play for nickels or dimes. I understand you're winning lots of those lately."

This made him smile.

Campbell was famous for his Scottish frugality and his nickel golf matches. My favorite story about him came from Harvie Ward, who once told me that Bill was the only guy who ever used the ball-washer on the first tee at Augusta. The story, of course, wasn't remotely true—to begin with, there are no ball-washers at Augusta— though Billy did carry a plastic sandwich bag full of gently used golf balls for important tournaments. Campbell was so scrupulous about maintaining his amateur status that he once sent Jack Nicklaus a check for the free box of balls he found in his locker at the very Memorial Tournament where he was being honored.

Lately, as Bill's strength ebbed, Paul Moran often took him over to the Greenbrier for the same kinds of putting matches Bill once played with his mentor Sam Snead near the end of Sam's life—only Bill and Paul putted extravagantly for dimes. In one of their recent matches, Paul had been five up when Bill began knocking down putts, and took the final dime on the last hole. According to Paul, he'd talked about his thrilling comeback win for days.

As far as I knew, a dime was the only money Bill Campbell ever made from golf. That alone made him almost unique in the wide world of the sport.

"So how is life in Pinehurst working out for you?"

"Just fine. Wendy's happy. The magazines are doing well."

"How about your golf?"

I shrugged and smiled. "Could be better. That's partly why I'm on this road trip—to knock off some rust and get back to my golf roots, to see a few folks and find my inner Golf Lad."

The reference to Pinehurst's official mascot prompted him to inquire what I thought of the double Opens, and whether No. 2 would hold up under the pressure of two Opens held back-to-back in the dead of summer. This was vintage Saint Billy. On the threshold of his own death, he was still interviewing me.

"Funny, I was planning to ask you the same thing."

He smiled again, and I was suddenly reminded of sitting with Opti the Mystic days before he slipped the bonds of this earth. At times he was so clear and graceful that you'd never have guessed he was passing away. That was a perfect phrase for it.

"But I asked you first," he said.

I told him I thought the double Opens were a novel idea, but I couldn't help wishing the USGA had chosen to grant Peggy Kirk Bell—fast approaching ninety herself—a fourth women's Open at Pine Needles. Mine was simply a lover's quarrel, however. I understood the intent of introducing a British Open–style golf course to the US Open, and that Pinehurst was perhaps the only place that could handle such a grand experiment. "Brown is the new green" was the marketing slug; Coore and Crenshaw had done a masterful job, and the course would probably be just fine—and tougher than ever. But I wasn't sure it would lure the reported eight million folks who'd dropped the game back to the course.

Bill took a deep breath, suddenly looking even more pale. Before I could thank him and move along, he made a final important point.

"The popularity of the game has always ebbed and flowed. Golf is a personal game that curiously tends to reflect the fluctuations of the society around it. Right now golf is in a fallow time. Fallow times are useful. They let you regenerate and take stock. My feeling is that there were a number of people around the game who viewed golf primarily as a financial opportunity, not a game for enriching their lives with friends and experiences. But the old game is still with us, and it always will be." He looked me in the eye. "Sounds like your road trip reminded you of this fact."

I agreed, leaving it at that.

"Where will you ramble next?"

I explained that I was taking Dame Wendy to Scotland in a month's time for her first visit, planning to finally catch the R&A's autumn medal competition and hopefully break 80 on the Old Course for the first time. After that I planned to "kiss the captain's balls" at the annual autumn induction dinner so that I'd no longer be the club's most delinquent American member. This made Saint Billy chuckle. He'd been one of those who supported my admission to golf's second-oldest club.

Over our last ten minutes together, we talked about a few things close to his heart—his last trip to Scotland (Joan and Bill always rented a house in Elie and took their family over); the night Wendy and I came to dinner at Three Valleys with Sandy Tatum and his wife; the time Sam Snead made him do early-morning push-ups and drove him home from his first West Virginia Open; how he loved driving visitors around the Greenbrier Valley in his father's restored 1953 Chrysler New Yorker; and how he once took Sir Michael Bonallack and a deputation of R&A honchos to play golf at a glorious local goat farm just to drive home the point that even in "the colonies" golf was a "yeoman's game at heart."

Bill's son, Colin, had silently appeared at the far end of the den, arms crossed but smiling, my cue to wind things up. He was his father's son, as gracious as he was dignified, too polite to interrupt and suggest that it was time to go.

I stood and shook Bill's hand, thanking him for letting me drop by. He held my hand with a firm Vardon grip, reminding me that he'd strengthened his rigid Hogan clubs and drivers with lead tape in order to make them even heavier, just like his mentor Sam Snead, whom he outdrove by three yards during the Long Drive competition at the 1951 Masters. "How the hell did you do that?" Sam demanded to know. "Easy," Bill replied. "I used your driver."

"Forgive me," he said, releasing my hand with a wry little smile, "if I don't say I'll see you soon."

═══ • ═══

Bill Campbell passed away twelve days later.

His memorial service was held at Lewisburg's stately Old Stone Presbyterian Church. Paul Moran and I sat together in a middle pew. The church was full, and I saw several old friends from the golf world, including Clark MacKenzie and USGA executive director Mike Davis. Bill was a past honoree of the splendid MacKenzie Cup, a two-day family event that had honored the likes of Sir Michael Bonallack, Reg Murphy, and Carol Semple Thompson for their valuable contributions to the game. Clark MacKenzie's papa was Roland MacKenzie, who played on the Walker Cup team with Bobby Jones. Clark himself was a former Maryland state amateur champion, whose maternal grandfather, William Clark Fownes, helped his friend George Herbert Walker create the Walker Cup in 1922.

"Keep this under your hat until we notify him," the always upbeat Clark said, gently taking my elbow as we climbed the steps of the church, "but this year we're honoring a good friend of yours—Rees Jones. Billy, I think, would be very pleased. You'd better be there again," he warned playfully. I assured him that I would be and thanked him for putting on the annual MacKenzie Cup, the sort of gracious event that distinguishes the MacKenzie family and their generational love of the game.

For me, the best part of Saint Billy's memorial was hearing the warm personal tributes from Bill's son, Colin, and daughter, Vicky, plus his three stepdaughters from his second marriage to Joan. They created the picture of a bighearted Renaissance man who took on a large family and made it thrive by dint of his wit, love, and old-world sense of humility. Colin's remembrance of how, when he was a boy, his father would come home from work and suggest that they grab their golf bags and play until dark was particularly moving. He told us about trying to hit shots into the darkness and his father pointing out that all you needed was the faith to believe you were making a good shot, and how they talked about their days as they walked along, a love affair not unlike the one I'd known with my father.

It was the perfect image to take away from the Old Stone Church. During the reception at Three Valleys that followed, I was able to chat with Colin and pay my respects to Joan, who patted my hand and thanked me for coming. She added, "There was something Billy wanted me to give you. But for the life of me, I can't remember what." She smiled and added, "I suppose it will come to me in time."

CHAPTER FIFTEEN

THE MAN WHO WOULD
BE KING

A funny thing happened on the road to St Andrews.
Donald Trump invited me to lunch.

Actually, that's not *exactly* what happened. Just days before my wife and I set off to see Arnold Palmer in Latrobe and then head to Scotland for her first trip to Golf's Holy Land, Donald Trump's public relations people tracked me down to say, bewilderingly out of the blue, that Mr. Trump wished to invite me to meet for lunch and golf at his new Trump National Charlotte Golf Club.

Truthfully, I'd never heard of Trump National Charlotte. But I thanked him for the invitation and pointed out that the day after Trump's event I was taking my wife to Latrobe for supper with Arnold Palmer, then on to Scotland to play in my first autumn medal competition at the annual R&A meeting. Due to the cost of sending four kids spaced two years apart through expensive private colleges, I hadn't been back to Scotland in ten years. Wendy had never been, so it was a chance to check off a pair of important RBL items.

Trump's PR man was on a mission, however. He phoned back

two days later to let me know that Jaime Diaz of *Golf World* magazine and Ron Green Jr. of the *Charlotte Observer* would also be on hand for the grand opening of Trump National Charlotte, as would Greg Norman, a friend from my *Golf* magazine days, and that Mr. Trump would personally appreciate it if I showed up to play golf and eat lunch. Because I had always enjoyed cordial relations with the Great White Shark and hadn't seen him in years, I suppose I waffled a bit.

"Mr. Trump likes your books," said his PR man enthusiastically. "You and your friends are going to love Trump National Charlotte. Mr. Trump is doing amazing things in the world of golf right now."

"I doubt Mr. Trump has read my books," I said. "He wouldn't know me from Greg Norman's housecat."

That evening as we were packing, Wendy pointed out how I'd recently made sport of Donald Trump's prematurely orange hair in my Sunday *Pilot* essay. "You should at least go and see what his club's like—if not his hair," she reasoned. "Maybe you can learn how he's saving the golf world."

So I went.

I arrived late to find Trump and *Golf World* editor Jaime Diaz entertaining fifty or so members of his new golf club in the practice tee area. The first surprise was to learn that Trump National Charlotte—which was thirty miles *outside* Charlotte—turned out to be the old Links at Lake Norman Club that Trump had purchased at a fire-sale price, then refurbished and made his own.

Greg Norman was standing off to the side with Ron Green Jr., one of the best golf writers anywhere, looking not entirely happy as the new owner boasted that he had transformed the clubhouse and Greg Norman's golf course into "one of the finest golf clubs in the state." Trump went on to assure his audience that the formerly troubled country club would eventually hold some "very, very important golf tournaments here, I kid you not—maybe even the Wells Fargo

Championship," which was currently conducted at Quail Hollow Country Club, one of the Queen City's premier private clubs.

Donald Trump, from everything I'd read and heard from friends in the golf establishment, clearly wanted to be the *new* King of Golf, which, I confess, made me perversely curious to see what he was really like up close and personal, as they say on TV, beneath all his yellow hair and windy self-promotion. I was determined to keep an open mind.

The playing arrangements called for Jaime Diaz and Ron Green and Greg Norman to play with Donald Trump for the first nine, with yours truly following with Trump's son Eric, director of his father's golf services; a big friendly fellow I took to be Trump's security man; and a local congressman named Robert Pittenger. At the halfway point, I was supposed to join Trump and Norman for the back nine before everyone sat down to lunch.

The gods seemed to have something else in mind, however. Greg Norman departed only a few holes in, and I never had the chance to speak to him. Then, as we stood on the ninth tee waiting to hit beneath rapidly darkening skies, a bolt of lightning announced the arrival of a biblical thunderstorm, which led to a race of golf carts back to the clubhouse. I was loading my clubs into the trunk, relieved to be heading home early to pack for Latrobe and Scotland, and resigned to perhaps meet the man who would be the new King of Golf another day, when a waiter jogged out with an umbrella. "Mr. Trump," he said, "really wants you to come inside and have a cheeseburger before you go." He added, "They're really *great* cheeseburgers."

A sucker for cheeseburgers, I went in.

I found my respected colleagues, a couple of Trump surrogates, and our host sitting around a large round table eating cheeseburgers and fries while Trump talked passionately about his recent extensive refurbishment of the venerable Doral Hotel in Miami, transforming it into "something truly incredible. I'm not kidding. The finest golf club in Florida, probably all of America, really fantastic, you won't believe it. The Tour players are already telling me it's their favorite course on the PGA Tour." To make his point, he whipped out his cell phone and dialed the Doral project manager and put him on speakerphone in order to confirm to us how unbelievable the transformation of Doral Hotel and Country Club and the famed Blue Monster golf course was. "Truly unbelievable," said his man in Florida. "Really incredible."

Dripping wet, I took a seat next to my friend Ron Green Jr. (whose daddy is also one of the finest sports reporters there is), and silently ate my cheeseburger as I listened. A funny moment came when Trump suddenly asked Jaime Diaz why *Golf World* had so little advertising these days, and Jaime thoughtfully replied that advertising was down across the board due to the Great Recession, and cleverly suggested that perhaps Donald Trump should buy the magazine and fill it up with advertising.

Trump laughed. "I might just do that. Someone's got to save golf," he declared. "Listen, seriously, check me out, I'm like the *only* guy doing anything to help golf right now. Show me anyone else who's investing as heavily in golf as I am. You can't do it!" Speaking in exclamation points, he went on to say that he believed golf should actually be an "aspirational game in America, a tool for people who aspire to be rich and successful" and that it should reward them with elite social status. This is why he was buying up distressed golf properties like the Links at Lake Norman Club, he explained, spending "millions and millions" to refurbish them while using the nation's bankruptcy laws to streamline their bottom lines and transform them into Trump holdings.

His passion for the game was undeniable. I just wondered if it was possible for him to make the game over in his own gilded image—at least here in the States. A couple of Scottish friends in the R&A had been keeping me up to date on Trump's swanky new private club in Aberdeen, Scotland, and the public firestorm his building it on cherished sand dunes had created among local burghers. All kinds of accusations and legal challenges had resulted from the untidy affair, and several key Scottish officials, who'd first welcomed the project, were now distancing themselves from it as a rising anti-Trump mood was reportedly sweeping Scotland. It would be interesting to see what came of Donald Trump's golf course buying binge, I decided as I politely finished my burger and got to my feet, thanking our host for the invitation to drop by.

Trump looked surprised. "Where are you going? Stay and eat. We've got some great desserts."

I thanked him again and explained that my wife and I were planning to get an early start for a drive to see a friend in Latrobe in the morning. It was three hours back to the Sandhills.

"Who do you know in Latrobe?" the Donald demanded to know.

When I told him, he grinned. "No kidding. You know, Arnold and I are like *this*." He showed me crossed fingers and hopped up with surprising vigor for a fellow on the near side of seventy. He surprised me by taking hold of my arm in an affectionate manner, as if we were old chums and he wished to convey an interesting confidence of some sort. He was a much bigger man than he looked on TV—and for the record, his hair looked genuine.

"You're the guy who writes the golf books. I haven't read your books," he confessed, "but I write books, too. Have you read *The Art of the Deal*?"

I admitted that I hadn't but said it was on my bedside table. He didn't seem to get the joke, but simply nodded.

"I'm sorry you didn't get to play the back nine or ask me any questions," Trump said. "I know all journalists have questions. Feel free to ask me anything you like."

For a second my mind went blank. I didn't know what to ask—

or what to quite make—of Donald John Trump. "Well," I said as a thought came to me, "are you planning to buy the Dormie Club?"

The Dormie Club was a terrific Coore-Crenshaw design that was built in the twilight years of golf's grand overreach, a perfect symbol of the industry's belief that golf is, in fact, a socially aspirational game meant only for the elite. But those days were long gone, and Dormie was presently enjoying life as a modest daily-fee course awaiting its latest sugar daddy—perfect low-hanging fruit, it struck me, for the man who aspired to become the new King of Golf.

"Yeah, you know, we're looking at it," he confirmed. "I'll tell you one thing, though—that course will never make a dime unless it has the Trump name on it." He smiled and invited me to ask him another question. "Really. Seriously. *Anything.*"

For a moment or two I was stumped for a second time. Then a good question came to me. I asked if he planned to run for president again.

Trump smiled and tightened his grip on me as we approached the door. "Funny you should ask that. Everywhere I go, people tell me, 'Trump, this country is completely fucked up. You're the only guy who can save it.' So what do you think? You agree? Think I should run?"

I explained to him that I was an old political hack who'd covered parts of three different presidential campaigns before golf saved me from a very different kind of life, for which I was ever grateful.

"Yeah," he agreed, "politics is such a nasty business. That's why people say I should run. We need a businessman who can cut through the bullshit and get the job done. Don't you think?"

In person, Donald Trump seems to have tremendous empathy. He can make you feel like he's someone you've known and trusted for years. He oozes golf-buddy charm and clearly wants to be liked. There are worse traits for a potential presidential candidate, I had to concede.

"You would certainly be fun to cover," I said.

Trump laughed. "Who knows, I might be the first guy to make money running for president."

I smiled and nodded, slightly appalled by that notion. "Think you'll do it?"

"I'm thinking about it," he admitted. We'd reached the door. "Okay—one more for the road. *Christ*, those were such softballs. Give me your best shot. Ask anything you want."

Oddly enough, at that instant I wished I'd gotten to play the back nine with Trump. He was such an engaging character, and clearly a natural-born salesman who believed in his pitch and was having the time of his life making pronouncements about saving the golf world, if not America at large.

But, figuring our paths would likely never cross again, a non-softball suddenly popped into my head.

"Fair enough. You're much friendlier and more down-to-earth than I thought you would be. My wife and I just watched your TV show for the first time. We were wondering if you're really as big an asshole as you seem, or you just play one on television."

Trump looked shocked, dropped my arm as if it had spontaneously caught fire, and stepped back a yard, making his famously animated Trump Tower gargoyle face. For an instant I thought he might even take a poke at me or—even better—yell "You're *fired*!"

Alas, he did neither. Instead, he doubled over with laughter, slapped me on the back, shook my hand, and boomed, "Yeah, it's *fun*, isn't it?"

═══ • ═══

Arnold Palmer also laughed when I told him this story the next night in Latrobe, on my first trip back since Winnie Palmer's funeral in November 1999.

He stopped laughing, however, when I told him Donald Trump was out to make golf an aspirational tool of the one percent.

"That's exactly what golf *doesn't* need at this point," Arnold grumbled, giving me a firm version of The Look. "The game of golf doesn't know or care how much money you have or who you know or do business with. It's a game that belongs to everyone, whether it's played at Augusta National or a nine-hole public golf course. Golf is the most democratic game on earth. If you don't believe it, go play in Scotland where the game started. You'll see exactly what I mean."

Coming from the most charismatic and influential golfer in history, the working-class son of Latrobe whose success had unleashed the tsunami of American sports marketing and prompted Orville Moody to remark that every pro golfer who followed him ought to give thanks for Arnold Palmer and pay him a dime for every dollar he made, this was both perfectly true and eloquent proof of the real King of Golf.

Besides my purely nostalgic reasons for being there, I was in Latrobe to have a conversation with Arnold for a *Masters Journal* story about his final major championship win, the 1964 Masters, where, trailed by forty thousand adoring fans, Arnold reached the tee of the seventy-second hole with a five-stroke lead and made a birdie to send his adoring Army into a frenzy, a moment he'd long dreamed about. "Can I do anything for you?" he asked his good friend and playing partner Dave Marr, who was in a battle for second place. "Sure, Arnold," Marr drawled. "How about take a *twelve*."

That moment was one for Arnold's own Range Bucket List— the first time he'd reached the final hole of a major championship with a completely insurmountable lead. "It allowed me to take a walk I'd dreamed of taking," he confided as we sat together in his memento-laden office adjacent to the modest house where he and Winnie had lived for half a century and raised their daughters, Peggy and Amy. "For the first time I was able to walk up a final fairway seeing faces I loved and saying thank you to fans. That was more special to me than anyone knows. It was my greatest win in golf."

It was also his last hurrah as a major champion. Whatever else was true, the key to Arnold Palmer's extraordinary popularity and longevity as one of the most beloved and marketable figures in American sports history was his genuine love of his fans and his authentic appreciation of his remarkable life. He was the happiest famous person I'd ever seen in his own skin. Unlike Donald Trump, whose presumptive ambitions to save golf and maybe America itself were based, at least in part, on what he could make *from* the game of golf, Arnold Palmer's ambition to perpetuate the best traditions and the fellowship of golf stemmed from what he could do *for* the game. Therein lay a world of difference.

Once upon a time, a group of powerfully connected Republicans corralled Arnold in a swanky hotel room and offered to stake him to a run for the presidency. Palmer listened to their pitch and politely turned them down by joking that he would need too much time off to play golf as commander in chief.

This conversation took place as Arnold and his second wife, Kit; Doc Giffin, Arnold's longtime assistant, and his wife, Bunny; and Wendy and I dined together that next evening at the Latrobe Country Club. It was a Tuesday night. We had the entire dining room to ourselves. Arnold seemed pleased when we changed the subject to Scotland and Wendy's first visit.

"He should be ashamed for waiting so long to take you there," he said, casting me a disapproving glance. "What took you so long?"

I explained that having four bright children spaced two years apart in age, all of whom chose private colleges over public universities, meant that we'd barely had lunch money most weeks, much less the funds for a proper tour of Golf's Holy Land. With our final child near the end of college, we could finally afford a trip abroad.

"I predict you'll love it," Arnold said to Wendy. "Hope you like haggis."

She smiled. "I'm eager to try it. I also can't wait to see Edinburgh and Saint Andrews and play golf there."

"How about you, Shakespeare?" he asked, looking at me. "Is Scotland still fun for you after all these years? How many trips have you made?"

"Don't know. Lost count. But it's been a decade, and it never gets old," I confirmed, adding that I would probably move to Gullane tomorrow if we could just pull up stakes and go. I explained this trip also had a couple of pieces of unfinished business at St Andrews, where I hoped to finally break 80 on the Old Course and go through the R&A's formal induction ceremony so I would no longer be the organization's most truant overseas member. I mentioned that I'd just been informed that my playing partner for the medal competition was someone near and dear to Arnold—namely his surgeon from the Mayo Clinic, a dapper fellow named Dr. Ian Hay. We had both been members for almost ten years but had never been through the piquant ceremony of "kissing the captain's balls," I added—"which makes us the *two* most rogue American members."

Kit looked mildly shocked, and I quickly explained that "kissing the balls" presumably meant paying homage with one's lips to a royal mace or maybe to Old Tom's ancient mashie niblick with the silver golf balls attached—something of that romantic nature. Or so I bloody well hoped.

Arnold chuckled. "Why am I not the least bit surprised to hear that you and Ian are paired? You'll enjoy him immensely. He's a true character. You two are a couple of peas in a pod and ought to have a good time—even if you don't break *ninety*."

Moments later, the true King of Golf looked even more pleased when a young assistant from the pro shop appeared at his side to report that Arnold's granddaughter Anna Wears, playing in her first high school golf match for Latrobe High—on the boys' team, no less—had just won her first nine-hole match, 2 and 1.

"Well, how about *that*!" bellowed the proud grandpa, looking as happy as I'd seen him in a long time. "Anna's an amazing girl. So are *all* my grandchildren, of course." He went on to explain that Anna was an outstanding student who deeply loved golf. "She'll be out there on the hottest afternoons, carrying her bag and working on her game. I can just see her down at Wake Forest soon, or—well—wherever *she* decides to go." He blushed and added, "It's really up to her, of course. It's her life. I'm just so proud of her. . . ."

The King of Golf was still glowing about Anna's debut the next morning when I sat with him in his cozy office and talked about his final Masters title. A stack of photos, flags, and other personal memorabilia sent by fans lay in front of him, waiting to be graced with the most important autograph in golf. By his own count, Arnold once told me he'd signed more than half a million autographs since his first Masters victory in 1958.

"So," he asked, "how's your Scottish mother-in-law these days—what is it you call her?"

"The Queen Mum."

Arnold's memory never failed to amaze me. During the nearly two years I traveled with him to open new golf courses or make public appearances, I frequently saw him surprise and delight scores of fans by remembering names and dates and family members who'd met him years before, an indication of his identification with the people who adored him. He'd never actually met Kate Bennie, my former mother-in-law and keenest book supporter, though Winnie had met her twice, and Arnold always found my nickname for her amusing.

"She's fine," I said, then corrected myself. "Actually, she's not doing so well." I explained that Kate was battling cancer, and that

I needed to drive up to Maine and visit with her sooner rather than later. I could see how this news touched him. He nodded.

"Well, when you do see her, give her my best."

Then he sighed and started on another photograph. "I'm getting pretty tired, too, to tell the truth. I'm actually thinking of not playing golf anymore—at least in public."

I'd heard him say this at least twice before, but never took him seriously. Arnold Palmer wasn't just addicted to golf—he represented everything that is good and enduring about the game, a living embodiment of golf's highest values. On the other hand, I knew the sands were running out. Winnie Palmer once privately confided to me that when the day arrived that Arnold couldn't fly his airplane or hit a golf ball, he wouldn't be "around much longer." To untold millions of people like me, a world without Arnold Palmer was almost unthinkable, a reality I simply wasn't willing to contemplate.

The reluctant King glanced up and smiled as his longtime secretary Gina Varrone brought in a fresh stack of items to sign. I sat quietly for at least a full minute more, trying to decide whether he was serious this time about giving up the game or was just pulling my leg after a bad outing across the street. Gina smiled at me and left as Arnold placed his distinctive signature on another fan's piece of memorabilia. He spoke without looking up. His tone was wistful.

"The truth is, Jim, time catches up to us all. You'll know what I mean soon enough—probably before you know it. That's why it's so important for you to take Wendy to Scotland and see if you can beat the Old Course—and to go see your Queen Mum, too. You get only a few chances to do these things. As a kid, I used to make lists of things I wanted to do in this life."

I knew this, of course, reminded of my own list inspired by him.

"Did you do them?" I asked.

He paused and gave me an almost tender look, thinking about my question, a king on the edge of winter.

"You wrote the book. You tell me!" he barked gently.

Then he winked, looked down, and carefully signed his name on a fan's photograph of Arnold Palmer at the Masters.

CHAPTER SIXTEEN

THE SANDS OF NAKAJIMMY

We began our trip on the rain-swept Mull of Kintyre by walking Machrihanish Golf Club in a wild Atlantic gale—the clubhouse was shuttered like a beach club at the end of the season—and followed that up by playing the nearby Machrihanish Dunes in a steady sideways rain the next afternoon. It was a true baptism into the Calvinist pleasures of golf in Scotland.

The former is an original Tom Morris course that's high on any Scotland-lover's list of must-plays, while the latter is a fascinating new creation on a protected Scottish heritage site laid out by talented young designer David McLay Kidd, son of my good friend Jimmy Kidd, the longtime superintendent at Gleneagles. Despite spitting rain and lashing wind, we fell in love with Machrihanish Dunes, a minimalist design full of bumps and dips that pleased many traditionalists but raised the ire of some who deemed it too wild and woolly. On her second shot in Scotland—a blind one, no less—Dame Wendy struck a fine three-metal shot that sent her ball scampering over a mounded bunker and along a tilted fairway, following the contours of the land as if it had eyes, nicking the flagstick

230 • The Range Bucket List

and stopping an eyelash from dropping into the cup. She saw me dancing a little jig on the hill and wondered what was up. When I pointed to the green where her ball lay beside the cup, she did her own little highland two-step and hurried up to the green before the wind could blow her ball away. She tapped in for a birdie and posed while I took a photo on her iPhone. After six holes in the tumult, we abandoned any hope of keeping a legible scorecard and played along just for the pleasure of hitting shots and seeing golf holes that looked as though they were made in agreement between the Almighty and the reserved hand of a talented young man.

To add to the pleasure of the outing, waiting for us at the cozy clubhouse pub afterward was none other than Jimmy Kidd, the designer's papa, whose opening comment as we shook hands was: "I heard there was a pair of crazy Americans out playing in this weather, and I hoped—even assumed—that might be you."

"I wanted her to have the full Scottish experience," I said, introducing him to my smiling and fully soaked wife. With that, we retreated to a warm corner of the pub for an excellent supper and good Scottish beer, a reunion that was much overdue.

The slashing rain followed us across the Highlands and down to Panmure, where Ben Hogan practiced for a fortnight before the British Open at Carnoustie in 1953, with John Derr tagging along almost every step of the way. The rain washed away our round there, but retiring club secretary Ian Gordon generously served us lunch and lured club historian Bill Dryden out for a lovely conversation about Hogan at Panmure.

The sun finally emerged at St Andrews, where I had just enough time to introduce Wendy to my old friend Sheila Donnelly at the Dunvegan Hotel, grab my clubs from the trunk of our rental, and hoof it to the first tee of the Old Course for my first-ever Royal & Ancient autumn medal.

Even if it wasn't the true and anointed Home of Golf, the game

having been played in some form or another there for at least five
hundred years, the ancient gray burgh of St Andrews would still
be a thoroughly magical place. Since medieval times, the town
has been a high seat of religion, learning, and sport, boasting the
remains of a cathedral founded in 1160 and one of the oldest universities in the world, an institution that granted Benjamin Frank-
lin an honorary doctoral degree in 1769. On a purely personal
note, two and a half centuries later, my daughter, Maggie, glad-
dened her papa's heart by applying and gaining early admission to
St Andrews University, only to change her mind at the last minute
and attend the University of Vermont. Naturally, I fully supported
her decision, though I secretly grieved for what Parents' Weekend
could have been like.

Any visit is a true journey of the heart, as indeed my first one
was in late August of 1977, just weeks after Tom Watson beat Jack
Nicklaus to the Claret Jug in an Open Championship at Turnberry
rightfully nicknamed the Duel in the Sun. I quit my job at the
Greensboro Daily News and took off for the Home of Golf with
a thousand dollars and my golf bag in tow, hoping to forget—or at
least to outrun—the recent murder of my girlfriend by a fifteen-
year-old boy, foolishly believing the very first place mentioned on my
list of "Things to Do in Golf" could somehow perform an exorcism.

Almost nothing went right. By the time I reached St Andrews,
I'd blown most of my money and had my golf bag stolen on a train
ride from Paris to London. My first glimpse of the Home of Golf and
its world-famous Old Course came on a cold and rainy September
afternoon. My gloom was so deep that it never even occurred to
me to try to rent golf clubs from one of the many golf shops along
the adjacent Links Parade Road in order to play the course my father claimed inspired his love of the game—and, by transitive logic,
mine. I went home even sadder than I had been at the beginning of
my pilgrimage, feeling that my childhood was officially over. Within

months I was working at the Sunday magazine in Atlanta, probing the heart of darkness in search of spiritual answers that were hard to come by.

It wasn't until I returned to St Andrews nine years later that I discovered the true magic of the place by playing the Old Course twice with a delightful caddie named Bruce Sorley, who became a good friend and regular companion over the next two decades whenever I happened to be in town. I never managed to break 80, but I did discover what Bobby Jones meant when he observed that each time one plays the Old Course, one's knowledge and respect for the simple-looking layout deepens immeasurably.

On this trip, as Wendy explored the shops on the High Street, I went around the Old Course with a barrister from Nairn named Stephen Booker-Milburn and the aforementioned Scottish-born American, Dr. Ian Hay, Arnold's physician from the Mayo Clinic in Minnesota. We had all arrived with high hopes and nine handicaps, and had a fine time talking and playing on the outward leg— probably a bit too much fun, in retrospect, to produce a decent score. To briefly review, despite a heavy wind off the Eden Estuary and an untidy bogey on the first hole—which boasts the widest fairway and the most publicly exposed tee shot in all of golf—I played surprisingly well early on, reaching the infamous par-three eleventh by the estuary just five over par and ready to turn and play my way home with the wind at my back.

This is the hole where young Bobby Jones, playing in his first Open championship in 1921, needed four to get out of the bunker, lost his cool, shredded his card, and stalked off the golf course— a show of youthful temper he regretted so intensely that he vowed to reform his behavior once and for all, becoming a model of sportsmanship going forward.

I took a double bogey on the hole myself, falling to seven over, and followed this up by scoring—and I am not making this up—an incredible 13 on the brutish thirteenth hole, managing to find four of the (aptly named) coffin bunkers that have undone so many legends and hackers alike over the ages. Despite the strong wind at our backs, my fellow players scarcely fared any better. We fell silently into a death march that brought us to the tee of the famous Road Hole, looking a little like pale-faced refugees from a shipwreck. By then I was actually thinking about poor Tommy Nakajima, the pleasant Japanese professional who had the Open within his grasp the year after my disappointing trip to St Andrews before arriving at the Open's seventy-first hole tied with Tom Weiskopf and putting his ball off the green into the Road Hole's cavernous greenside bunker, resulting in a quintuple-bogey nine that left him in seventeenth place for the championship. It was one of golf's greatest disasters, prompting the cruel British wags to designate the moment the "Sands of Nakajima."

By the time we reached the seventeenth tee, I'd made my own separate peace with the masterpiece of folly I'd authored on thirteen, essentially falling apart at the seams for the next three holes, piling on double bogeys and emphatically proving that the Old Course is always in control of a player's destiny. As such, I decided to call my painful undoing the Sands of Nakajimmy and was just happy to see my bride waiting for me by the Road Hole green wearing a new wool sweater and a big smile. "How's it going?" she couldn't resist asking, grinning like an expectant Tour wife. Like an idiot, I'd gamely predicted a 78 and an important box finally checked off my Range Bucket List.

"We're having a contest to see who can at least break a hundred," I cheerfully explained. She thought I was joking until we showed her our cards.

Ironically, I settled down enough to make a rare and welcome par on the infamous Road Hole, widely regarded as one of the toughest holes in the world.

As we waited for the group ahead of us to clear eighteen, Wendy asked me why I was smiling. I replied that I was remembering what happened to our friends Bob and Holly on their couples trip to St Andrews.

My companions—equally relieved that our ordeal was nearing its end—were eager to know the details, so I told them the funniest story I'd ever heard about a visit to the Home of Golf.

Some years before, our good friends Bob and Holly—not their real names, mercifully—and another American couple from Philadelphia got the clever idea to rent a new recreational vehicle that slept four and would enable them to motor all over Scotland. According to their plan, while the husbands golfed, the women would shop and visit local heritage sites and museums—all without having to unpack a bag more than once.

The plan worked beautifully. Wherever the foursome roamed, according to Bob, their fancy recreational rig attracted local crowds, who greeted them warmly. Their finale brought them to St Andrews, where Bob managed to park their home on wheels in a parking lot just off the Links Parade Road in sight of the eighteenth tee. When Bob and his buddy arrived on the tee during their round on the Old, however, they saw a large crowd gathered around their vehicle and decided to hop the fence to go see what was up.

To their horror, they discovered that the large mirrored bathroom window of their bus—just off the showroom floor—had been accidently installed backward. The crowd was watching Holly step from the shower and take a seat on the toilet. "I couldn't believe what we were watching," Bob related to Wendy and me over dinner months later. "We thought it was a full-length bathroom mirror. Instead, we'd been flashing people all over Scotland. There was even a fellow filming it with his video camera."

"What on earth did you do?" I asked Bob.

"The only honorable thing to do," he replied. "We hurried back to the eighteenth tee and finished the round as if we had no idea who those crazy people in the bus were. I didn't tell Holly about it until we were home."

My suffering companions seemed to enjoy this story immensely. We sat together that evening at the annual supper and had a great time listening to the amusing speeches by R&A captains from all over the world, and happily went through the peculiar ceremony of "kissing the captain's balls"—silver golf balls, as I'd hoped, attached to a vintage wooden club—before doing our share of damage to the Fairmont Hotel's finest claret.

Laughter is healing, and one of the game's greatest virtues. The impossibility of beating Old Man Par fosters both humility and good humor. When I described our day's adventure on the Old to my former *Golf* magazine boss, George Peper, he smiled, patted me on the back, and said, "That's just St Andrews saying welcome back— you've stayed away too long."

=== • ===

The next day, we wandered Edinburgh's Royal Mile in a light drizzle and then played in the mixed alternate-shot event at David Kidd's Castle Course before moving on to the golf-mad village of Gullane, where my old friend Archie Baird gave Wendy a tour of his popular golf museum and joined us for supper at the delightful Old Club-house Pub across from the village "wee" links. Our last round was at North Berwick, a fabulously eccentric links that members claim may actually be older than the Old Course, though nobody can say for sure. Golf's origins are wonderfully mysterious, which seems only right and proper.

As our flight home lifted off, Wendy took my hand and thanked me for bringing her to Scotland at long last. "I've decided to start my own Range Bucket List," she explained.

I was pleased to hear this. "That so?" I then asked what things were on her list.

She smiled and glanced out the window at rainy, green Scotland disappearing below the clouds.

"A second trip to Scotland."

CHAPTER SEVENTEEN

A PROPER GOOD-BYE

Suddenly it was the middle of October, the beginning of the end of golf and gardening season in Maine. A golden afternoon was slowly expiring when I pulled into Kate Bennie's modest cottage above a dark-water cove just blocks from the Bowdoin College campus.

We'd been home less than a week from our Scottish travels when word came from Alison, my former wife, that the Queen Mum was failing—and that I shouldn't delay much longer if I wished to say a proper good-bye. "It would really lift her spirits to see you," Alison added, and I could hear in her voice how difficult this reality was for her.

Someone once said that life is the complicated stuff that happens between hello and good-bye—so make it all count. One of the deepest truths I've learned from living long and loving much is the importance of a proper good-bye. Whenever the end of a life approached, a physician friend of mine always made a point to thank his dying patients for allowing him to care for them—the care of a soul, he believed, being even more important than that of a body. Not surprisingly, it was the good old Queen Mum, the no-nonsense Pink Glaswegian who loved golf and good English gin, pointing out to me that the word "farewell" is an ancient blessing that derives from Middle English and simply means "Fare thee well along the path, wherever it shall lead," the ultimate pilgrim's blessing. This is the same woman, I should add, who wept gently during Evensong at St John's Chapel in Cambridge when the choir sang "Old Hundredth."

Not to put too fine a point on the subject, but I often have my own metaphysical feelings about golf and gardening, my life's two competing outdoor passions. Gardens provide the lovely illusion of consorting with the gods, while golf reminds you that you are simply a foolish mortal for thinking you can play like one. Candidly, I find both experiences to be as close to heaven as one can get on this earth, which perhaps explains why I find myself thanking favorite trees and golf holes, knowing both will long outlive me. But please don't spread that around, though.

Not surprisingly, I found the Queen Mum propped up and clear-eyed in her cheerful, sun-splashed bedroom. Several books sat on her nightstand, including the latest by A. S. Byatt. I saw a pair of bird feeders outside the window nearest her full of black-headed chickadees and a lone goldfinch, who was feeding like crazy.

"Hello, James," she said with her prim Glaswegian accent as Alison led me into the room. "How good of you to come. How was your drive?"

Hers was such a familiar and almost formal greeting that it was hard to believe she was in the final stages of the cancer that precluded her rising from bed. But that was just Mum.

I told her it was fine, though not nearly as much fun as the one Wendy and I had just taken across her homeland.

She smiled, pointing to the empty chair beside her bed. I sat.

"Alison explained that you two were moseying around Scotland. How did Wendy find it?"

She listened with amused interest as I described the highlights, from Machrihanish Dunes to my comic disaster on the Old.

"Returning to Scotland is now on top of Wendy's Range Bucket List," I said.

This made the Queen Mum smile. "You and your lists. I remember you always talked about moving there someday."

She asked about life in the Sandhills.

I told her it was fine, but I missed Maine.

"I thought by now you would be safely back in Greensboro," she said.

I admitted that was still in the cards as well—to finally get all the way to my hometown. Then I changed the topic to her favorite subject: her grandchildren, seven boys and one alpha girl. It didn't surprise me at all when she explained that my daughter, Maggie, the oldest of the brood, checked in with her by phone every day, sometimes twice, and Jack phoned at least twice a week. Our two, Alison's and mine, were Kate's first and closest grandchildren. Not for the first time, she commented on how proud she was of their character and work ethic.

"Well," I said, "they had a tough old Scottish lady for a grandmother who set a good example—even for their parents."

We talked for another half hour, mostly about books and the recent referendum in Scotland about whether to break away from Great Britain or stay in the Union. I assumed—incorrectly—that the Queen Mum would have voted to leave the Union ASAP. But the old Glaswegian was still full of surprises. When I mentioned recently having had lunch with Donald Trump, she shook her head, and when I added that I'd shortly thereafter dined with Arnold Palmer, she actually smiled.

"That was such a lovely night we had with Mrs. Palmer," she remembered, meaning the night Winnie took us to see Tony Bennett perform with the Boston Pops and introduced us to him backstage afterward. "Thank you for that."

"No need to say thanks," I said. "I'm here to say thanks to you."

I could see Kate suddenly growing tired. But she still summoned one of her stern superintendent looks—not quite a match for the Arnold Look, but in the same ballpark. "For what, for goodness' sake?"

Here's where my voice gave out. I sat for a moment and composed myself before I thanked her for taking a homesick southern boy into her family and being not only the first and most ardent reader of my early books but also the glue that held our extended family together through life's most wonderful and challenging years, the true matriarch of our clan who'd made a point to advise me, in the disorienting days following my divorce from her daughter, "James, you broke a very fine window just to get into this family. Don't for a minute think I'll let you out that easily."

Hers were words I'd come to cherish, because they lifted my spirits and brimmed with the kind of plainspoken optimism my late father—with whom, not surprisingly, Kate had shared a strong friendship—expressed till his dying day.

Perhaps sensing my difficulty, she reached over and touched my hand and pointed upward to the top of the door directly behind me. I turned my head and felt the waterworks begin anew. On a lone shelf above her bedroom door were half a dozen of my books—the six she'd read before anyone else—standing together.

"So, where are you headed next, James? You know I've always lived through your travels."

Recovering a bit, I explained that I was going over to Brunswick Golf Club for a late-afternoon round with my old friend Terry Meagher, Bowdoin's legendary hockey coach. Before striking out for home tomorrow, I intended to drive up to Natanis Golf Course in Vassalboro to play a few holes with a trio of golf-mad ladies named

Alexandra, Marsha, and Charlotte, old friends I'd promised to tee it up with even if the first snowflakes were in the forecast. I'd also made plans on the drive home to investigate an event called the Punchbowl at Yale Golf Club, a year-ending tournament put on by the Outpost Club, an organization that might hold one of the keys to the future of golf in America. In lieu of belonging to a single club, members of the Outpost were able to gain access to many of the world's finest layouts, a membership model based loosely on Britain's concept of society golf, the brainchild of Yale golf coach Colin Sheehan and his golf pals Will Smith and Quentin Lutz. Some felt this approach might be especially appealing to time-strapped millennials who, studies showed, were reluctant to join clubs and organizations of any kind. Only time would tell.

"I shall expect a report," Kate said quietly.

I rose and kissed her on her cool, pale cheek.

"I won't say good-bye," I whispered to her, "just farewell till we meet again."

This seemed to amuse her. "Tell me something, James," she said with a smile. "I've been meaning to ask for years. Did you ever make a *real* hole in one?"

"No, ma'am," I replied honestly. "Just yours."

═══ • ═══

The porch light was on, and a tall box was standing beside the door. Rufus the cat appeared out of the azaleas and followed me up the steps. It was well after midnight. The wild women of Natanis and the Outpost Club had provided a much-needed lift to my spirits. But Kate Bennie had been on my mind all the way home.

The box looked like it might contain golf clubs. I used my car key to open it.

Inside, bubble-wrapped, was a set of well-used Hogan irons. There was a handwritten note from my friend Paul Moran.

Dear Jim,

Joan thought you might like to have these. Bill would insist.

All the best,
Paul

The clubs had belonged to Saint Billy Campbell.

Sometimes the golf gods take away. And sometimes they give back.

CHAPTER EIGHTEEN

OPEN SEASON

A few weeks before the historic back-to-back men's and women's 2014 United States Open Championships came to Pinehurst, a young historian friend named Josh Evenson invited me to join him and a buddy for a round of golf at the National Golf Links of America, C. B. Macdonald's tribute to British golf on Long Island's Sebonic Bay, a destination long on my Range Bucket List.

Better yet, he invited me to bring along a friend.

I immediately thought of my son, Jack, a recent college graduate who was working his first job in Manhattan at a documentary film company. His interest in golf, like his old man's, was fueled early in life when he helped me lead a special father-son trip around Scotland for PerryGolf. Jack was only ten at the time, officially too young to play most of the famous courses we visited, though he gamely caddied and read greens impressively well for his proud old man in several fun matches with other dads and sons. During the last two days of the trip, he finally got to play his first full championship golf course with a caddie at the newly opened Kingsbarns. Back home in Maine a year or so later, he'd attempted to establish a golf team at his junior high school, then went on to help anchor his high school golf squad, at one point establishing a nine-hole record on a golf course I helped design in his hometown. By then he had a powerful swing and a very fine short game, and we often chatted about returning together to Scotland someday to play the courses he'd only been able to caddy for me. In college, however, Jack had wisely chosen to pursue journalism over golf, perhaps proving that apples really don't fall far from their trees. I wasn't the least bit disappointed by this decision, figuring that golf would always be waiting, as a wise fellow named Barnes once told me, if and when he decided to resume the game. He was currently deeply involved in research for an Alex Gibney film about the life of Steve Jobs, the founder of Apple.

That's why, when I phoned him to extend the invitation, his response was such a nice surprise. "Cool, Dad," he said, sounding genuinely interested. "But you'll have to bring up my clubs—if you can find them." Then he laughed. "I think they're deep in your garage." The clubs were Callaways, sent to him by Arnold Palmer. By my calculus, he hadn't touched them in at least four years, maybe five. I assured him that I could find them and might even bring along a special set of my own, explaining about the remarkable gift I found on my doorstep after seeing his grandmother, hoping their magic might translate.

A week later, we arrived at the National in a cold and misty fog bank, a late-spring Monday morning that promised periods of wind-whipped showers off the sound. But that did nothing to dampen my excitement. On the drive out to Southampton from Jack's Brooklyn apartment, I even reminded him of our plan to return to Scotland in order to play the courses upon which he'd caddied.

Jack patted my knee. "Sounds good. We'll do it."

Meantime, there was Macdonald's masterpiece with which to contend.

Charles Blair Macdonald was American golf's first Renaissance man. A native of Chicago who fell in love with the game while a student at St Andrews University in 1872—inspired by observing a match between Old and Young Tom Morris, he later wrote—Macdonald returned to his hometown determined to be in the vanguard of golf evangelism in the New World. Three years before James Tufts made his fateful trip to investigate the healing properties of the Carolina Sandhills in 1892, Macdonald laid out his first nine-hole golf course for the Chicago Golf Club and soon expanded it, creating the first eighteen-hole course in America. Three years later, the club moved to its present site in Wheaton, where Macdonald designed a new eighteen-hole championship layout.

Though an outstanding player who won the first US Amateur Championship and helped found the Amateur Golf Association of the United States, which soon evolved into the USGA, Macdonald is best remembered as a skillful course designer who worked for no fee, making his income principally as a stockbroker in Chicago and New York. Among other things, he conceived the Walker Cup and coined the phrase "golf architect," creating his masterpiece, the National, on Sebonic Bay in 1911. It was immediately hailed as the finest new course in America and inspired a generation of budding designers like Ross, Arthur Tillinghast, and Seth Raynor and his partner Charles "Steam Shovel" Banks. Macdonald, Raynor, and Banks went on to collaborate on a dozen of America's most heralded courses, including the Course at Yale University and the Greenbrier's Old White. Upon its official opening in 1913, the National was described by Ben Sayers, the much-respected head professional at Scotland's famed North Berwick Club, as "the finest golf course of the world." The first Walker Cup matches were staged there in 1922, with an American squad that featured Bobby Jones and his pals Jess Sweetser, Chick Evans, W. C. Fownes, and Francis Ouimet. They were a formidable team; all eight participants had won the US Amateur, and two—Ouimet and Evans—had won the US Open.

(Jones would win his first Open the next year.) The *Times* of London dispatched Bernard Darwin to write about the matches. Fresh from a look at the newly opened Pine Valley Golf Club in eastern New Jersey, Darwin wrote: "I will not describe that delightful spot [the National] again. It is one of the best and most enchanting of courses, ideal for a match from the player's point of view, but rather too remote for the spectators'." The superior Americans won in a lopsided romp over their British visitors.

In both spirit and design, Macdonald's remote but magical layout was informed by a pair of tours he made to Britain's greatest linkslands, his course an unapologetic replication of features and natural elements that powerfully echoed the best of classical Scottish design—rolling mounds of native fescue, a sandy wasteland terrain that buckled and heaved, land exposed to the vagaries of weather, and constant wind off the water. His National Golf Links also featured numerous blind shots; redan-style, punchbowl, and double-plateau greens; a Cape hole; an Alps hole (inspired by Prestwick); a Road Hole tribute to St Andrews; and so on. Did I mention three-hundred-plus fiendishly placed bunkers? Not polite American "sand traps," mind you, a phrase guaranteed to curl the mustache of a true golfing Scotsman. These were bunkers, meant to inflict psychic pain and wound the unwary.

"Which tees shall we play?" the genial Josh Evenson wondered after breakfast in the baronial clubhouse and a warm-up session in the mist. His friendly partner, Henry, turned out to be a player from the Web.com Tour.

"Whichever you guys prefer," I replied, without thinking it over. Jack hadn't played a lick of golf in more than five years, but his swing on the practice range looked surprisingly smooth, producing several prodigious drives. My Carolina Golf Association handicap at that moment in time was a highly questionable ten, assuming the moon, tides, and stars were all in proper Copernican alignment.

To be on the safe side, I'd wisely left Bill Campbell's clubs at home, having decided my only hope of a good score lay with my own well-worn Hogan irons and Titleist driver.

"Sir," our caddie spoke up, clearing his throat, "if I may ask . . . how old are you?"

"Sixty-one," I answered, trying to put something Sam Snead once told me out of my mind: namely that sixty is the most danger-ous age for a lifelong golfer, because that's typically when something happens—sudden injury, illness, or loss of interest fueled by pre-cipitously declining skills and loss of power—and your mortality is on display for all to see. Or, as Slammin' Sam said, with his typical bluntness: "Sixty's when most good golfers become weekend duf-fers. Sad to say, and worse to see. But it's damned true."

Our caddie seemed to be channeling his inner Sam. "Well, if I may say so, with no disrespect to you, there aren't many sixty-year-old members of this club who would play from the tips. It can be a very difficult walk."

"Not to worry," I said. "My son has very strong shoulders."

Everyone laughed. I laughed, too. Alas, it would be my last laugh on a golf course anywhere for a very long time.

The National's first hole is a sweetheart, a short siren of just over three hundred yards. Showing no apparent rust from his lengthy layoff, Jack nearly drove the green and halved the hole with a clutch par putt. More impressively in my book, he did the same thing on the next hole, a fiendishly engineered one called Sahara, which fea-tures a blind tee shot over a sandy wasteland with unseen bunkers and a sliver of a green somewhere over the hill. No designer today would dare to build such a hole, I daresay, because Sahara's mystery teases the brain with pure uncertainty, even if one understands the proper driving line, which is just to the right of the National's fa-mous wooden windmill.

Using his driver, Jack unleashed a monstrous draw that quickly turned into a hook that had the temerity to ricochet off the side of the sacred windmill and fly back onto a grassy patch one hundred or so yards from the putting surface. He wedged up and just missed making birdie.

The once and future duffer in our group contributed exactly one par that halved the eighth hole during the outward leg, hardly carrying his not inconsiderable weight but thrilled to finally see the National in her late-spring underwear, and awfully proud of his only son.

Josh and Henry played superbly, finally taking a lead they would keep by the turn. That's where my happy fortunes turned as well. In one of Macdonald's lordly cross-bunkers, I attempted to hit a fairway wood and felt the firm sand under my left foot shift on the downswing—sending a sharp pain shooting through my left knee. The ball loped about ten yards beyond the bunker. By the time we reached the green, I was limping and wondering what the hell I'd done to my "good" knee.

On the tee at thirteen, Jack asked if I was okay. I assured him that I was, shrugging off the injury. The spectacular par-three is called Eden, a beautiful tribute to the eleventh hole at the Old Course, where Jones blew up in his first Open championship. As Jack teed up his ball—both of our opponents already had decent birdie opportunities—I lost my composure when I heard Henry chatting to Josh while Jack set up. Whether consciously or not, he'd been chattering all round long whenever one of us was about to play.

To tell the truth, I'm a bit of a chatterbox myself on the course— but never when a friend or adversary is playing a shot. Jack, on the other hand, didn't appear to be bothered by the chatter, but I couldn't stop myself from speaking up and asking him to pause a second or two before he pulled the trigger.

Jack looked at me, and I glared at our opponents before launch-

ing into a hot little speech about proper sportsmanship that I regret
to this day. It was perhaps the only time since I buried that Bulls Eye
putter in the green at Green Valley in 1966 that I'd fully lost my cool
and shown my rear end on a golf course.

Our opponents looked stunned, to say the least. Jack did, too,
mumbling, "Dad, really, it's okay . . ."

Josh and Henry quickly apologized, and Jack hit his ball onto the
green as his old man stewed and tried to ignore his throbbing knee.
But both mood and match effectively ended right there. I hit an
anemic shot into the facing bunker and was never the same, dump-
ing my tee shot into a creek on the beautiful hole that followed and
hobbling along toward the imposing clubhouse that overlooks the
bay. Finally, at the brilliant punchbowl sixteenth, I took a moment
to apologize to my playing mates, pointing out that I was simply
"old-school" about certain things and regretted speaking my mind
with such vigor. They apologized again, and we all shook hands, the
goodwill mostly returning. We were closed out on the hole, 3 and 2.

After enjoying the National's famous lobster lunch and snoop-
ing around its spectacular clubhouse to look at historic photographs
and plaques, we shook hands again and said good-bye. I congratulated Josh on his handsome forthcoming tribute book to St Andrews
and promised him golf and supper at Mid Pines on his next trip
through the Home of American Golf. He was hoping to come for the
historic twin Opens, asked for the umpteenth time about my knee,
and heard me assure him that the knee would be fine by the time
we next met.

The skies opened on the drive back to Brooklyn.

"That was really fun," Jack said. "I've missed playing golf." He
looked over at me and added, "How's the knee? You okay?"

The knee was killing me, swelling by the minute. But I assured
him I was fine, which in one respect I absolutely was. By finally see-

ing the National and playing golf with my son again, I'd managed an RBL two-fer in a single day. It's small moments like these that golfing papas live for.

We chatted about his work. He told me about his research on Steve Jobs and mentioned that he was thinking about applying to an elite documentary and investigative filmmaking program at the Columbia School of Journalism, adding that he would borrow the money to pay for it. I liked the idea, commended him on his independence, and said we would discuss the finances when the moment arrived.

More importantly, I apologized to him for being such an old fart on the thirteenth tee, temporarily spoiling the mood of the round.

He patted my remaining good knee. "Dad, really, it's not a big deal. They probably didn't realize it was poor behavior until you called them on it." He smiled. "Besides, I've never seen you do that sort of thing on a golf course. It was kind of funny; so out of character for you."

"Glad to amuse you. It's the only thing I have in common with Bobby Jones. We both lost our cool on the Eden hole. The difference is, he was just nineteen. I'm sixty-one and feeling every inch of it."

I told him the story, one of the great turning points in Jones's life—and golf's. The story seemed to stir something in my son.

"We really should go to Scotland and play sometime," he mused as we turned down his residential street in rainy Brooklyn. "The way you and Granddaddy did."

"I would love that," I admitted. "Just say when."

"Maybe next year," he said, still looking at me. "Dad, *seriously*—how's the knee? You look kind of pale. Are you okay to drive all the way home?"

"Better than okay," I said with a small lump rising in my throat à la Arnold Palmer, who cried at the drop of a golf cap. I wasn't talking about my injured knee, however.

I gave him a kiss on the cheek, and he kissed me back.

"Be careful driving. And get that knee checked out, will you?" he said, hopping out into the deluge.

"No problem," I told him, blinking back tears.

═══ • ═══

The historic twin US Opens at Pinehurst a fortnight later were, for me at least, both a true eye-opener and a walking nightmare. To try to preserve the restored waste areas and fairways, the USGA had dramatically shrunk the spectator viewing areas and removed several key crosswalks that made walking a real chore for spectators on opening day. I hobbled through the sweltering heat of week one with the aid of a medical knee brace and a bottle of maximum-strength Advil. Somehow I produced six columns that week for our *Open Daily* team, which was partnering with *Global Golf Post*, but to this day I can hardly recall a word I wrote. That first week was a blur of pain and dust.

A bittersweet moment came late on Thursday afternoon when I glanced up from my desk in the Media Center and saw Dan Jenkins standing alone in the cavernous space. He looked as gray and out of place as his old friend Ben Hogan might have appeared in the same circumstances. I walked over to say hello to golf's Voltaire. He seemed pleased to see me. We shook hands, and he told me he'd come for one day just to get a glimpse of the Open circus, joking that at his age it might be his last chance to visit a championship site. "This is just too much now," he added. "I'm going home to watch it on TV."

On Sunday morning, in honor of Dan and needing to rest my bum leg, I skipped a visit altogether and watched German Martin Kaymer putt his way to our national championship on TV, a somewhat anticlimactic finish on both our parts. The real winner that week and the next proved to be Crenshaw and Coore's revised

No. 2, which not only held up spectacularly but provided an emotional finish when Michelle Wie finally got the monkey off her back by winning the seventy-third Women's Open.

Maybe the nicest moment of the fortnight for me occurred late on Saturday afternoon, when Wendy and I bumped into Dame Peggy Bell and her daughter, Peggy Ann, by the eighteenth green. I'd made no attempt to hide my lover's quarrel with the USGA for passing up Mrs. Bell's Pine Needles Resort in favor of the back-to-back experiment at Pinehurst No. 2. Pine Needles, after all, had hosted three outstanding Women's Opens and ranks high on the list of favorite venues among veteran LPGA players, but the actuarial odds of Ma Bell—then ninety-three—being around to host a fourth Women's Open weren't good. Few, if any, can match Dame Peggy's role in popularizing golf among American women; she was a pioneer of the early LPGA whose innovative teaching methods and popular "Golfari" schools have brought literally thousands of women into the game. I think of her, in fact, as the Arnold Palmer of women's golf.

After we'd exchanged our usual neighborly pleasantries and discussed her handicapping of the women's field—Ma Bell was keen on Michelle Wie by a wide margin—she asked why she hadn't seen us around Pine Needles lately. After nine decades of life, she pulled no punches, and demanded to know, before I could reply, "And why on earth are *you* limping so badly?"

"He twisted his knee on a golf course up north," Wendy stepped in to explain. "I'm making him finally get it checked out next week."

"Well, you'd *better*," Mrs. B. snorted at me. "That's exactly the kind of thing that can ruin your golf game. And once you leave golf at your age, you may never come back. I want you to get that looked after right away."

Peggy Ann just smiled at me. "You heard Mama," she said with a laugh.

I smiled and changed the subject, asking Dame Bell about her grandchildren and if there was any truth to a rumor I'd picked up in the media center that week that the USGA was planning to award Pine Needles a fourth Open Championship in 2020.

"If so," she replied with a coy little smile, "I'll probably be too old to play by then."

═══ • ═══

A month after the Opens left town, I finally saw my first orthopedic surgeon. He surprised me by suggesting a full knee replacement— maybe two, given the fact that my right one was bone-on-bone from an old football injury from high school years. When I inquired how long it would be before I could walk a golf course, he replied: "Realistically, nine or ten months, with the right therapy; maybe a little longer."

I preferred the opinion of the second doctor I consulted. A top surgeon who worked with UNC football players in Chapel Hill, he admitted that "injured knees are something of a mystery to modern medicine," adding that in his opinion I was "too young" for a new knee and might be better served spending a full year getting rest and therapy to strengthen my leg muscles. He did, however, mention something about a radical new therapy that involved injecting pulverized chicken beaks—if I heard correctly—into the injured joints, though it was frightfully expensive and not yet covered by most medical insurance, leaving me to wonder if I should next consult a witch doctor or faith healer.

As that long, hot, and painful summer drew to a close, my pal Rees Jones invited me to meet him at East Lake Country Club in Atlanta a couple of weeks before the year-ending PGA Tour Championship and FedEx finale was to be played there.

I'd spent weeks up till then riding a stationary bike and having physical therapy on the knee, with little to show for it, and seriously wondered whether I was up to a walk around historic East Lake.

Thanks to my dark passage through the hometown of Bobby Jones, I'd managed, like a reformed alcoholic who carefully avoids bars, to not return to Atlanta for more than three decades, save for a brief stopover at CNN to promote *Final Rounds* in late 1996. Yet the idea of someday returning to see the golf course Charlie Yates and Tommy Barnes and others had saved from the bulldozer—the place that inspired my first golf writing and rekindled my love affair with the game—had long been something I intended to do.

Rest and therapy, I decided, could wait. I was excited to finally see Rees's restoration work and the neighborhood resurrection job that Atlanta developer Tom Cousins had wrought when he not only underwrote a complete redo of East Lake's Gothic clubhouse and golf course in 1992 but also spearheaded the formation of a revital- ized club and foundation that launched an even broader revival of the surrounding East Lake community, providing low-income hous- ing, employment, and magnet schools that now ranked among the city's highest-performing public institutions. Gone were the barbed- wire fences and "Little Vietnam" slums. Nowadays, East Lake was held up as a model for what private and public collaboration could do to revive an entire community.

Naturally, I didn't bother to tell Rees about my injury until he spotted the problem as we followed our caddies along the first fair- way. He asked if I was okay, and I quipped that it was just the price for an unforgettable day with my son at the National, nothing a cou- ple of Advil and a fancy new knee brace couldn't handle. He looked doubtful and pointed out that we could stop at any time.

Rees and I are old golfing pals who've played a great deal of my favorite kind of golf together over the years—more talk, less score— discussing everything from our favorite golf courses to presidential politics and, most important, the ongoing adventures of our growing children. For years I've been after him to write his memoirs. Not only is he the youngest scion of America's leading golf course dynasty but he inherited the title of "Open Doctor" from his pioneering papa, Robert Trent Jones, for revising more than a dozen major championship layouts. Like many of us growing long in the tooth and short on time, he worries about the values of fellowship and sportsmanship that we may or may not be passing along to the next generation of golfers. He also has stories aplenty about the characters of the modern game. With luck, and enough prodding from his friends, he may someday get it down on paper.

After a rough start that included a triple bogey followed by a double, the Advil kicked in, and I was able to enjoy the walk, happy to listen as Rees explained his thinking during his comprehensive renovation of the course. I was intrigued to learn that he'd followed an original routing plan that Tom Bendelow created for East Lake when it opened for play on Independence Day in 1908, followed by a revision by Donald Ross in 1913 and a comprehensive redo of East's second golf course in 1928. Decades later, George Cobb added his own updates before the Ryder Cup of 1963, when Arnold Palmer served as team captain. Rees rebuilt and strategically shifted several greens, adding new tees and considerable length and dramatic bunkering and bringing the water closer into play on several of the crucial back-nine holes. He also had the benefit of Yates and Barnes to help ensure the authenticity of the restoration work.

"They walked the course with me, telling stories and remembering where everything had been in Jones's day, details you just never could have picked up from the drawings of the golf course. Being with them was like taking a walking seminar in the history of the club, a step back to the Golden Age," Rees said. "Their insights were very important to the restoration of this place."

Sadly, I only managed to reach the fourteenth tee before my left knee began barking at me like a chained-up yard dog from Little Vietnam. While Rees and the others played on to the concluding uphill holes, I limped over and sat on the empty Tour Championship bleachers that stood ready beside the seventeenth fairway, admiring the view of the lake and clubhouse on a warm summer afternoon in the city where I left my childhood behind for good but rediscovered a game that changed my life. My caddie, whose name I recall being Doug, came and sat with me and told me about his own early life in California, growing up almost in the shadow of the Los Angeles Golf Club, though he never played golf until he came east for college and got hooked on the game. He'd even been something of a journeyman on the satellite pro tours and still played in pro-ams from time to time, but believed caddying was what he was born to do.

"That's the great thing about golf," he said. "Anyone can find their place in the game." Then he chuckled. "Even when you can't play it the way you once could." He blushed and added, "I don't mean *you*, of course. I meant me. My game is fading fast. That's why I love caddying. I have years of experience in my head. That's now my place in the game."

This was a lovely thought. I told him what Tommy Barnes once said to me, not far from where we dangled our legs off the bleachers—that the game is always waiting for us to come back.

"So this isn't your first time here?" he said.

"No," I said. "I had a life-changing afternoon here thirty years ago. I'm just tying up loose ends—completing a personal circle of sorts."

I told him something a playing partner once said to me as I struggled with my game. "Golf is the only game where those who can't master it love it more than those who can. That's the true glory of the game. Maybe that's why we keep coming back."

Doug nodded and smiled. "I agree with that. Mind if I use it?"

"Feel free. Someone gave it to me."

Following our round, Rees and I grabbed a bite in the beautifully restored club room and took a walking/limping tour of the club-house, looking at framed Jones memorabilia and photos of generations of famous players who'd made the pilgrimage to Bobby Jones's golf home. The sprinklers were shooting plumes of water into the evening air as we parted company, and I struck out for home, driving through my old neighborhood just to see if it had changed as much as I had over the last thirty years.

I drove past the ballpark where I once coached the rambunctious Highland Park Orioles, and even stopped at Woody's Cheesesteaks, across the street from Grady High School stadium, for a steak sandwich and a chocolate milkshake, pleased to discover it was still hopping after all these years with young folks, kids, and neighborhood families.

In the absence of golf, coaching a racially mixed baseball team for two unforgettable summers had saved my sanity during the height of the terrifying "Missing and Murdered" crisis that gripped Atlanta for more than a year, when young African-American kids began disappearing and being found murdered. Eventually, a freelance photographer named Wayne Williams was arrested and convicted of the crimes. But it seemed to place a fitting coda on my dark passage as a reporter through the City Too Busy to Hate.

When we won our second league championship in a row, the team trashed my aging Volvo, and the dudes at Woody's—who always complained whenever I brought my Wild Bunch in for post-victory meals—gave us free cheesesteaks and milkshakes on the house.

Those were the happiest moments of my life in Atlanta.

Until now.

CHAPTER NINETEEN

PURE ONE-DERR

One evening six months later, not long after the holidays had come and gone, John Derr, the legendary CBS broadcaster, came for one of his occasional Sunday-evening suppers at our house. For a fellow who'd recently hit ninety-five, he was in exceptional form, regaling our dinner party, which included a couple of awestruck young folks, with lively tales about Hogan and Snead and his friendships with Mahatma Gandhi and dalliances with a young actress named Grace Kelly.

Some of us locals called John the "Living One-Derr" because he was as mentally sharp as a man half his age, a splendid raconteur and walking encyclopedia on sports and American history in the twentieth century, essentially blind in one eye but still regularly playing golf—though as he pointed out to the table that evening, he hadn't "made an ace since I was ninety-three."

"You know, James," he mused, looking out at the Christmas lights as I drove him home to his condo, "it's been an amazing life. I never imagined where golf would lead me. But I feel things could finally be winding down."

The Living One-Derr had recently finished a treatment for bladder cancer. At supper he'd eaten very little, save for a slice of Wendy's locally famous old-fashioned caramel cake. She'd sent him home with a large wedge of it for breakfast.

"Nonsense," I said. "You need to stick around to witness *my* first legitimate ace with your remaining good eye."

He was right about one thing, though: he'd had an amazing life in golf.

When Hogan won his last major championship at Carnoustie in 1953, John was with him every step of the way, accompanying the Hawk as both a journalist and a trusted friend, from Hogan's first secluded practice round at nearby Panmure Golf Club to the final hole, where the surging crowds prompted Hogan to grab Derr's belt and ask him to "plow a path" through the jubilant galleries. Following the presentation of the Claret Jug in a gathering rain, Hogan gave his winning Titleist ball to John for his infant daughter, Cricket. Moments later, in a maintenance shed hastily transformed into broadcast booth, as rain pelted the corrugated roof, John did the first live broadcast interview with Hogan after his victory. Afterward, Ben confided to his friend, "I think that's it, John. I'm going home to start my equipment company." He asked Derr to keep this information under his hat.

Like Harvie Ward and Opti the Mystic, John was a self-made son of the Old North State, born into an athletic family with a malformed knee that left him unable to play baseball and basketball like his brothers and sisters. His father, feeling sorry for John, constructed a two-hole golf course for his son that ran from the backyard apple orchard down the hill to the creek and back up again. "Golf became my salvation. I got my hands on a seven-iron and a putter and, oh brother, wore them out." At seventeen, when he finished high school, he had no means of attending college, yet wrangled a job working as a stringer covering high school sports for his hometown Gastonia newspaper, and soon made a deal with the local headmaster at Belmont Abbey College to work as the Catholic school's public relations man in exchange for evening classes in English composition.

That same autumn he convinced his editor to let him report from the Duke–Georgia Tech football game in Atlanta, where he found himself seated beside O. B. Keeler, the famed sportswriter from the *Atlanta Journal-Constitution* and Bobby Jones's literary collaborator and biographer. "Mr. Keeler asked me if I liked golf, and I told him about the two-hole golf course where I taught myself to play. 'Well,' he said, 'you should convince your boss to let you come down to Augusta in the spring and write about a new tournament Bobby Jones is starting up. We need some press attention. I think you'd like it.'"

This was 1935, the second year of the Augusta National Invitational.

The first person he spoke with after paying his two-dollar entry fee was O. B. Keeler, who immediately took John to meet Mr. Jones and Mr. Roberts, the tournament's founders. He also introduced him to legendary sportswriters Grantland Rice, Damon Runyon, and the rest of the northern scribes who'd come south to cover the tournament purely because Jones's name was attached to it. "This was the bottom of the Great Depression, mind you, and there was a lot of concern not just about the tournament but also about keeping the club going," Derr explained.

Jones in particular took a shine to the upbeat Carolinian, starting a long friendship that endured until his death in 1971. But Derr was initially more interested in the sportswriters than the players, which explains why he was hanging out in the second-floor pressroom when word came that Gene Sarazen had double-eagled Augusta's fifteenth hole. "No one believed it, of course. Runyon told the caddie who brought the news that he must have meant a two on the sixteenth, the par-three. But ten minutes later Jones himself confirmed the shot—which he'd witnessed." Sarazen went on to beat Craig Wood by five strokes in a Monday playoff. Years later, while playing golf with Sarazen in Florida, Squire Sarazen expressed amazement at the number of people who claimed to have witnessed his albatross at Augusta, the "shot heard round the world," as every newspaper in the land began calling it. "In fact, he told me that there were only twenty-two people around the green that afternoon, and he knew all their names. Still, it was exactly what Augusta National and the fledgling Masters and maybe golf in general needed to give the game a boost. It basically guaranteed there would be a *third* Masters Invitational."

John attended every Masters after that for the next six decades, deepening his friendships with Roberts and Jones and the cream of American sportswriting, right up to and through America's entry into the Second World War in 1942.

Due to his media experience, he wound up being attached to the personal staff of a four-star general named "Vinegar Joe" Stilwell, the hard-shell commander of the China-Burma-India Theater, assigned to post news of Allied successes and occasional interviews with key newsmakers of the region. Closer to John's heart, and for troop morale purposes, the young One-Derr convinced his boss to let him fly from New Delhi to St. Louis to report on the World Series of 1944. *Time* magazine called it the "longest sports assignment in history." At war's end, CBS Radio hired him to work as a writer for Red Barber's *Sports Magazine of the Air*, Barber being the first of several famous bosses who included Edward R. Murrow and Arthur Godfrey. By the late 1940s, John Derr was running CBS's new sports division and overseeing live radio broadcasts of college football and other sporting events from around the country.

"After the war, the coming of television was really the big story," he'd explained to me during one of our many long lunches on the terrace of the Holly Inn in Pinehurst. "Those of us who were doing sports on radio knew it was only a matter of time before television took over covering baseball and football, and maybe even golf."

In 1948, John inked the deal that permitted the first TV broadcast of the Rose Bowl. The next year, he signed up the Kentucky Derby. During these years he hobnobbed with sports and Hollywood royalty, got married to an editor of the *Ladies' Home Journal*, and had a baby daughter. His close friendships with Sam Snead and Ben Hogan spoke volumes about his understanding of golf, for neither man could tolerate lazy journalism. John often shared rides to tournaments with Sam, and they went on vacations together with their wives. Hogan liked John because he was a self-made man who conducted himself with dignity and charm and had impeccable journalistic instincts—he always knew what question to ask and when to ask it. It didn't hurt that Cliff Roberts and Bobby Jones had taken a fancy to Derr, either.

Roberts wasn't convinced that television was right for the Masters. "His belief was that if golf proved to be popular on TV, attendance would be hurt. It took several more years for those of us who believed TV would be a good fit to actually convince him. Basically, two things changed his mind."

One was amateur Billy Joe Patton's colorful rise from nowhere in 1954, a story worthy of a Frank Capra film. The witty lumber salesman from the mountains of western North Carolina just missed making the Monday playoff with Hogan and Snead, competing for a final green jacket in the twilight of their careers, which Sam won. "That Masters was the last hurrah for Ben and Sam," Derr explained, "and the fact that a hillbilly named Billy Joe almost beat them both made Cliff reconsider his belief that golf had no future on television. The press went crazy over Billy Joe. He wound up on the covers of several national magazines. Here was a true amateur nearly beating the greatest players of the age—almost like Ouimet at Brookline with Vardon and Ray." John paused, then added: "But the real earthquake began to occur quietly that same summer when a handsome young fella from Latrobe, Pennsylvania, won the National Amateur. His name was Arnold Palmer."

The Masters debuted on CBS television in April of 1956 with John Derr anchoring the fifteenth tower and racing off to Butler Cabin to serve in the role that Jim Nantz ably handles today, introducing the winner and conducting post-tournament interviews. That same spring, ironically, John raised the ire of his new bosses at CBS by accepting a last-minute invitation from President Eisenhower to scoot down to Washington late on a Thursday afternoon in order to play golf with reigning US Open champion Jack Fleck at the Congressional Golf Club. When John reported to work on Monday morning, his boss was fuming, demanding to know why he failed to show up for work on Friday. Despite his reasonable explanation that he'd not only informed his secretary of his whereabouts but was responding on CBS's behalf to a direct request from the president of the United States, he was relieved of his TV duties by the president of CBS Sports, though he kept his radio anchoring duties. A promising young broadcaster named Jim McKay took John's slot in the television booth.

When Edward R. Murrow—another Carolinian—learned that Derr had been replaced as the head of the network's sports division, he reportedly kicked his office wastebasket across the room and declared, "They just got rid of the one guy who really knows anything about sports in this goddamned company!"

The living One-Derr would anchor the network's radio broadcasts for the next two decades, covering the Masters for CBS until his retirement and move to Pinehurst in 1982. In 2007, the members of Augusta National presented John with their coveted lifetime achievement award for his sixty-two years of service. In my book, nobody ever deserved it more. By that point, John was a resident of four different sports' halls of fame.

═ • ═

"Did I ever tell you how we *really* got the TV contract at CBS?" John asked me as I was driving him home from supper that night.

"I don't believe you did," I said.

John smiled. "Well, that's not surprising. I haven't told many people this. But at ninety-six, I suppose we don't have too many more conversations left. The Bible talks about counting your days like the hairs on your head. Problem is, I'm almost completely bald."

"Don't be ridiculous," I said. "Wendy says you're the only ninety-something on Facebook. And lest you forget, you promised to speak at my retirement dinner in twenty or thirty years. I plan to hold you to that."

John gave a long sigh and glanced out the window at the prettily illuminated houses of Midland Road. "Oh, young brother, I just don't know. I think it's almost time I shuffled off to be with old friends." He added, "I've had a good long run."

This kind of talk was worrying, doubly so on the heels of having lost the Queen Mum, Billy Campbell, and Arnold Palmer having given up playing golf and flying his plane.

"So tell me the story you never told me—how CBS really acquired the Masters."

"Love," he said simply.

"Love of the game?"

"That, too."

The day after the Masters ended in 1955, John asked his friend Cliff Roberts once again about televising the Masters. Roberts informed him that a decision had been made to move ahead with the project for 1956—televising just a few closing holes. Naturally, John was delighted, though Roberts explained that since NBC Radio had

long held the primary radio broadcasting rights, they would be offered the first option to televise the tournament and given thirty
days to submit a bid. Months later, a letter from Augusta National
arrived on John's desk at CBS in New York.

"The letter began 'Dear Tom' and went on to explain that the
committee had decided to offer the television rights to the Masters
and he—Tom—would be given thirty days to submit a bid. It was
very strange. And then I realized there'd been a big mistake. The
letter was obviously meant to go to Tom Gallery, the head of sports
over at NBC. But for some reason, Cliff's very able secretary had
mistakenly sent it to me instead." He paused, and then added, with
the faintest note of nostalgia: "She and I were very close in those
days. She was always rather sweet on me. I think it was probably
just an honest mistake."

Derr set the letter aside and basically forgot about it. "I think
I may have informed Cliff's secretary about the mistake, though I
can't be sure. In any case, a month or so later, I phoned Cliff to
ask how the television rights were coming along. He was surprised
that NBC hadn't even responded to the club's offer, and informed
me that we at CBS were invited to submit a bid for the TV rights.
I did so immediately. And *that's* why the Masters is on CBS to this
day."

John had a roguish smile on his face as he told me this story.

"Everything happens for a reason, dear boy. Live long enough,
and you'll realize this is the gospel truth. To this day I believe CBS
was fated to have the Masters telecast. It's worked out pretty well,
hasn't it?"

═ • ═

As we pulled into his driveway, the living One-Derr said, in a voice
that sounded like his old commentator's tone, "You know, Jim, I
think your father would be very pleased you decided to come on

home to North Carolina. He'd be pleased with your books for sure, but also very proud of those magazines you've created."

I thanked him for saying that and got out to help him into his house, taking his arm. I took this moment to also thank him for two new sets of golf clubs that had recently shown up on our doorstep. For years he and Tom Stewart had needled me about my loyalty to my forged Hogan blades, until one day the director of TaylorMade's state-of-the-art fitting center in Georgia got in touch to say that a fitting appointment had been made for both Wendy and myself. When I asked who arranged the fitting, I was informed it was the work of John Derr. The clubs were his gift to us. We couldn't have said no.

"Wendy is over the moon with hers," I told him. "She took them straight over to Pine Needles and came home beaming."

"How about you?"

"They're great. I can't thank you enough." In my first outing with them at a wonderful private club in Wilmington called Eagle Point, I'd shot an unexpected 76, proving golf really is a mystery wrapped in a riddle. I didn't have the heart to tell him, however, that owing to my knee injury I hadn't been able to play a full round of golf in almost six months. Unable to finish a full swing, I'd basically shelved my brand-new clubs beside Bill Campbell's beloved ones until rest and therapy showed tangible improvement.

He nodded, pleased. "If you have a moment, come inside. I have something else to give you—two things, in fact."

John's kitchen table was covered with stacks of papers neatly organized into piles, his oversized life reduced to a small mountain range of papers. His dining room table and most of his living room furniture held boxes of papers, letters, and newspaper and magazine clippings of every sort, a paper trail from one of the most celebrated professional careers in American sports, the long and well-lived life of a national treasure. There were also a couple of boxes of his newest book sitting on the floor, the introduction of which I'd been honored to write.

"Ah, here's what I want you to have. Maybe you'll know what to do with them."

He handed me a zippered pouch full of personal letters. I opened the pouch and saw hand-scripted letters and notes from Sam Snead, Bing Crosby, and the chairman of *Time* magazine, along with a creamy note bearing the seal of the White House, and many others.

"Is the letter from Cliff Roberts to NBC in here?" I asked playfully.

John smiled. "Could be. I don't know exactly who or what's in there. I just know I'd like you to take those letters and do whatever you think should be done with them."

I told him they should be in a university library somewhere, preferably either up in Chapel Hill or maybe back at Belmont Abbey, where he bartered his words for an education. They were, after all, not only a record of his remarkable career from an apple orchard to Augusta National but also a revealing window into postwar American life. He liked this idea and asked me to look into it.

Still burrowing in boxes, he asked me what important things I'd learned from my own travels through golf.

It was exactly the sort of thing Opti the Mystic might have asked me. I told John about a small notebook I'd recently found that contained a list of eleven "Things to Do in Golf."

He glanced up, amused, his hand still in a box. "Did you do them all?"

"Pretty much, except for two items. I've yet to make a real hole in one, and I haven't played golf in Brazil."

"Why Brazil?"

"No idea. There was a pretty girl in my eighth-grade class from Brazil, however."

"The oldest motivation of all," John said, and chuckled. Recently

One-Derr had informed me that if I regrettably predeceased him, he planned to "waste little time moving in on Wendy, if she'll have me."

He was rummaging again. I was tempted to ask him about the current state of the game and the new crop of promising youngsters who had replaced Tiger at the top of PGA tournament boards, an appealing bunch who, refreshingly, appeared to play with genuine camaraderie and joy. Derr and his late friend Herb Wind were the first to point out to me that throughout the game's history, whenever golf was dominated by two or more players—ideally three—the game's popularity soared, its growth surged. Maybe Day, Fowler, and young Jordan Spieth could provide the competitive energy the pro game sorely needed, with Tiger on the sidelines and golf's popularity in flux.

"Ah!" he declared triumphantly. "*Here's* what I was looking for . . ." He handed me a sheet of paper with something written on it in elegant script. "You're finally old enough to enjoy this now."

It was, of all things, a poem.

Golf After Sixty

My muscles are flabby, I can't hit a drive.
My mind often doubts if I am really alive.
My chipping is lousy, I never could putt.
I guess I'll stay home and just sit on my butt.
My iron play is awful; my woods are as bad.
I'm describing my game as a shade short of sad,
So the outlook today is for grief and for sorrow.
Say! Who can we get for a fourth for tomorrow?

"I wrote that when I was your age," he explained.

"May I copy this?" I asked, thinking how appropriate a gift it was.

John gave a particularly endearing laugh and patted my arm.

"Absolutely! The original is for you. The point, dear boy, is that life passes in an instant, but golf will always be your friend. Put that in your golf bag just to take some solace from it when either your legs give out or those new clubs aren't working worth a toot anymore."

He walked me to his garage door, still holding my arm. I thanked him again for the new clubs and for the poem. I could have thanked him for so much more, but that would have to do for now.

"Just one final request," he said, with that same glint in his eyes. "When you speak at my memorial service, as I'm sure you will, please go last and be sure to give the crowd a good laugh. Tell them my favorite joke. You know the one I mean. As Arthur Godfrey used to say to me, always best to leave them smiling."

═ • ═

Six months later, just weeks after John Derr came to our house for supper a final time, he was watching the Belmont Stakes, the third leg of horse racing's Triple Crown, hoping to see someone gallop home to the first Triple Crown in forty years. According to his daughter, Cricket, who arrived at his condo a few moments after the race, she found her father sprawled backward in his easy chair, arms thrown out as if embracing the sky.

"I think the excitement of seeing the Triple Crown was too much for his heart," she explained. "He even looked happy."

At summer's end, I was the last to speak at John's crowded memorial service at Pine Needles. I followed Jaime Diaz, Tom Stewart, Les Fleisher, and a delightful archivist from Raleigh who'd been helping John get his decades of memorabilia catalogued and stored. They spoke movingly about his remarkable life and career, his zest for living, and even his uncanny number of aces.

When it was my turn to speak, I shared a few personal thoughts about the man who, after Opti the Mystic and Arnold and the good

Queen Mum, had shaped my golf-writing life most notably. Per the honoree's firm instructions, I concluded with a One-Derr-ful joke.

An old man lay in his upstairs bedroom, waiting for the end to come, his strength ebbing by the minute, when he suddenly smelled fresh-baked chocolate-chip cookies wafting up from downstairs. Warm chocolate-chip cookies were his favorite thing in the world, and the smell of them prompted him to get out of bed and wobble out of the bedroom and down the stairs on fragile legs, the smell of cookies growing stronger with each step. Staggering into the kitchen, he was thrilled to see a large platter of chocolate-chip cookies cooling on the counter and reached for one, only to have his hand sharply slapped by his wife.

"Put that cookie back," she declared. "Those are for the memorial service!"

No One-Derr the audience roared.

CHAPTER TWENTY

SOMETHING BRINGS YOU BACK

Three weeks after having knee surgery to repair a torn meniscus, as my eleventh spring in the Sandhills dawned, I slipped away from the office late one beautiful March afternoon and drove to Mid Pines Golf Club with Bill Campbell's clubs in my new MacKenzie Walker bag, picturing the perfect way to work my way back into the game. Campbell's clubs, after all, clearly had magic in them, and my repaired left knee was feeling better than it had since my injury.

Silly old me. Emphasis on "old."

After making a triple bogey on the first (and easiest) hole of the golf course, I topped a six-iron on the uphill par-three second, felt a sharp stab of pain in my left knee, and limped back to the clubhouse hoping I hadn't done serious damage to the handiwork of a talented surgeon named Glen Subin, realizing neither knee nor golf swing was ready for even a duffer's evening stroll.

═══ • ═══

There's a popular saying in golf that *something* always brings you back to the game—a memorable shot that redeems an otherwise mediocre round, a lucky break that reverses the flow of a match, a good unspoiled walk with a friend, or simply a golf course at dusk or dawn that awakens your sense of being alive.

Something is different for every golfer.

In my case, there were several small *somethings* that happened in remarkable sequence over the late spring and summer that finally brought me fully back to a game I'd loved since I was a kid making his first golf to-do list. They also reminded me that life is full of chapters, and a new one was opening for me and forty million baby boomer golfers like me.

The first *something* occurred as I was driving home from a monthly editorial meeting with my magazine staff in Wilmington. It was the Friday of Masters week, and I was taking a familiar back road home to Southern Pines, passing through a small village outside of Fayetteville called Lumber Bridge, when I saw a sign for a public golf course curiously named Scothurst. I was intrigued by the name and curious to check it out, in case Scothurst might be a contender for my Top Fifty Glorious Goat Farm List.

That's the list I began quietly making for fun when I moved back to North Carolina in 2005, inspired by Saint Billy Campbell's own love of modest public golf courses. Such humble golf courses have always owned a large piece of my heart, for these are the places most golfers begin their love affairs with the game, and sometimes where they wind them up. Besides, as I like to tell my snobbier golf friends, there's something to love about any golf course, if only the friendly staff and the nifty rotating hot dog rack in the pro shop. My friend David Woronoff had enthusiastically offered to join me on a protracted tour of our home state's Glorious Goat Farms, and I knew my pal the Irish Antichrist was always up for playing a new GGF in the elusive hope of finally beating me at my own game.

At that hour, already pushing suppertime in Lumber Bridge,

there were only a dozen vehicles in the course's gravel parking lot—seven pickup trucks and five cars—and the first tee stood open.

Inside the shop, I found a friendly older gent manning the counter while the Masters telecast played behind him on the wall.

"Who's leading?" I asked.

"Spieth has a two-shot lead over Danny Lee. Sergio and Poulter are close behind."

"Think I could play a few holes?"

He explained that the evening golf league had just teed off on the front side, so I might wish to play the back nine, but I was "free to play till you run out of daylight." He took ten bucks from me, the best deal of the day.

I'd almost forgotten what it was like to play until darkness.

"Cart or walkin'?" he asked, interrupting my little reverie.

"Cart, I'm afraid. Hope to be walking soon, though."

He didn't ask why, and I didn't provide my usual whine about a bum knee. He simply smiled, handed me a cart key, and said I could park the cart by the shed if everyone happened to be gone by the time I came back. I thanked him and hurried to fetch my clubs.

I parred Scothurst's tenth hole, a short par-three. I parred the next hole, too, a handsome par-four with a small pond guarding the left flank of a large kidney-shaped green. My repaired knee held up okay, but my golf swing felt strangely alien and wobbly, as if I'd forgotten where my arms were supposed to go.

My good fiend Laird Small, who directs the Pebble Beach Golf Academy, always urges his pupils to aspire to "a state of NATO," which means Not Attached To Outcome. The older I get, the more sensible Laird's approach seems to me. But old habits die hard. It's tough to remove one's ego from a game you've spent half a century measuring yourself against and trying to master.

Even so, for the moment at least, I forgot about trying to knock the accumulated rust off my swing and just enjoyed the sights, smells, and sounds of a gorgeous Carolina spring evening settling over an honest little golf course that was alive with waking nature. Scothurst was like thousands of country golf courses in America—designers unknown—where the game was still nurtured without fuss or pretense. During evening club talks, I often ask for a show of hands of members who began their golf journeys at municipal golf courses or simple public layouts like Scothurst. Typically two-thirds raise their hands, all the proof I need that if golf is ever to resume growing at a sustainable rate in America, public courses and Glorious Goat Farms like Scothurst will be in the vanguard of the long-awaited grassroots revival.

Playing along the fourteenth fairway, I passed a middle-aged African-American couple tooling along an adjoining fairway; they waved, and I waved back. Soon I caught up to a trio of teens shouldering their bags, chatting away about whatever teenage boys talk about with one another these days. They invited me to play through and politely watched as I (mercifully) struck a half-decent nine-iron to the green on the fifteenth hole.

By the end of the first nine, my golf swing was still pretty sorry—almost every shot, for one thing, was coming up ten yards shorter than before my injury—but the pleasure of being alone on an unknown golf course and bumping into a fragrant spring evening over Scothurst's modest Bermuda fairways, getting off a respectable swing every fifth shot or so, was reason enough to continue.

As dusk crept over the course, I saw a hawk cruising on evening thermals above the tops of ancient longleaf pines and a doe and her spotted fawn feeding on new grass behind a perfectly still irrigation pond. The sound of spring's first crickets and frogs made me marvel at how quickly my life had passed and how far I'd come since I'd buried that Bulls Eye putter at the long-gone Green Valley Golf Club exactly fifty years ago. What a wonderful and unexpected journey it had been.

Chinese lore holds that crickets are sacred creatures that remind us of life's bittersweet impermanence. Indeed, the sound of those crickets made me think about my friend Bill Duff, who'd recently passed away. Bill was my age exactly, part of a lively group of guys from Raleigh who played something called the South Hawkins Invitational Tournament—or SHIT, for short—every summer at a glorious goat farm of a country club hard by the Pamlico River down in Little Washington, North Carolina. Bill and his brother-in-law, Whit Powell, an old friend who introduced me to the event, were the SHIT's larger-than-life creators, promoting an event founded on "bad golf, inappropriate humor, lots of good food and wine, and wives who insist on crashing the party," as Whit once summed it up. Bill Duff was the SHIT's guiding spirit. One day he felt a small pain in his lower back and went to get it checked out. He put up a game and classy fight against cancer, always relentlessly upbeat whenever I saw him, but passed away within a year. His funeral service, at an Episcopal church in Raleigh, was an overflow affair. The rector told stories about Bill's deep love of family, friends, and golf, reminding us how one life invariably touches so many others. There wasn't a dry eye in the house. Those crickets reminded me how I was going to miss Bill Duff and his wonderful SHIT.

Somewhere around the fifth hole on the front side I finally ran out of daylight and trundled back to the clubhouse, where I found the friendly shop attendant closing up. I accepted his offer of a scribbled-out rain check and promised that I would return soon and bring my golf-loving bride along.

"Hope you liked what you found," he said.

"Almost like being a kid again," I answered truthfully.

========= • =========

A month later, another lovely *something*.

I caught a dawn flight to New York City, where—unable to secure a taxi or figure out how to work my newly installed Uber app—I decided to give the repaired knee a significant test by hoofing the seventy-five or so blocks from the airport shuttle drop at Grand Central Station all the way to Columbia University's central quad at 116th Street, where my son, Jack, was graduating from the journalism graduate school with a dual degree in investigative journalism and documentary filmmaking.

The knee complained a bit, but held up better than expected. I arrived sweating and only twenty minutes behind schedule, just missing the keynote address by the UN's Ban Ki-moon but somehow finding my son and his pretty girlfriend, Henriette, and her parents in the ocean of Columbia-blue graduation robes and beaming families.

Jack looked pleased to see me, but his expression changed to anxious surprise when I explained that I'd walked all the way from Midtown to Columbia.

"*Seriously?* Is that good for your knee?"

"Who knows? But it was good for me." We were off to find a quick lunch before the graduate school commencement festivities in the afternoon. "Besides, my knee passed an important test," I said, pointing out that the distance from Grand Central to Columbia turned out to be 5.1 miles, or roughly the length of Pinehurst No. 2.

This made him smile and pat his old man on the shoulder. "That's great, Dad. I guess we'll have to plan that trip back to Scotland after all."

I assured him that few things would give me greater pleasure, vaguely wondering when "something" might actually happen, because Jack had a busy summer of researching and writing a film on

America's debtor prisons ahead of him, a prelude to a career that would undoubtedly take him on his own journey over the horizon. But that was nature's way, and it was perfectly fine with me. If it was meant to be, golf would be waiting for Jack to come back—that much I'd learned from my own long trek. And if Scotland factored into the deal, all the better. His old man would be ready to drop all and steal away for a final golf trip to the game's birthplace, just the way I'd done with Opti the Mystic.

Henriette's folks were a delight. They hailed from Jaffa, Israel, and were Palestinian Christians who couldn't have been more fun to get to know. Her father owned a popular grocery store back home, and her mother spoke perfect English, having been educated at a Scottish school. We talked about their children, Middle Eastern foods, and the three-ring circus of American presidential politics. They admitted to being baffled and not a little concerned by the bluster of Donald Trump, but seemed to find my account of the strange afternoon of golf and cheeseburgers with Trump amusing, if not reassuring.

We parted in a swirl of blue Columbia robes on the crowded sidewalk on Broadway after we'd all gone to get drinks at a café following the grad school commencement. Flushed and happy, Jack and Henriette were heading off to a party with some of their pals, and I took photos of everyone on my phone to send to Wendy and Jack's mama (unavoidably absent due to graduation exercises at the college where she works in Maine). Jack showed me how to properly operate my new Uber app, and we hugged good-bye as a black Toyota pulled to the curb moments later. I slept during most of the flight back to Raleigh, arriving home well after midnight. But what a day it had been.

=== • ===

A third *something* happened a month later when my neighbor Max "Grumpy" Morrison invited me to play what turned out to be my first *full* round of golf in almost two years at the Southern Pines Golf Club, a red-letter day on a Donald Ross gem that sits only a few blocks from the *Maison du Golf.*

Max was making his own way back to the game after an unexpected hiatus, recovering from recent heart surgery that hadn't allowed him to play for the better part of a year. At eighty-five, a year younger than Arnold Palmer, he'd made a reasonably quick return to his locally famous veggie garden, but had played only a couple of rounds of golf with his regular weekday group on the heels of a long recovery.

I loved playing golf with Grumpy Morrison, in part because his game was such a comic masterpiece, an affront to Archimedean physics. Maxie played right-handed but putted left-handed with an old Bulls Eye putter exactly like the one I once buried in an innocent putting green. His preferred driver was an ancient Orlimar number, his golf swing a hilarious three-part affair that resembled a farmer cracking a bullwhip at a stubborn mule, somehow resulting in surprisingly long, straight tee shots. Grumpy being a true Scot, the rest of his clubs were a hodgepodge of inexpensive knockoffs purchased over the Internet. His large leather cart bag was monstrously heavy, filled with hundreds of BIFs ("Balls I Found") that the bag's frugal owner relentlessly pulled from creeks and ponds wherever he happened to be playing.

Needless to say, cheap was key to Grumpy Golf, which explained why he was wearing the same faded knit shirt he'd won in a golf tournament at the Country Club of North Carolina not long after I came to town. He and I had actually ham-and-egged it beautifully to tie for first place with two other teams in the autumn "Dornocher" tournament but lost out in a coin flip for the top two prizes, taking home only a couple of logoed CCNC golf shirts. Mine was orange enough to position a telecommunications satellite by, so I promptly gave it to Goodwill. Grumpy's was Carolina blue (where he attended med school), so he wore it to this day—and *on* this very day.

"You know," he confided as we trundled to the first tee in a cart (as usual, Max had to drive), "this is where I took up playing the game before we joined CCNC. It was about five dollars to play here. I've always liked this course. I'm thinking of playing more golf here. It's good to go back to where you have good memories, I suppose."

I asked whether this was before or after the War of 1812. As usual, he ignored my friendly jibe. "Probably around 1963," he said. "That was the year we arrived here and I opened my practice down on Main Street. I had a few golf lessons over at Pine Needles from Harvie Ward, and we joined the Elks Club so the kids would have a place to swim and I could play golf. This was the place to be before they opened up CCNC. We moved over there in 1968. My dues for a family membership were less than thirty dollars a month. Can you believe that?"

"What are they now?"

"About twenty times that." Noticing that the first tee stood open, he grumbled, "Are we going to play golf or sit and gab all day? It's not getting any cooler out here."

He was right about that. Though it was only midsummer, intense heat lay over the Sandhills like a steamed barber's towel, soaking the skin within minutes. Once you spend a summer behind the Pine Curtain, it's easy to understand why the Tufts family traditionally shut down their golf resort and bolted for the coast of Maine until October. The advent of air-conditioning changed that scenario in the late 1960s. It seemed to me, however, that summers had grown noticeably longer and hotter since I'd lived there, but I wasn't about to bring up the touchy subject of global warming with my beloved neighbor, who believed it was an elaborate hoax perpetuated by the liberal media and "tree huggers" like me. It said something nice about our friendship, however, that Grumpy Morrison and I could hold divergent views on everything from presidential politics to turkey carving at the holidays and remain such good friends who loved to needle each other at golf—further proof of the game's commendable democracy and genius for making unlikely friendships.

As a reluctant concession to injury and age, I'd decided it was finally time to move forward to the middle tees and switch to "distance" golf balls and a new driver with a "regular" graphite shaft, instead of my beloved Tour-shafted Titleist driver of many years, more or less confirming Lee Trevino's famous quip that "the older I get, the better I *used* to be." I also dug out my trusty Ram Zebra putter, which for years had carried me over some of the world's best courses in Britain and rarely let me down.

Despite these changes, and a special new knee brace to boot, I foozled along to a discouraging opening nine-hole score of 45. My golf swing felt nearly as out of sync as it had at Scothurst, the new distance ball was a complete dud, and the fancy new driver was about as reliable as a badminton racket. Grumpy Morrison, on the other hand, cobbled together a quite respectable 44, roughly half his age.

As we gulped ice water at the turn, both of us dripping with sweat, I popped a couple of Advils, and Max needled me about needing pills to play golf, adding that he could probably make room for me in his regular "Tuesday group of elderly duffers—those who haven't already given up the game or just gone off and died." He chuckled at his own joke. I told him he'd better not give the gods good ideas.

On the other hand, maybe those same golf gods simply felt sorry for a sweaty, struggling senior citizen trying to find a new place in an old game. For it was at that moment that I had another helpful revelation—namely, that I actually had nothing to prove to anyone in golf, least of all Grumpy Morrison, but merely had a desire to keep playing for the pleasure of playing a game I'd loved since I was knee-high to a ball-washer, if only for the fellowship and exercise it provided, and the occasional magical *something* that brought me back.

So I laughed at Grumpy's jest and eased my grip in more ways than one. As a result, something sweet and wholly unexpected happened on the back nine of the Elks. I went around in thirty-five strokes, while Grumpy faded to forty-five, still finishing an impressive three strokes north of his age, a worthy achievement on any elder-golfer's RBL.

"I didn't think you could play that well anymore," Maxie commented with an evil chuckle as I hoisted his massive BIF-filled golf bag into the flatbed of his Chevy pickup truck. This was his sweetly contrarian way of offering congratulations.

"Not bad, I guess, for a Ray-Ray round of golf," I agreed, pointing out that this was my first legit eighteen-hole round in more than two years since my misadventure at the National. Now all I had to do was actually walk a golf course again with my shouldered bag.

"What's a Ray-Ray round?"

Ray Charles on the front, I explained, and Ray Floyd on the back.

Grumpy Morrison gave what passed for a real smile. "Come on over to the house," he said. "I'll make you and *both* Rays an iced-down bourbon to celebrate our triumphant returns to the game." Then he actually grinned, which always telegraphed another Grumpy barb on its way. "Better not get too cocky, though. You'll soon be playing Grumpy Golf, too!"

═══ • ═══

Something special happened on Father's Day weekend.

For many years I've hosted a Father's Day/US Open weekend event for Pinehurst Resort built around *Final Rounds* that attracts more than a hundred fathers and sons, golf pals and couples, singles and families from all over the country for three days of casual golf and fellowship on historic No. 2 and the resort's other fine courses. The event includes an opening dinner during which I welcome returning participants and newcomers with well-worn jokes, followed by a Saturday-night dinner conversation with interesting figures from the world of golf. For that year's edition I'd brought my good friend Howdy Giles and his wife, Carolyn, to Pinehurst. Howdy was Arnold Palmer's longtime dentist and de facto photographer. Between us we had lots of untold Arnold Palmer stories to share, complemented by Howdy's photo documentation of Arnold's epic career.

At the end of Friday evening's welcome dinner, a man named Kevin Reinert and his wife walked up to say hello. Kevin offered me a strong military handshake and an earnest gaze. He turned out to be a retired Air Force colonel living in Greensboro. "This is my first year here. I just want to say thank you for saving my life," said Colonel Reinert.

I smiled, waiting for the punch line. But there was none.

Instead, he told me one of the most harrowing stories I've ever heard—a powerful reminder to cherish every day.

One evening the previous October, Kevin slipped out after work to play some golf at Starmount Forest Club in Greensboro, something he loved to do on warm summer evenings. He hoped to get in a full eighteen holes before a club fund-raiser scheduled for six o'clock. "I breezed around the course and was pushing my cart up the path to the eighteenth tee," he explained, "kind of lost in my own happy world, when I heard an engine roaring and looked up. I didn't believe what I was seeing."

What he saw was a Kia Rio with smashed side mirrors barreling directly toward him on the cart path, a stolen car being driven by a man who was on a crime spree across the city and being chased by

the police. He'd mistakenly turned into the club's main entrance—
Sam Snead Boulevard—but quickly found his only potential escape
route to be the lovely golf course where Snead won half of his record
eight Greater Greensboro Opens.

"I had just enough presence of mind to try to jump out of the
way," Kevin recounted. "So I jumped, hoping—I don't know—that
I'd land on the hood and roll over the top like you see guys do in
the movies. I didn't get quite high enough," he added with a laugh.

The car—later estimated to be going about 40 mph—struck
Kevin at the knees and knocked him thirty feet through the air. He
landed facedown on the eighteenth tee. "My first thought, as I lay
there, was a kind of stunned disbelief. I saw that one leg was lying at
a ninety-degree angle from my body, and when I tried to lift myself
up, my arm wouldn't work."

Workmen from a nearby house hurried over, dialing 911. A
threesome walking ahead on the final fairway ran back to help. By
the time head professional Bill Hall brought out a maintenance cart
equipped with a flatbed—due to recent heavy rains, the EMS crew
couldn't drive onto the golf course without fear of getting stuck—
Kevin Reinert was wondering if he would ever walk again.

Both Reinert's knees were crushed. He also suffered a shattered
femur, a broken tibia, a broken right ankle, and a fractured right hu-
merus bone, the upper bone of his arm. There was a deep laceration
on his face, but otherwise his head was remarkably free of injury.

The next morning he underwent six hours of surgery. This was
followed by four more surgeries in the ensuing weeks. "The doctors
were totally noncommittal about my chances of walking again—to
say nothing of playing golf."

After eighteen days in the hospital, Kevin was sent home. His
wife, Jean, happened to be the head of nurses for the same hospital
where he was treated. His daughter, LeeAnne, was also a nurse. He
began intensive therapy three days a week.

"The hardest part was not knowing what was ahead. I was haunted by the idea that I might never be able to walk or play golf or referee lacrosse again." Kevin had just begun a new career as a' college-level official. "I sat and tried to watch TV, but the news was so discouraging that I turned off the set and decided to try to read books instead. By nature, I'm a very upbeat guy. But this was so depressing, the toughest thing that had ever happened to me."

An old friend from Long Island who introduced him to golf during their college years sent him a box of his favorite books. The one that grabbed Kevin's interest was my 2004 biography of golf's most elusive superstar, *Ben Hogan: An American Life*. "I read it over a week and couldn't believe the similarities of our injuries."

At the peak of his playing career in 1949, Hogan and his wife, Valerie, were involved in a head-on car crash with a Greyhound bus that nearly killed Hogan and all but destroyed his legs. Facing a similar prognosis that he might never play golf or even walk again, Hogan was inspired by an avalanche of unexpected letters of support from thousands of fans to begin a furious rehabilitation routine that resulted in him returning triumphantly to win the 1950 US Open at Merion in a playoff that transformed Ben Hogan from golf champion to American sports legend. He went on to capture three more major championships, concluding with the British Open at Carnoustie, before retiring in 1954 to create a golf equipment company that became legendary in its own right.

"Reading your account of how he did this completely inspired me," Kevin explained. "I vowed to Jean and my kids that I, too, would get back to the game within a year—just like Hogan did."

A month before Kevin and Jean drove to Pinehurst for the Father's Day weekend, Kevin returned to the eighteenth tee at Starmount Forest, where he and his son, Phillip, a captain in the Air Force, teed off and walked the final hole while a bagpiper on the hill played "Scotland the Brave" and a large crowd of more than one hundred friends and fellow club members followed along.

"I needed to finish that golf round. I could barely see to hit my shot, I was so choked up," Kevin admitted. He "finished" with a bogey, officially recording 88 strokes.

Now, weeks later, he and Jean had come to the Father's Day event to play *his* first full eighteen holes of golf in eight months at the Home of American Golf—and to thank their choked-up host for his account of Hogan's resurrection.

The next day, Kevin Reinert accomplished this task heroically—playing the difficult Pinehurst No. 4 with Howdy Giles and Pinehurst president Tom Pashley while sharing a cart with me. We had a great time talking about everything from the adventures of our grown kids to why we both loved Greensboro, and found inspiration in the stories of so many severely wounded veterans who were turning to golf to find their way back to something resembling a normal life. Kevin seemed pleased when I mentioned that I'd spoken at a number of events raising funds for disabled veterans.

"You never realize how short life's walk is until something like this happens," he said at one point. "I will never take any of it for granted again."

"Amen to that," I agreed, thinking of Bill Duff and his SHIT.

I forget exactly what we scored. We lost the card, not that it mattered to either of us. More important, I was once again being sent a message from the firmament to savor even the most bittersweet of moments, because, as Opti the Mystic long ago advised, the round ends too soon.

The next day, Kevin walked No. 2 with a caddie. Afterward, he told me, sweating but flat-out glowing with exuberance, "This was the greatest weekend of my life. Next year, my son, Phillip, will be coming with me."

I promised him I would try to lure my son, Jack, back to the Sandhills. We would make the perfect four-ball.

═══ • ═══

The Aiken Golf Club had been on my radar since a summer afternoon not long before I injured my knee. Tom Stewart and I showed up there to see an old friend of his who ran the Kalamazoo Open for years, and to play the Palmetto Golf Club, a beloved layout designed by Alister MacKenzie and partner Perry Maxwell shortly after they completed work on Augusta National.

Palmetto turned out to be everything we'd hoped for, a gem of classic Golden Age craftsmanship presided over by a dandy Stanford White clubhouse, a famous playground of presidents and movie stars, amateur champions and Masters winners as long as your arm. During Masters week and the week following, the course hosts some of the finest players in the world, and its annual Palmetto Invitational is the stuff of South Carolina legend.

But it was the modest Aiken Golf Club, a mile or so away, that proved to be the real eye-opener on that trip, unexpectedly capturing our hearts. I'd recently read a column by my friend Michael Bamberger calling AGC the "most charming golf course in America," and we wanted to see if it, too, lived up to that billing. So after our round at mighty Palmetto, we dropped by Aiken Golf Club just to see what it was all about.

By the time Tom and I reached the cute wooden snack shed between the eighth and ninth holes, we were both echoing Bamberger's sentiments, which made meeting eighty-eight-year-old Ellen McNair even more of a revelation. She sold us Powerades and dollar slices of her homemade banana bread and gave us enough of the club's intriguing history to leave us hungry for more.

Miss Ellen told us, for instance, how she and her husband, Jim, purchased the course in 1959 from the city of Aiken for "something like twenty thousand dollars, or about what we paid for our first house"—a bargain, she added, because the course was in such poor shape. Jim McNair spent the next forty years of his life bringing the course back to life and giving golf lessons to local residents. She told us the course dated from 1912 and was constructed to serve as an amenity for a fancy hotel on the neighboring hill called the Highland Park, designed by a man named John Inglis, with input from Donald Ross.

The stock-market crash of 1929 dealt both the hotel and the golf course near-fatal blows. The hotel hung on until 1941, at which point it was torn down. By then the town of Aiken had taken over the course and changed the name to the Aiken Golf Club, using WPA workers to create, among other things, an extraordinary set of stone steps on the sixteenth hole that became a signature feature. "Fred Astaire loved to play here in those days. He belonged over at Palmetto but had a son in the local school," Ellen McNair said. "They tell the story that he once danced down those steps with a golf club."

I wanted to hear much more of this delightful tale, but a trio of local golfers was closing fast on our heels, which prompted Miss Ellen to suggest we find her son, Jim Jr., after our round. "He knows all the history because he totally rebuilt the course himself after his father died. His daddy would be so proud. This place was the first course ever to have women's tees, you know. You should ask him about that."

Unfortunately, Jim McNair Jr. turned out to be away from the property that warm spring Friday, working on a newly acquired sister course across town called the Cedar Creek Golf Club.

On the ride home to the Sandhills I confessed to Tom that Aiken might be my new favorite golf course anywhere, and I couldn't wait to go back for a closer look.

Which explains why Wendy and I chose to go there for our fifteenth wedding anniversary two years later, a dual celebration of our marriage and my surgically repaired knee.

Sweetening the return, Wendy somehow wrangled us the remaining guest room at the cozy Willcox Hotel, a historic property listed among the world's finest boutique hotels and booked to the rafters this particular summer weekend with a large, boisterous wedding party. Since the room was available for one night only, and the grounds were crawling with wedding preparations that appeared to be for Gamecock royalty, we checked in and headed straight to the golf course, where Jim McNair Jr. had left a message saying he would meet us for drinks and a chat following our round. We teed off just ahead of a large Friday shootout of local members and had, despite the intense heat, one of our most memorable afternoons ever on a golf course.

I won't burden you with the details. Suffice it to say, we both had fine rounds, and I even did a true redneck two-step down the sixteenth's famous stone steps in memory of Fred Astaire. Wendy has the embarrassing photograph to prove it. Mostly, though, it was the layout's modest but ingenious routing scheme and wonderful shot values, its beguiling quirks, artful bunkering, timely blind shots, gorgeous natural waste areas, and absolute originality that wooed my seasoned golf heart. Introducing Ellen McNair and her magical banana bread to my wife was a bonus. In sum, Aiken was a pure joy to play, and cured whatever psychic aches remained from my long hiatus.

Jim Jr. was waiting for us in the air-conditioned snack bar when we rambled in, soaked to the bone by Aiken's one-hundred-degree blanket of heat. He couldn't have been more engaging as he filled in the gaps of Aiken's remarkable story, a tale full of surprising connections that proved that American golf really is one big family affair.

Jim the Younger had done volumes of archival research on the golf course that he'd brought back from the brink of extinction.

John Inglis, we learned—who played a role in building Shinnecock Hills—had served the club as its first head professional and was the man who most likely laid out the original routing plan developed by Donald Ross for the Highland Park Golf Club, as it was known upon its founding in 1911. More surprising was to discover that the hotel and course were part of an ambitious vision Pinehurst's Richard Tufts and his family had to create a string of fine luxury golf resorts down US Highway 1 from Pinehurst to Camden to Aiken, which in those days were the winter playgrounds of the Northeast.

"Inglis was a remarkable fellow, a true unsung hero of American golf and an especially passionate teacher of women," Jim said, explaining how Inglis grew up with Chick Evans and knew the golf-rich Turnesa family and had all sorts of connections to the wider golf world that was exploding at that time. When the female manager of the hotel approached him in 1916 to suggest that women who wanted to play the game needed their own individual tees, Inglis created the first ladies' sets of tees in America, a fact verified by the USGA.

Despite the Depression bringing hotel trade to a trickle, Inglis also created a major Women's Invitational that attracted the likes of Babe Zaharias, Patty Berg, and even a retired grand dame named Glenna Vare to Aiken as the troubled decade drew to a close. In 1939, the City of Aiken purchased the course and ran it until Jim McNair Sr. purchased it two decades later.

McNair Sr. was another unsung hero of golf. He was the best player on a Duke University golf squad that included the likes of eventual Masters winner Art Wall and future PGA star Mike Souchak, and he never lost a match as a collegian. Even more telling, he beat both Harvie Ward and Billy Joe Patton to claim the Carolinas Amateur title—twice.

Lacking the funds to try the professional tour after graduating in 1948, the elder McNair took a club job in Florida, and soon wound up as head professional at Charlotte Country Club. He always dreamed of owning his own golf course, though, and when the City of Aiken ran out of course funding, he negotiated a deal to buy the club for $23,000 in 1959.

"The course was in awful shape. The city had covered up the steps on sixteen and filled in most of the bunkers," Jim Jr. remembered. "My father loved this course, though, and ran it brilliantly on a shoestring budget for the next three decades, doing much of the maintenance himself. He built a swimming pool and renamed it the Highland Park Country Club. That move probably saved the place."

Following his own college golf career at Clemson, where he played against the likes of Curtis Strange and other stars of the early 1980s, Jim Jr. returned to Aiken and joined his father in the golf-course business. Jim the Younger started a local bed-and-breakfast, and a decade later decided something bold had to be done to elevate the appeal of the golf course to a new generation. So he wrote to Ben Crenshaw and Bill Coore, inviting them to come see and share their thoughts on the Golden Age relic Jim had inherited.

"I think I became something of a pest," McNair allowed with a sheepish grin, "but eventually Bill Coore did come and ride around the golf course with me. I think he was pleasantly surprised by what he saw, noting elements that were clearly Ross concepts. He agreed with me that it was worth restoring. But the real surprise came when he said, 'Jim, you should do this work yourself. You're a golf person. You don't need a big design company. Who knows this place better than you? It's all right in front of you.'"

So Jim the Younger borrowed enough dough from a local bank to fund a three-man construction crew that included himself and a couple of occasional local volunteers and completely rebuilt the course using Donald Ross's original routing scheme, uncovering and restoring the famous stone steps in the process. "I like to think this golf course has a lot of Donald Ross's ideas and my soul in it," Jim said with a smile and visible emotion. "This place is my life's work, my family's home. My father's spirit still resides here." Gone is the swimming pool, replaced by a nifty eighteen-hole putting course named in honor of his papa. The semiprivate club remains the site of the City of Aiken's Golf Championship, which has been won by a stream of Palmetto State prodigies.

"Is it true that Fred Astaire once danced with a club down those stone steps?" I had to ask before Wendy and I headed back to the Willcox for showers and a firm eight o'clock dinner reservation.

Jim smiled, giving a little Delphic shrug. "That's what they say. There's supposed to be a photograph of that, but I've never seen it. My dad used to say those were the kind of steps Fred Astaire couldn't have resisted dancing down, though."

=== ● ===

At dinner with my bride a couple of hours later, I confided that I felt like an important circle had finally been closed.

"How do you mean?"

I told her that I finally felt I'd made it all the way back to golf, even if my shots were ten yards shorter and my legs weren't fully up to walking eighteen holes in the hundred-degree heat. Still, that day was surely coming soon.

"That's great to hear," she said, sipping her wine. "But I think there's another circle to complete—one even more important than golf." I looked at my beautiful golf partner. She was still wearing the glow of our incredible day at Aiken Golf Club. Before I could ask, she said: "The one you've been trying to complete for at least ten years, maybe more."

Dame Wendy is a woman who knows her mind—and mine, most of the time. We both knew exactly what she was talking about.

"I think it's time to start looking for a house in Greensboro."

"Are you sure?" I said. "Give up the *Maison du Golf*?"

"Yes. It's time for you—for us—to go all the way home. I've already started checking out houses in your old neighborhood."

Why wasn't I the least bit surprised to hear this? "Anything grab you?"

"A couple of really nice ones. We should go look."

I nodded in agreement, flooded by something I couldn't quite give a name to, a powerful feeling of gratitude and peacefulness that had as much to do with my wife's uncanny sense of timing as the excellent wine we were drinking.

"And one more thing," she added, glancing over at the lively wedding party going on in the lobby.

"Yes, ma'am?"

"I want to come back here every wedding anniversary to play golf at Aiken Golf Club and stay here. This place is now a permanent thing on *my* Range Bucket List."

CHAPTER TWENTY-ONE

SAFELY HOME

There was yet another important circle I needed to close. At summer's end, a few weeks before his eighty-seventh birthday, I found the man who inspired my original "Things to Do in Golf" list sitting in his handsome rustic den in Latrobe watching an episode of *Gunsmoke,* one of the most beloved TV shows in America when Arnold Palmer ruled the world of golf. A few feet away stood a metal walker.

Ostensibly I'd come to research a tribute piece about Arnold for the 2017 edition of *Masters Journal,* though there wasn't really much I needed to ask him about his extraordinary life and times. I'd come mostly to see a good friend of many years who wasn't doing very well. In the back of my mind, as with the Queen Mum and Bill Campbell, I suppose I'd also come knowing in my heart that it would probably be my last chance to say a proper good-bye to someone who had enriched my life immeasurably.

Arnold's body was frail, but his mind was sharp. "I had a bad time over at the range this afternoon," he confided as we sat in the den while his wife, Kit, made us drinks. "I couldn't even get the club back to take a full swing. Can you believe it?" He shook his head, glanced at the TV set, and switched it off. This news reminded me of Winnie Palmer's comment that when Arnold Palmer could no longer hit a golf ball or fly his airplane, he wouldn't be around for long. He'd quit flying his plane in 2012.

"I've got a couple of girls coming in tomorrow morning from the hospital to work with me, physical therapists. Maybe that will help."

I assured him it would, and hoped I was right. But I had my doubts. The key to Arnold's golf swing was his powerful legs, and his legs were clearly gone. He was also recovering from a serious shoulder injury suffered from a recent fall.

During supper with Kit and Arnold and his longtime assistant Doc Giffin at the Latrobe Country Club across the street a little while later, however, we talked about happier things, almost like old times—his grandchildren and my children and his grandson Sam's continuing efforts to make his way onto a PGA Tour that his grandpa transformed. We even ventured briefly into the current presidential campaign, which had become so difficult to witness that the only thing Arnold could bear to watch was classic westerns. The world Arnold Palmer knew and loved—and that loved him back—seemed very far away indeed.

"Aren't you glad you got out of the political game and into golf?" he teased me at one point. "Much safer world."

I agreed, but reminded him that he once entertained—albeit briefly—thoughts by some friends of his buddy Eisenhower to mount a run for the nation's highest office. "It's probably not too late," I returned fire. "If golf doesn't work out for you, maybe you could be the next Donald Trump."

Kit laughed. Arnold gave me The Look. I noticed, however, that he was hardly touching his meal. "I wish you'd brought Wendy along. I always liked her *much* more than you," he said with a wink. "Are you two in Greensboro yet, or still in Pinehurst?"

As always, the man's memory astonished me. Only once, as best

I could recall—and two decades earlier, at that—had I made brief mention of my hope to someday return to my hometown, joking that golf and life were, in the end, both circular affairs. The idea of a Carolina boy permanently settling down in the north woods of Maine seemed to amuse him.

As a matter of fact, I explained, Wendy and I had been quietly looking at houses in Greensboro for a while. Nothing had grabbed our imagination until we learned that the Corry house was up for sale. Ironically, it sat two doors down from the house where I grew up, in an old Gate City neighborhood called Starmount Forest, a block from the country club of the same name. Al and Merle Corry had been my parents' best friends, and their three sons were close pals of mine. I knew almost every room of their house, which was my favorite in the neighborhood.

"Wouldn't that be something," Kit was moved to say, "if you wound up back where you grew up."

"I love Greensboro," Arnold put in wistfully. "So many of my friends were from Greensboro and Winston-Salem. I almost won the tournament there twice, you know." He was eating a little vanilla ice cream with fudge sauce, his preferred dessert.

"I know," I said. "I was there both times."

═══ ● ═══

The next morning, a sunny, cool Tuesday, I showed up early at the offices of Arnold Palmer Enterprises to briefly visit with Doc Giffin and his staff before the boss arrived.

Doc had recently been honored at Jack Nicklaus's Memorial Tournament for his incredible half century of service as Arnold's executive assistant, running Arnold's complex golfing life and handling an insatiable world media with the aplomb of an orchestral maestro.

At one point, Jerry Palmer, Arnold's younger brother, popped in to say hello. We had a nice half hour catching up until I heard the boss's voice gently barking in the next office. "We'd better get in there," Doc said.

Arnold was already seated at his desk in the handsome office, with its photo- and memento-laden walls of a life well spent in golf. As usual, he was autographing items for fans from a neat stack on his big desk. Also in the room were two perky young women dressed in sneakers and workout clothes.

Arnold motioned me to a chair by his desk and introduced me as the writer who had helped him write his autobiography.

"They're going to help me learn to hit a golf ball again—aren't you, girls?"

"That's right, Mr. Palmer," the therapy girls chimed more or less in unison. They looked so young. Arnold must have been thinking the same thing.

"They never saw my golf swing in action," he said.

"They will after they work you out a bit," I said, suggesting to the therapy girls that they not go easy on him.

"I think we have a remedy for that," Doc said, calling to Gina Varrone to bring in a DVD that had recently arrived, a newly released colorized film of the 1960 Masters.

Doc placed the DVD in the video player. The therapy girls positioned themselves directly behind Arnold, with Doc standing off to the side. The monitor was right beside me. I had a side view of the screen and a direct view of their faces.

Suddenly there was Jim McKay's familiar voice narrating the afternoon's drama from Augusta National. Ken Venturi finishes with a par on eighteen to hold the lead in the clubhouse at 283. Trailed by his mammoth Army, a charging Arnold Palmer arrives at the seventeenth tee one stroke behind his nemesis, with two holes to play. He unleashes a massive drive with his famous corkscrew swing. "Did you see that?" Arnold asked quietly, almost in a whisper.

"That's so great, Mr. Palmer," chirped one of the cheerful therapy girls.

The boxy TV camera actually shakes a few moments later when Arnold drains the long cross-green putt for birdie on seventeen. The roar is deafening. Then he's on to the dangerous eighteenth, hitching up his pants as he strides, needing one more birdie to win his second Masters green jacket. You can hear the excitement building in Jim McKay's voice. You can see it growing as Arnie's Army swarms Augusta's eighteenth tee to try to get a glimpse of the King's final tee shot.

We watch Arnold tee up and lash the ball.

"There it is, girls! *That's* my swing!" cries Arnold.

But I'm no longer looking at the screen—I'm looking at Arnold's handsome old face. His eyes are bright with joy, and there are tears pooling in the corners. There are tears in my eyes, too.

The film cuts from his approach to his final eight-foot putt. The gallery rings the green, silent as a church. He makes his famously hunched, wristy putting stroke and curls the ball into the cup and complete euphoria breaks out. He is only the second wire-to-wire Masters winner in history.

The film ends, and we are all left a little breathless.

═══ • ═══

The therapy girls went next door to get ready for their workout session with the King, and Doc went back to his office. Arnold and I were left alone for a few minutes.

"Well," I said, "I should probably be moving along, too."

"Where are you going?" he asked; he was already back at it, signing items on his desk.

I reminded him that I planned to meet Wendy and a real estate agent at the Corry house at around seven o'clock. "If I leave now, I can just about make it."

He nodded. "I have a feeling that's the house for you two." He finished writing and glanced up at me. "So what can I do for you, Shakespeare?" he asked. This was a familiar question from Arnold Palmer, one he often asked his friends.

"Nothing," I replied. "You did everything when you asked me to collaborate on your book. That changed my life."

Arnold frowned. "It's *our* book."

"Which reminds me," I said, "there *is* something you can do for me." I pulled a first-edition copy of *A Golfer's Life* from my shoulder bag, the first copy I received from our publisher. I handed it to him. "I always meant to ask you to autograph a book. Guess I just forgot."

The room fell silent as he wrote. It seemed to take a small eternity, giving me time to study the walls, the many family photos, the tributes, and the awards for a final time, the artifacts of an ordinary man's extraordinary life.

He finished, shut the book, and handed it to me.

"Don't open that till you get safely home," he commanded.

I smiled and promised I wouldn't.

"I'd better see you again soon," he said.

I nodded, momentarily losing my voice, and reached across the desk to shake his hand. He took my hand in his and placed a second massive hand on top of mine.

"But don't come back again without Wendy. *Understood?*"

This made me laugh. I needed a laugh. Otherwise I might have cried.

═══ • ═══

It was just getting dark when I reached the Corry house. Wendy was running late. Somewhere around the Maryland state line, I confess, like a kid who couldn't stay out of the Halloween candy, I cheated while gassing up the car, opening my book to see what he'd written.

It hit me hard. But then, like my old friend Arnold Palmer, I'm prone to crying at anything from a favorite church hymn to the opening of a Wal-Mart.

Now, as I waited for my wife and the real estate broker to arrive, I opened the book to read his inscription for a second time. The waterworks returned in force.

Dear Jim,

Thanks for all your wonderful words. You are the greatest friend I could have.

Arnold

Wendy pulled up moments later, smiling, visibly excited to see the Corry place and eager to hear details from my visit with Arnold and Kit. She asked me if I was okay. I handed her the book.

She touched her throat, clearly moved. "Oh my goodness. I think this is exactly what he would say to his millions of fans. He's saying it through you."

═══ • ═══

Arnold's memorial service at Latrobe's stately Saint Vincent Basilica on the fourth day of October befitted a King of Everymen. The service was titled "A Life Well Played—A Celebration." My only regret was that I was forced to go solo because the service fell on a day when Wendy was leading a team at a national human resources conference in Philadelphia. She was texting me roughly every half hour for updates, though.

Everyone in golf except for Tiger Woods, however, seemed to be in attendance, including hundreds of ordinary Arnie fans who lined the public areas around the basilica just to watch the invited guests arrive and depart. I spoke to one man and his wife who'd driven all night from Chicago just to stand and pay their respects. The man was holding a hand-lettered sign that read GOOD-BYE, ARNIE—THE ONE AND ONLY KING. The Golf Channel provided all-day coverage, with Kelly Tilghman interviewing luminaries as if a head of state had passed—which indeed one had.

Sam Saunders, Arnold's grandson, spoke movingly about the influence his grandpa had had on his life; Russ Meyer, the long-time CEO of Cessna Aviation, remembered Arnie's pioneering life in the air. Jim Nantz of CBS gave a beautiful account of his growing friendship with Arnold through television, PGA Tour commissioner Tim Finchen spoke of Arnold's seismic impact on golf and sports in general, and Peter Dawson of the R&A told of Arnold's role in reviving popular interest in the British Open. Jack Nicklaus beautifully euologized "My Rival, My Friend," and Vince Gill performed a haunting version of James Taylor's "You've Got a Friend."

I sat behind Arnold's old friend Dow Finsterwald, next to Howdy and Carolyn Giles. After the choir sang "The Battle Hymn of the Republic" and the Coast Guard color guard retired the colors, the thousand or so family, friends, and invited guests clustered on the steps of the basilica beneath a deep-blue autumn sky that featured a lone white cloud and watched as Pete Luster, Arnold's longtime copilot, flew a pair of low passes over the basilica in Arnold's beloved Citation X, soaring heavenward after his final pass and disappearing into the clouds.

We all walked down the hill to the Fred Rogers Reception Center, where—fittingly—guests were served iced Ketel Ones as well as other nonalcoholic refreshments. It was exactly the kind of homecoming Arnold Palmer would have loved. I paid my respects to the King's daughter, Amy, and wife, Kit, and visited for a spell with Barbara Nicklaus. I chatted with my old friend, former LPGA commissioner Charles Mechem, the memorial's emcee and Arnold's close friend and personal advisor of many years, and spoke to a dozen others I'd met on my own long journey through golf.

A short time later, I slipped out a bit earlier than planned, leaving time to drive past the Latrobe golf course and Winnie's barn a final time before heading east on the Lincoln Highway.

==== • ====

Late on a chilly Friday afternoon a few weeks later, I dropped by the Gillespie Park Golf Course on the east side of downtown Greensboro, a nine-hole municipal course that owns a forgotten piece of American social history.

The course was designed and built in 1941 by Perry Maxwell, perhaps the last great designer of America's Golden Age of Golf, about the time Maxwell also designed Winston-Salem's magnificent Old Town Club and made spectacular refinements to eleven of the eighteen holes he and his late partner Alister MacKenzie designed and built for Augusta National.

Not long after Gillespie Park opened for play as a public facility, and shortly before he enlisted in the Army Air Corps, a young ad salesman and aviation columnist for the *Greensboro Daily News* named Brax Dodson played his first-ever round of golf there with buddies, using a borrowed set of clubs. To hear him tell it later, my old man quickly became hooked on the game. He found a second-hand set of Bobby Jones Spalding clubs and read every book on golf he could find at the Greensboro Public Library, already making a plan to someday visit St Andrews.

By the time I knew of its existence in the late 1960s, Gillespie Park—named for a Scottish-born hero of the American Revolutionary War who had owned the land where the course was built—was a run-down facility in the toughest part of town. I remember my father remarking as we once passed it, "That used to be a very fine golf course. That's where I first played golf. So did half of Greensboro. Shame what happened to it."

Back in December of 1955, the same week the Montgomery Bus Boycott was launched in the wake of Rosa Parks's defiance of segregation laws in Alabama, a Greensboro civil rights activist and local dentist named Dr. George Simkins, head of the local chapter of the NAACP, and five African-American friends showed up at Gillespie Park aiming to desegregate the facility. Peacefully demanding their right to play, they put down their seventy-five-cent greens fees and teed off despite the objections of the manager, who advised them that Gillespie was a "private course for members only."

The six men were arrested for simple trespassing. Two months later, Simkins and the others were convicted of trespassing and fined fifteen dollars plus court costs. In a second trial, which was ordered because the original arrest warrants had erroneously described Gillespie as a "club leased by the city" rather than a "public golf course," a white middle-district judge from North Wilkesboro issued a favorable declaratory judgment in favor of the "Greensboro Six," calling the city's "so-called lease" of a private facility an invalid claim.

In October 1956, while the initial trespassing case was still working its way through state courts on appeal, Simkins filed suit in the US District Court for the Middle District of North Carolina against the city of Greensboro for racial discrimination in maintaining a public golf course for white citizens only. He was joined by nine others, including the original five golfers who had been with him in December 1955. On March 20, 1957, the court ruled in favor of Simkins, stating in its ruling opinion that the city of Greensboro could not escape its legal obligation to provide equal privileges to all citizens to enjoy city functions. The case was immediately appealed to the Fourth Circuit of Appeals, which affirmed the District Court's ruling and ordered the city to discontinue operating the course on a segregated basis.

Eventually, Simkins's suit even found its way to the US Supreme Court, where, missing the key facts from the amended lower-court brief, the high court ruled against the plaintiffs by a 5–4 margin, with a strong dissent by Chief Justice Earl Warren. Days later, however, North Carolina governor Luther Hodges commuted the sentences of the Greensboro Six.

By then, Gillespie Park was almost only a memory. Two weeks before the middle-district judge issued his favorable ruling, Gillespie's historic clubhouse—the original farmhouse belonging to the Gillespie family—mysteriously burned. A short time later, the city council voted to get out of the recreation business and shuttered the facility, quickly selling off nine of the holes.

"It was a pivotal moment in the history of this city," Greensboro's beloved longtime mayor Jim Melvin told me over lunch a few days after I returned from Arnold's memorial service. We were sharing Arnold Palmer stories from Melvin's years running the GGO and wound up talking about Gillespie Park, where the former mayor had grown up just across the street and earned his first pocket money by caddying on weekends. Melvin pointed out that it took another seven years, a strong public backlash, and a newly elected city council to reopen Gillespie Park Golf Course as a public nine-hole facility in 1962, two years after the historic sit-down demonstration occurred at Woolworth's in downtown Greensboro, a moment historians view as a touchstone of the civil rights movement.

In its seventy-fifth year, Gillespie Park had also managed to come full circle. With funding from Melvin's Bryan Foundation and the support of the Wyndham Championship, Perry Maxwell's old course was ably restored by Greensboro-based designer Chris

306 • THE RANGE BUCKET LIST

Spence, a Donald Ross expert who added a fine new practice area
and short course that became home to the First Tee of the Triad.
An acclaimed South Carolina sculptor, according to Mayor Melvin,
was in the process of creating a bronze statue of George Simkins to
eventually stand somewhere in the city. "It's about time we honored
the Martin Luther King of Greensboro," Melvin told me. "A lot of
us, black and white alike, owe our love of golf to this little course."

And so, of course, did I.

Jim Melvin was amazed when I admitted that I'd never played
the course—especially since I was once again a legal resident of
Greensboro, living with my wife in my favorite house in Starmount
Forest.

"In that case, you'd better go play it immediately," Mayor Melvin
instructed.

So that afternoon, as another golf season drew to a close, I paid
my fifteen-dollar greens fee, shouldered my MacKenzie Walker bag,
and set off on foot to see the course the way my father might once
have seen it.

I didn't bother keeping a scorecard. I just hit balls and admired
Perry Maxwell's clever routing scheme as I walked along, thinking
about Arnold and my father and how life and golf truly are circular
affairs of the heart, how right Tommy Barnes had been when he told
me that the game is always waiting for us to return.

Maybe best of all, for the first time in a very long time, I walked
completely free of pain.

That made this moment a true Range Bucket List two-fer—
maybe even a rare RBL *three*-fer, when you considered that, as a
king decreed, I was finally all the way safely home.

G ratitude, as the French proverb goes, is the heart's memory. This book—my little love letter to the game—was shaped by many hands, beginning with Opti the Mystic and ending with Arnold Palmer. Likewise, I am deeply indebted to the late Glenna Vare; Herbert Warren Wind; Kathleen Bennie and her wonderful daughter, Alison Bennie; and the irrepressible John Derr for years of guidance and encouragement. Ditto Pat Robinson, a beloved Dartmouth bookseller whose longtime passion was a blessing to my writing life. My former colleagues at *Golf* magazine had a strong hand in this yeoman's tale, including—and especially—former editor George Peper (now of *Links*) and senior editor Mike Purkey (*Global Golf Post*), whose love of golf writing continues to elevate the game. Former mentors and old friends Jud Hale, Mel Allen, and Tim Clark of *Yankee Magazine* and legendary southern editor Lee Walburn also have my everlasting gratitude. Additionally, I thank Doc Giffin and Gina Varrone of Arnold Palmer Enterprises for many years of help and friendship.

Life in the Carolina Sandhills provided enduring friendships, beginning with publisher David Woronoff and his uncle Big Frank Daniels, who own the award-winning *Pilot* newspaper and North State Magazine Group, where I'm fortunate to serve as editor. Neighbors Max and Myrtis Morrison and daughter Jean, longtime pals Ran and Fritz Morrisette, Dame Peggy Kirk Bell and family, Dr. Walter Morris, Tom Pashley of Pinehurst Resort, and the Rev. Bill Waterstradt will always be extended family. Ditto Andie Rose, the gifted art director of our magazine group and a valued partner, and longtime neighbors Stephen and Barbara Boyd and Chris Larsen. To have former *Golf World* stalwarts Jim Moriarity and Bill Fields recently join our magazine group is a gift from the gods. For their guidance and many years of friendship, I also thank Barney Adams, photographer Joann Dost, and Laird Small, true icons of the modern game.

To my longtime brothers of the game—Patrick McDaid, Nick Niles, Tom Stewart, Whit Powell, Rees Jones, Howdy Giles, Chris Buie, and Dewsweeper Jon Sager—long may we hobble after the game in one another's company. Ditto my gifted friend John Hopkins, longtime golf columnist for the *Times* of London, who was kind enough to read the manuscript and offer valuable suggestions and changes.

And to my longtime agent and friend Jay Mandel, who had the wisdom to introduce me to Jofie Ferrari-Adler, a talented young editor whose passion and stewardship brought this tale to the page, I offer sincerest thanks. That gratitude also extends to the great team at Simon & Schuster that includes publisher Jonathan Karp, associate publisher Richard Rhorer, marketer Stephen Bedford, publicist Elizabeth Gay, production editor Al Madocs, copyeditor Benjamin Holmes, and Jofie's indispensable assistant, Julianna Haubner.

My good friend and fellow hacker Harry Blair, an award-winning cartoonist, was kind enough to offer his wry illustrations to the narrative. And to the members of the stately Biltmore Forest Country Club, whose annual Jess Sweetser Invitational perfectly symbolizes the spirit of the game as Bobby Jones intended, I must say thank you—for many years of fellowship and fun. Especially "Golf Shop" Sheila Fender and Charlie Price.

Finally, persuaded that having a partner who is uncannily in tune with the ways of the universe is the key to a long and productive life, I thank my wife, Wendy, a feisty twenty-five handicapper who shoots well under par in the art of living well and inspiring those around her.

That's why this tale, first and last, is dedicated to her.

James Dodson is a two-time winner of the United States Golf Association's Herbert Warren Wind Award for best golf book of the year. He is the author of ten books, including *Final Rounds, American Triumvirate, A Golfer's Life* (with Arnold Palmer), and *Ben Hogan: An American Life*. He lives with his wife in North Carolina.